You Shall
Have
My Word

You Shall Have My Word

Exploring the Text of the Doctrine and Covenants

*edited by Scott C. Esplin,
Richard O. Cowan,
and Rachel Cope*

**THE 41ST ANNUAL
BRIGHAM YOUNG UNIVERSITY
SIDNEY B. SPERRY SYMPOSIUM**

The Sperry Symposium is sponsored annually by Brigham Young University and the Church Educational System in honor of Sidney B. Sperry. In the course of his forty-five-year career as a religious educator, Dr. Sperry earned a reputation for outstanding teaching and scholarship. The symposium seeks to perpetuate his memory by fostering continuing research on gospel topics.

Copublished by the Religious Studies Center, Brigham Young University, Provo, Utah, and Deseret Book Company, Salt Lake City, Utah.

© 2012 Brigham Young University

All rights reserved.

Any uses of this material beyond those allowed by the exemptions in U.S. copyright law, such as section 107, "Fair Use," and section 108, "Library Copying," require the written permission of the publisher, Religious Studies Center, 167 HGB, Brigham Young University, Provo, Utah 84602. The views expressed herein are the responsibility of the authors and do not necessarily represent the position of Brigham Young University or the Religious Studies Center.

DESERET BOOK is a registered trademark of Deseret Book Company.

Visit us at DeseretBook.com

Library of Congress Cataloging-in-Publication Data

Sperry Symposium (41st : 2012 : Brigham Young University)

    You shall have my word : exploring the text of the Doctrine and Covenants : 41st Annual Sidney B. Sperry Symposium / edited by Scott C. Esplin, Richard O. Cowan, and Rachel Cope.

        pages cm

    Includes bibliographical references and index.

    ISBN 978-0-8425-2819-1 (hardbound : alk. paper) 1. Doctrine and Covenants—Criticism, interpretation, etc.—Congresses. 2. The Church of Jesus Christ of Latter-day Saints—Doctrines—Congresses. 3. Mormon Church—Doctrines—Congresses. I. Esplin, Scott C. (Scott Clair), 1974– editor. II. Cowan, Richard O., 1934– editor. III. Cope, Rachel, editor. IV. Title.

    BX8628.S72 2012

    289.3'2—dc23   2012017916

Printed in the United States of America

Malloy Lithographing Incorporated, Ann Arbor, MI

10 9 8 7 6 5 4 3 2

Contents

Preface vii

1. You Shall Have My Word: The Personal Ministry of Jesus Christ in the Restoration
   Elder Gary J. Coleman 1

2. "That They Might Come to Understanding": Revelation as Process
   Steven C. Harper 19

3. "I Will Send You Elijah the Prophet"
   Kenneth L. Alford 34

4. "Commissioned of Jesus Christ": Oliver Cowdery and D&C 13
   Mark L. Staker 50

5. The Lord's Supper in Early Mormonism
   Justin R. Bray 64

6. Sacramental Connections: Deliverance, Redemption, and Safety (D&C 27)
   Matthew O. Richardson 75

7. Gathering the Lord's Words into One: Biblical Intertextuality in the Doctrine and Covenants
   Lisa Olsen Tait 92

8. Isaiah in the Doctrine and Covenants
   Terry B. Ball and Spencer S. Snyder 108

9. "Let Zion in Her Beauty Rise": Building Zion by Becoming Zion
   Scott C. Esplin 134

10. Revealing Parables: A Call to Action within the Doctrine and Covenants
    Amy Easton-Flake 149

11. A Culmination of Learning: D&C 84 and the Doctrine of the Priesthood
    Matthew C. Godfrey 167

12. The Olive Leaf and the Family of Heaven
    Samuel Morris Brown 182

13. "Health in Their Navel and Marrow to Their Bones"
    Kate Holbrook 192

14. Illuminating the Text of the Doctrine and Covenants through the Gospel of John
    Nicholas J. Frederick 205

15. Treasures, Witches, and Ancient Inhabitants (D&C 111)
    Craig James Ostler 220

16. From Obscurity to Scripture: Joseph F. Smith's Vision of the Redemption of the Dead
    Mary Jane Woodger 234

Index 255

Preface

In March 1829, a full year prior to the official organization of the Church, the Lord declared to the Prophet Joseph Smith—then engaged in the process of translating the Book of Mormon—"This generation shall have my word through you" (D&C 5:10). Two months later, Joseph's brother Hyrum traveled to Harmony, Pennsylvania, to see if he could assist with this work. During this visit, Joseph received a revelation for his brother, which instructed him, "Wait a little longer, until you shall have my word, my rock, my church, and my gospel" (D&C 11:16). In the succeeding years, Joseph indeed received numerous revelations that fulfilled each of the promises the Lord had given Hyrum; many of these are included in the Doctrine and Covenants, "a collection of divine revelations and inspired declarations" through which the Lord invites all to come unto him (Explanatory Introduction).

As readers engage with the Doctrine and Covenants, they will recognize its Christ-centered message, a message that expands our understanding of the Lord's purposes for each of us. By studying it, we learn more about the nature of God, the divinity of his Son, and the reality of the Holy Ghost, while also coming to recognize more completely the work they are accomplishing on the earth today. This sacred text crystallizes our understanding of the plan of salvation, which includes pre-earth life, the purposes of mortality, and the reality and nature of life after death. Furthermore, it expounds the importance of temple covenants, the eternal potential of families, and the power whereby these units can persist beyond the veil. Ultimately, it teaches us about the possibilities of fulness, indeed of exaltation.

The Doctrine and Covenants also testifies of the blessings God's grace brings to humankind; it teaches us how to become active agents and wise stewards. While shifting our thinking from event to process, the concepts of consecration, worship, and sanctification become more powerful and meaningful as we connect them to Christlike living and our desire to establish Zion. Organizationally, the Doctrine and Covenants clarifies the order and function of priesthood, details the duties of specific priesthood offices, and describes the role of presiding councils. Historically, it chronicles the opening of the heavens and the events of the Restoration. Indeed, the word of the Lord on these and many other topics, together with "the testimony that is given of Jesus Christ—his divinity, his majesty, his perfection, his love, and his redeeming power," makes the Doctrine and Covenants "of great value to the human family and of more worth than the riches of the whole earth" (Explanatory Introduction).

Studying the word of the Lord contained in the Doctrine and Covenants yields great blessings, including the desire to be transformed through the grace and power of Christ. Prefacing "the book of [his] commandments," the Lord explained that he "called upon . . . Joseph Smith, Jun., and spake unto him from heaven, and gave him commandments . . . that every man might speak in the name of God the Lord, even the Savior of the world; that faith also might increase in the earth; that [the Lord's] everlasting covenant might be established; that the fulness of the gospel might be proclaimed by the weak and the simple unto the ends of the earth" (D&C 1:6, 17, 20–23). Hearkening to these words, the reader will "come to understanding" (1:24). Those who err as well as those who sin will "be chastened" by the Lord's revelations, "that they might repent" (1:27). Those who seek wisdom from these pages will "be instructed," while those who humble themselves because of its words will "be made strong, and blessed from on high, and receive knowledge from time to time" (1:26, 28). These blessings and many more are available for all who "search these commandments" (1:37) and then choose to act upon them.

Inviting you to embark on this search, the forty-first annual Sidney B. Sperry Symposium at Brigham Young University focuses on the text of the Doctrine and Covenants, exploring significant messages, teachings, doctrines, and themes given by the Lord and his prophets in this modern book of scripture. Elder Gary J. Coleman, emeritus member of the Seventy, begins the publication, analyzing the Lord's personal ministry throughout the earliest revelations. Examining the Lord's use of personal pronouns, Elder Coleman testifies of the Savior's loving-kindness, as demonstrated by his words to the early participants in the Restoration. Chapters throughout the remainder of the publication are organized to coincide with corresponding sections in the Doctrine and Covenants. They discuss the process by which the Lord delivered his word, the restoration of priesthood authority, and ordinances associated with the restored gospel. Chapters on Zion, the eternal nature of families, and the Word of Wisdom will enlighten you to doctrinal depths and application found in modern revelation. Literary analyses examine connections between the Bible and the Doctrine and Covenants, especially the influence of the language of Isaiah and of John the Beloved throughout the text as well as the Lord's use of parables. Finally, historical assessments of specific revelations clarify difficult passages and introduce the story behind the Lord's words. All is done in an effort to help you appreciate the power and meaningfulness contained in this sacred text and know, as President Joseph F. Smith declared, "the book of Doctrine and Covenants contains some of the most glorious principles ever revealed to the world, some that have been revealed in greater fulness than they were ever revealed before to the world."[1]

As a Sperry Symposium committee, we express gratitude to the authors and presenters who participated in the conference, the external reviewers who shared their expertise, and the editors at Brigham Young University's Religious Studies Center and at Deseret Book Company who clarified the writing. The faculty members of the committee acknowledge the special contribution of Patty Smith, who provided administrative support for both the symposium and the publication. Finally, we express appreciation for the word of the Lord revealed throughout the Doctrine and Covenants, a text that represents "the mind of the Lord, . . . the word of the Lord, . . . the voice of the Lord, and the power of God unto salvation" (D&C 68:4).

> Scott C. Esplin
> Richard O. Cowan
> Rachel Cope
> Patty A. Smith
>
> Sperry Symposium Committee

Note

1. Joseph F. Smith, in Conference Report, October 1913, 9.

1

You Shall Have My Word: The Personal Ministry of Jesus Christ in the Restoration

Elder Gary J. Coleman

In each of the three books of scripture in the collection often referred to as the triple combination, we find a page of introduction. We will briefly examine references from the introductions specifically in the Book of Mormon and the Doctrine and Covenants. The introduction to the Book of Mormon says that "the crowning event recorded in the Book of Mormon is the personal ministry of the Lord Jesus Christ among the Nephites soon after his resurrection." The Explanatory Introduction to the Doctrine and Covenants says, "In the revelations one hears the tender but firm voice of the Lord Jesus Christ, speaking anew in the dispensation of the fulness of times; and the work that is initiated herein is preparatory to his second coming, in fulfillment of and in concert with the words of all the holy prophets since the world began."

The Doctrine and Covenants is another witness of the personal ministry of Jesus Christ to the children of God in these latter days. The multitude of personal pronoun phrases from the first nineteen sections of the Doctrine and Covenants will clearly illustrate the Savior's loving ministry to the Prophet

---

Elder Gary J. Coleman is an emeritus member of the First Quorum of the Seventy.

Joseph Smith and his colleagues prior to the organization of the Church in April 1830. Through these verses, we learn that the work of the Restoration of the gospel is truly the work of the Lord Jesus Christ.

Section 18, given to the Prophet Joseph Smith, Oliver Cowdery, and David Whitmer in June 1829 in Fayette, New York, gives us a clear example of how personal that ministry can be for each individual Saint. Jesus speaks of His words, His voice, His Spirit, and His power to be revealed in the restoration of all things. He declares in verse 34, "These words are . . . of *me*," and in verses 35 and 36, "For it is *my* voice which speaketh them unto you; for they are given by *my* Spirit unto you, and by *my* power you can read them one to another; and save it were by *my* power you could not have them; wherefore, you can testify that you have heard *my* voice, and know *my* words" (emphasis added to first-person pronouns in this chapter).

This powerful declaration was stated similarly three years later in Doctrine and Covenants 84:60 when the Lord said, "Verily, verily, *I* say unto you who now hear *my* words, which are *my* voice, blessed are ye inasmuch as you receive these things."

These powerful declarations from the Lord Himself are no doubt the reason the Explanatory Introduction concludes with the following: "Finally, the testimony that is given of Jesus Christ—his divinity, his majesty, his perfection, his love, and his redeeming power—makes this book of great value to the human family and of more worth than the riches of the whole earth."

In the four verses noted above, there are two references to *me* and eight references to *my*. We will find dozens of other personal pronoun references to the Savior as we explore the pronouns *I*, *my*, *me*, and *mine* in the personal ministry of Jesus Christ leading up to the Restoration of the gospel and the organization of the Church in 1830. I have learned over the years of pondering and teaching the scriptures that we may apply the words of the Lord on an individual level where appropriate. For instance, in following the pattern available in Doctrine and Covenants 18:34–36, one could personalize the words as follows: I testify that these words are of Jesus Christ and not of man. His voice speaks them to me. They are given to me by His Spirit. By His power I can read them for myself and to others. I could not have the words except by His power. I can testify that I have heard His voice and that I know His words.

I have taught missionaries to read the scriptures so that they personalize and internalize the holy words for themselves, and it strengthens their own faith and confidence in the words of the Lord. In this application of the scripture to ourselves (see 1 Nephi 19:23), we can truly feel the love of the Savior for each of us. We can know He will visit us and manifest to us His will through a voice of love, of invitation, and of expectation. We can then respond and follow Him as He reveals to us the path we must walk to return to Him and His Father. Elder Dallin H. Oaks has taught, "Revelation from God to man comes for different purposes and in different ways. It should be a reality for every Latter-day Saint, because each has the gift of the Holy Ghost."[1]

The Doctrine and Covenants is a latter-day testament of the ministry of Jesus Christ to the children of God through prophets and servants of God, and it illustrates the divine pattern of revelation that guides the Church and its members today. The Church of Jesus Christ of Latter-day Saints truly is the Lord's Church. Through the revelations of the Restoration and the continuing spread of the gospel over the whole earth, we may come to a personal knowledge of His divine influence. It may not come quickly and easily, but I testify that it will come! President Dieter F. Uchtdorf spoke of this quest as follows:

> The truth is, those who diligently seek to learn of Christ eventually will come to know Him. They will personally receive a divine portrait of the Master, although it most often comes in the form of a puzzle—one piece at a time. Each individual piece may not be easily recognizable by itself; it may not be clear how it relates to the whole. Each piece helps us to see the big picture a little more clearly. Eventually, after enough pieces have been put together, we recognize the grand beauty of it all. Then, looking back on our experience, we see that the Savior had indeed come to be with us—not all at once but quietly, gently, almost unnoticed.[2]

The Doctrine and Covenants is a grand illustration of the personal ministry of Jesus Christ to all who would seek to know Him and come unto Him. My own journey of conversion is filled with the grand process of putting pieces of the divine tapestry of the restored gospel together and coming to know over and over again of the sacred steps to my personal knowledge of the Savior and His magnificent work for each of us.

The essence of my message is focused on the first nineteen sections of the Doctrine and Covenants. These sections about the preorganization of the Church give ample testimony to the Lord's use of personal pronouns such as *I*, *my*, *me*, and *mine*, and they suggest a close personal relationship to the reader. For the most part, these sections were given in chronological order from September 1823 to March 1830. Section 1 was given in November 1831 and serves as a preface to the book. Section 10 was given in the summer of 1828. In the first five sections, we note the following significant personal pronouns referring to the Lord Jesus Christ.

Section 1:

My church (v. 1)
Mine authority (v. 6)
My servants (v. 6)
I the Lord have decreed (v. 7)
I the Lord, knowing the calamity (v. 17)
My servant Joseph Smith, Jun. (v. 17)
Mine everlasting covenant (v. 22)
My gospel (v. 23)

I am God and have spoken it (v. 24)
I, the Lord, am well pleased (v. 30)
My Spirit (v. 33)
I am no respecter of persons (v. 35)
What *I* the Lord have spoken, *I* have spoken (v. 38)
Mine own voice (v. 38)

Section 2:

I will reveal (v. 1)

Section 3:

My work (v. 19)

Section 5:

I have caused (v. 3)
I have commanded that you should (v. 4)
My words (v. 5)
I have committed unto you (v. 7)
I will show (v. 11)
I will give them power (v. 12)
I tell you these things (v. 20)
I command you (v. 21)

I grant unto you eternal life (v. 22)
I speak unto you (v. 23)
I foresee the lying in wait to destroy thee (v. 32)
For this cause *I* have said (v. 34)
Stop, and stand still until *I* command thee (v. 34)
I will provide means (v. 34)

Let me illustrate further the importance of personalizing and internalizing holy words with this scripture: "Stop, and stand still until I command thee, and I will provide means whereby thou mayest accomplish the thing which I have commanded thee" (D&C 5:34). This sentence entered my mind in a hallway of the Covina California Stake Center, where our mission was to have a fireside for members and nonmembers. I noticed a young father standing ill at ease near the back of the cultural hall, holding a small child. The Spirit prompted me to speak to him. His name was Eddie, and he was there with his wife, Beatrice, and their baby son, Daniel. He was a less-active member, and his wife was not a member. After greeting them and assuring them they were most welcome, my wife and I escorted them to the chapel for the viewing of the video *Together Forever*. As the video began in the darkened room, I heard the cry of a small child. I quickly moved to the mother. It was Beatrice with Daniel. I asked if I could hold him in the adjacent foyer while the video was shown. She felt Daniel would not come to me, as he had not let others hold him previously. "You need to hear the message of the video with your husband," I assured her. "Daniel and I will be just fine." I held the little fellow for the next half hour, and we conversed in the celestial language of a tiny spirit less than a year from his heavenly home. The mother walked into the foyer immediately following the video and rejoiced that Daniel and I were doing just fine.

At her baptism three weeks later, administered by her husband, Beatrice thanked us again for the opportunity to feel the Spirit of the Lord on that previous occasion with her husband in the chapel. She said, "I can't believe you helped me with my baby." I thanked the Lord for His prompting, "Stop and stand still, and I will provide means for you to accomplish my work." Truly this was a powerful example to me about having His word and His voice to help me bring about His purpose.

In sections 6–9 we find additional evidences of the personal instruction and counsel of Jesus Christ. Remember, in these sections, it was still a year before the Church would be organized. The young Prophet must have been truly amazed at the truths he was being taught.

Section 6:

- Give heed unto *my* word (v. 2)
- If you will ask of *me* (v. 5)
- *I* will encircle thee in the arms of *my* love (v. 20)
- *I* am Jesus Christ (v. 21)
- *I* am the same that came unto *mine* own, and *mine* own received *me* not (v. 21)
- *I* am the light (v. 21)
- Did *I* not speak peace (v. 23)
- If they reject *my* words, and this part of *my* gospel and ministry (v. 29)
- As *I* said unto *my* disciples, where two or three are gathered together in *my* name (v. 32)
- Built upon *my* rock (v. 34)
- Look unto *me* in every thought (v. 36)
- The wounds which pierced *my* side (v. 37)
- Prints of the nails in *my* hands and feet (v. 37)
- Keep *my* commandments (v. 37)

There are many personal pearls of great price to Joseph in this section. One that has struck me as comforting and inviting to the members of the Church and new converts is verse 13, which reads, "If thou wilt do good, yea, and hold out faithful to the end, thou shalt be saved in the kingdom of God, which is the greatest of all the gifts of God; for there is no gift greater than the gift of salvation." I hear the Savior saying, "I will save you in *my* kingdom!" Can the human mind fully comprehend this proclamation of promise to all future members of the Church? Oh, what gifts God has in store for His covenant people!

Section 7:

Until *I* come in *my* glory (v. 3)
Bring souls unto *me* (v. 4)
Come unto *me* in *my* kingdom (v. 4)
I will make him as flaming fire (v. 6)
I will give this power and the keys of this ministry until *I* come (v. 7)

Section 8:

I will tell you in your mind and in your heart (v. 2)

Section 9:

I have entrusted unto him (v. 1)
I will give unto you power (v. 2)
It is wisdom in *me* (v. 3)
I have dealt with you (v. 6)
Supposed that *I* would give it unto you (v. 7)
No thought save it was to ask *me* (v. 7)
Then you must ask *me* if it be right (v. 8)
I will cause that your bosom shall burn (v. 8)
Neither of you have *I* condemned (v. 12)
Work wherewith *I* have called you (v. 14)

These simple references to *I*, *me*, *my*, and *mine* stir my soul with devotion for Jesus, our Savior and Redeemer, who is willing to fill us with His love and grace if we will but seek to find Him and follow Him throughout our lives. We are already seeing fulfilled in these opening sections of the Doctrine and Covenants the promise made in the aforementioned lines from the Explanatory Introduction as to the evidence of the "tender but firm voice of the Lord Jesus Christ." He is unfolding the glorious work of the plan of God for all of His children to the young Prophet Joseph. This is a time of wondrous anticipation for the human family.

Section 10 gives us a clear and precise look into the value the Savior places upon the work underway to prepare the publication of the sacred Book of Mormon. The Lord seeks to assure Joseph that the coming forth of another testament of Jesus Christ is a work that will test and try the Prophet's very being because Satan will viciously oppose this key to the Restoration of the gospel. Section 10 continues with personal pronouns used by the Lord to impress upon Joseph the majesty of the work he will undertake to bring forth the Church of Jesus Christ and the plan of God in the latter days.

Section 10:

I will not suffer that Satan shall accomplish his evil design (v. 14)
I will confound (v. 42)
I gave unto them [*my* gospel] (v. 48)
I bring this part of *my* gospel to the knowledge of *my* people (v. 52)
I do not bring it to destroy (v. 52)
I will establish *my* church among them (v. 53)
I say this to build up *my* church (v. 54)
I am Jesus Christ (v. 57)
I am he who said (v. 59)
Other sheep have *I* (v. 59)
I will show unto this people (v. 60)
I will bring to light (v. 61)
This *I* do that *I* may establish *my* gospel (v. 63)
Him will *I* establish upon *my* rock (v. 69)

One senses the flow of spiritual power to Joseph as the restored gospel of Jesus Christ is opened to the Prophet. Could he, or we, even comprehend the seventeen words of verse 55? Remember, this was given nearly two years before the organization of the Church: "Therefore, whosoever belongeth to my church need not fear, for such shall inherit the kingdom of heaven." To me, the Lord seems to be saying: "Brother Coleman, I have prepared a place for you in my kingdom."

Hundreds of years prior to these instructions and revelations to the Prophet Joseph in the Doctrine and Covenants, Jesus had accomplished His personal ministry among the Nephites soon after His resurrection. He had used the pronouns *I, me, my,* and *mine* profusely among His people in the Americas. This pattern was used during His ministry to the Nephites in 3 Nephi of the Book of Mormon. Between 3 Nephi 9 and 3 Nephi 28:12, there are 531 verses, and these verses contain over 700 personal references to Jesus. Some of these references are given here.

Third Nephi:

> *I* will declare unto you *my* doctrine (11:31)
> *I* am Jesus Christ (9:15)
> *I* was with the Father (9:15)
> *I* am the light and life (9:18)
> *I* have come unto the world (9:21)
> *I* have laid down *my* life (9:22)
>
> How oft will *I* gather (10:6)
> *I* have suffered (11:11)
> *I* bear record (11:32)
> *I* speak (16:2)
> *I* fulfil the covenant (16:5)
> *I* will remember (16:12)
> *I* have prayed (18:16)

Section 10 is very similar to the Book of Mormon account of the personal ministry of Jesus Christ to the people of the covenant in the use of the pronouns *my* and *me*. We know that the Lord personally visited, taught, ministered, prayed, and wept with the people. Can we not feel His intimate concern for us in these personal expressions to His people in all generations? He is using the same loving and compassionate phrases for the children of God in the latter days as He did in former days. I feel His love for me and for my family.

As we continue searching through 3 Nephi, we continue to find instances of personal pronouns that collectively characterize the Savior.

Third Nephi:

> *My* face (9:5)
> The Father [is] in *me* (9:15)
> *My* own received *me* not (9:16)
> By *me* redemption cometh (9:17)
> Their faith in *me* (9:20)
> Laid down *my* life (9:22)
> Taking upon *me* the sins of the world (11:11)
> Come forth unto *me* (11:14)
> *My* side (11:14)
> *My* hands (11:14)
> *My* feet (11:14)
> Baptized in *my* name (11:23)
> *My* rock (11:39)
>
> *My* sheep (15:24)
> *My* gospel (16:10)
> *My* covenant (16:12)
> *My* joy is full (17:20)
> *My* Spirit (18:7)
> *My* commandments (18:14)
> *My* wisdom (21:10)
> *My* flesh and blood (18:28)
> *My* church (27:8)
> *My* people (18:31)
> Points of *my* doctrine (21:6)
> Do it in *my* name (27:7)
> Call the church in *my* name (27:7)

Section 10 prepared the followers of Christ for the reason that the keystone of our religion, the Book of Mormon, had to be published before the Church was reestablished on the earth to welcome the coming Restoration of the true gospel of Jesus Christ. The Book of Mormon contains words, phrases, doctrine, and plain and precious parts of the gospel that are always clear to the understanding of all mankind. The Book of Mormon teaches the divine harmony between the true gospel of Jesus Christ in former days and the Doctrine and Covenants of the latter days. How blessed we are to have these eternal principles repeated generation after generation, from former days to latter days through all eternity.

Section 10:

- *My* gospel (v. 45)
- *My* holy prophets (v. 46)
- *My* disciples (v. 46)
- Build up *my* church (v. 54)
- Whosoever belongeth to *my* church need not fear (v. 55)
- Bring to light the true points of *my* doctrine (v. 62)
- Establish *my* gospel (v. 63)
- Points of *my* doctrine (3 Nephi 21:6)
- This is *my* doctrine (v. 67)
- The same is *my* church (v. 67)
- He is not of *my* church (v. 68)
- Whosoever is of *my* church (v. 69)
- And endureth of *my* church (v. 69)
- Establish upon *my* rock, and the gates of hell shall not prevail against them (v. 69)

The first reference to "rock" had been mentioned in section 6, verse 34. Section 10 often quotes the Lord as referring to "*my* rock." I am a witness of this sure foundation, the rock of our Redeemer. I know that Jesus is the Christ, the Son of God, upon whom we should establish our foundation.

Some years ago, I was asked to find a building large enough to house six hundred single adults during a three-day conference. I sought the St. Michael's facility, just north of Spokane, Washington, which was quite large and had once housed three hundred seminarians who were preparing themselves for the ministry. In 1974 the building was virtually empty, quiet, and cold. Where were those young men who had once filled its halls?

I inquired of an old priest who took care of this great facility if our Church could use it. It took me a while to convince him of the great atmosphere that could be there once again, but he finally accepted. The event was such a success that our Church used this building during several years, filling the rooms on each floor during youth and single adult conferences.

One day I went alone to the unoccupied basement, lighting my way with a flashlight into a hallway several hundred feet long. In the middle of the hall I saw a great basalt rock that protruded from the middle of the cement floor. On the rock there was a bronze plaque. I read the words on the plaque, which said, "And I say also unto thee, That thou art Peter, and upon this rock I will build my church; and the gates of hell shall not prevail against it" (Matthew 16:18).

This caught my attention. Their church had been empty, silent, and cold for several years. It no longer housed young seminarians; it was abandoned. The facility had been built upon the wrong rock! The Latter-day Saint youth were the ones to fill the church that day. The Church of the Restoration, the Church built upon His holy and continuous word, prevailed there that happy day. These youth filled those walls with their songs, testimonies, laughter, happiness, and joy. Why? Because we are built on the true rock, upon "a sure foundation, a foundation whereon if men build they cannot fall" (Helaman 5:12). The youth were feasting upon His word and living by it. They had His gospel, His Church, His rock, His power, and His doctrine among them. It was a time and place of rejoicing for all.

The prophet Helaman was right in his day of 30 BC. The Lord declared who He was during His mortal ministry in northern Israel on the mount, and the Prophet Joseph learned of the Rock of our Redeemer, who is Christ, the Son of God, in the glorious latter days. I add my witness to these former-day witnesses.

We have only begun to tap the vast reserves of the personal ministry of Jesus Christ to the Prophet Joseph and the Restoration of the true Church upon the earth. Section 11 is truly a marvelous work. It was given by revelation through Joseph Smith to his brother Hyrum Smith in May 1829. The Book of Mormon was soon to be ready for publication, the Aaronic and Melchizedek Priesthoods were coming forth, and it was less than a year before the Church was to be organized. Nuggets of great import are to be gleaned from this section.

Section 11:
- *I* am God (v. 2)
- Give heed to *my* word (v. 2)
- *I* say unto you (v. 2)
- Keep *my* commandments (v. 6)
- Believing . . . in *my* power which speaketh unto thee (v. 10)
- It is *I* that speak (v. 11)
- *I* am the light (v. 11)
- By *my* power *I* give these words unto thee (v. 11)
- This is *my* Spirit (v. 12)
- *I* will impart unto you of *my* Spirit (v. 13)
- *I* command you (v. 15)
- Wait a little longer, until you shall have *my* word, *my* rock, *my* church, and *my* gospel, . . . *my* doctrine (v. 16)

Wait a little longer! Glorious days are ahead! The restoration of the Melchizedek Priesthood was only days away. I sense excitement and anticipation of coming events. For hundreds of years following His own sacred ministry in Israel and the pure gospel being taught for 200 years following His visit to the Nephites, the Savior had waited nearly 1,600 years for the Restoration of His gospel. Verse 16 suggests that the long-awaited time of restoration was due to overthrow the foolishness and vainness of man in usurping His power and authority through apostate priestcrafts, in preaching doctrines that were not purely His, and in perverting His holy ordinances with ungodly and unauthorized practices. Verse 21 speaks of "seek first to obtain *my* word, and then . . . you shall have *my* Spirit and *my* word." Further, "study *my* word which shall come forth" (v. 22) and "build upon *my* rock, which is *my* gospel" (v. 24) and "I [will] give power to become the sons of God" (v. 30). Joseph and his associates must have been thrilled with the anticipation of coming days of revelation. Oh, how grateful we ought to be for the intimate counsel and guidance the Lord provides for His servants. The dawning of the long-foretold day of restoration of all things was imminent.

Sections 12–14 provide similar phrases and pronoun use as noted in previous sections, such as "I am God," "*my* word" (D&C 12:3), "I am the light and the life of the world" (D&C 12:9), "*my* commandments" (D&C 14:7), "*my* name" (D&C 14:8), "I am Jesus Christ" (D&C 14:9), and "I must bring forth the fulness of *my* gospel" (D&C 14:10). Joseph was just a few years away from the wondrous First Vision of the glorious personage of God the Father, who spoke to him and said, "This is My Beloved Son. Hear Him!" (Joseph Smith—History 1:17). There he learned that the work of the Father is the work of the Son. The doctrines of men that he had experienced as a youth were being replaced by true doctrine. The creeds that were an abomination in the sight of the Lord were fast fleeing from his mind. The manmade doctrines having a form of godliness were toppling into the pit of error with every passing revelation from the Lord Jesus Christ. The powerful doctrine of eternal life was again spoken of in section 14, still ten months before the Restoration of the Church. Would Joseph have heard and pondered upon these words in awe? "And, if you keep my commandments and endure to the end you shall have eternal life, which gift is the greatest of all the gifts of God" (D&C 14:7). Listen, Latter-day Saints! This is the tender but firm voice of Jesus to all of us. As Elder Quentin L. Cook recently expressed, "Thankfully, 'the key of knowledge' has been restored and the doctrine of the Father is upon the earth again!"[3]

In sections 15 and 16 we are introduced to a profound truth regarding the doctrine of the Godhead. The Savior refers to "the kingdom of *my* Father" in each of these sections. I testify that this is a most precious doctrine of the Restoration. A knowledge of the Father is the key to all other gospel knowledge. This was a major doctrine He taught to the people in 3 Nephi during His ministry in the land of Bountiful.

These excerpts from 3 Nephi provide further examples of personal pronoun use:

> *I* . . . have glorified the Father (11:11)
> *I* have suffered the will of the Father (11:11)
> It is the doctrine which the Father hath given unto *me* (11:32)
> The Father beareth record of *me* (11:32)
> Whoso believeth in *me* believeth in the Father also (11:35)
> He that doeth the will of *my* Father who is in heaven (14:21)
> The Father hath commanded *me* (18:14)
> Ask of the Father in *my* name (18:20)
> Pray in your families unto the Father, always in *my* name (18:21)
> Father, *I* thank thee that thou hast given the Holy Ghost unto these (19:20).

Following are three of the dozens of references in the Book of Mormon concerning the Godhead:

> *My* doctrine, ... the doctrine the Father hath given unto *me*, ... the Holy Ghost beareth record of the Father and *me* (3 Nephi 11:32)
>
> Baptized in *my* name, ... that ye may witness unto Father, ... ye shall have *my* Spirit to be with you (3 Nephi 18:11)
>
> The Father hath given *me* fulness of joy; ... and the Holy Ghost beareth record of the Father and *me* (3 Nephi 28:10–11)

Additionally noted are several other references as to personal counsel the Lord gives to individuals.

Section 15:

> *I* speak unto you with sharpness and with power (v. 2)
>
> *I* will tell you that which no man knoweth save *me* (v. 3)
>
> *My* words which *I* have given unto you (v. 5)
>
> *I* say unto you, that the thing which will be of most worth (v. 6)

Section 16:

> Same uses of *I* and *me* and *my* as in section 15

There are occasions when the Lord chooses to bless His servants in like manner in our day. While I was serving as a mission president in California, Elder Thane Ottley asked me to assist his companionship with the teaching of Patoch, a minister of the Hungarian Reformed Church. Upon leaving for the appointment, I began praying about my role in the discussion. I was impressed that he would ask me two questions: why he should submit himself to being taught by these two young men who were not schooled or trained in religion as he had been, and how he would manage his affairs if he joined the Church and lost his income as a minister. I pondered these impressions and thought about scriptures that might help resolve these concerns.

Upon arriving at the minister's home in Covina, California, the elders and I were graciously received. After the prayer, the elders began to teach the fourth discussion, and I listened. Suddenly, Mr. Patoch turned to me and stated, "I am a trained and ordained minister. Why should I submit myself to being taught by these two young men who are not trained in theology as I have been?" I marveled at the question and proceeded to review several scriptures that had been on my mind earlier during the drive to the appointment. He seemed satisfied with the explanation, and the elders proceeded with the discussion. In a few moments, he again turned to me and asked, "If I join this

Church, how will I manage my life and obtain an income? I will be forced to give up my ministry." Again I thought of the prompting received earlier and reviewed a few scriptures with him that related to the problem. Satisfied, he asked the elders to proceed, and they concluded the discussion.

Several days later, Elder Ottley called me and asked if I was available on Saturday morning at eleven. "Brother Patoch would like you to attend his baptism." Yes, I know from my own experiences that the Lord will tell His servants "that which no man knoweth."

Section 17 introduces us to the uses of *I* and *my* as follows: "And *I*, Jesus Christ, your Lord and your God, have spoken it unto you, that *I* might bring about *my* righteous purposes unto the children of men" (v. 9). Surely we are eternally grateful for His kind and loving guidance that helps us to partake of all the blessings He has promised us.

As we review section 18, a revelation given to Joseph Smith, Oliver Cowdery, and David Whitmer in June 1829, we find some three dozen references to *my*, over a dozen references to *I*, and continued use of *me* and *mine*. Necessary priesthood had been restored. The Book of Mormon had been translated and the printing of the book was under way. The priesthood and the Book of Mormon were to be the foundational reference points for "*my* church, *my* gospel, and *my* rock" (D&C 18:4).

Section 18 begins with "*I* give unto you these words," with a steady litany of personal references to Jesus Christ to follow.

Section 18:

- *I* give unto you a commandment (v. 3)
- *My* church, *my* gospel, *my* rock (v. 4)
- *I* command all men everywhere to repent (v. 9)
- Great shall be your joy with him in the kingdom of *my* Father (v. 15)
- One soul that you have brought unto *me* into the kingdom of *my* Father (v. 16)
- How great shall be your joy if you should bring many souls unto *me* (v. 16)
- You have *my* gospel before you, and *my* rock, and *my* salvation (v. 17)
- Ask the Father in *my* name, in faith (v. 18)
- As many as repent and are baptized in *my* name (v. 22)
- Called to declare *my* gospel (v. 26)
- Ordained of *me* to baptize in *my* name (v. 29)
- *I* speak unto you, the Twelve (v. 31)
- *My* grace is sufficient for you (v. 31)
- You are they who are ordained of *me* (v. 32)

I would like to return to the special witness given by the Lord in verses 34–36. They have had a powerful effect upon my ministry over the past several decades:

> These words are not of men nor of man, but of *me*; wherefore, you shall testify they are of *me* and not of man;
>
> For it is *my* voice which speaketh them unto you; for they are given by *my* Spirit unto you, and by *my* power you can read them one to another; and save it were by *my* power you could not have them;
>
> Wherefore, you can testify that you have heard *my* voice, and know *my* words. (D&C 18:34–36)

We rejoice in the Lord's simple ways and express our deepest gratitude when He gives us words of comfort or guidance in our assignments in His holy work.

I served as the president of the California Arcadia Mission from July 1987 to July 1990, and I met Lee McElhaney my first week there. I found a way to visit him monthly over the next thirty-six months. His wife and children were members of the Church, and his oldest son entered the Provo Missionary Training Center in June of 1990. Our backgrounds were similar, and his Catholic resolve was evident. Every set of missionaries assigned to his ward had taught him and his family year after year. One Sunday, June 3, 1990, just four weeks before my release, I was impressed one more time while praying about Lee, with the simple words of the Spirit: "Invite him to the meeting tonight." It was an institute graduation, and I was the speaker. I did invite him, and he responded courageously that he would attend. My remarks were directed toward him, though there were several hundred persons in attendance. Still following the impression to be bold with him, after the meeting I challenged him to be baptized on Father's Day, just two weeks away. Many persons, including priesthood leaders, spoke words of faith and assurance to him in the coming days. There was doubt and opposition, but loving leaders were there to help. On Father's Day, June 17, 1990, in the presence of five former bishops and over one hundred friends and family members, Lee was baptized. I called the Provo MTC and informed the president that Elder McElhaney had his first baptism, though performed by others, and it was his father. Lee asked me to ordain him a priest the next Sunday. We left the mission the next week. Now he serves as a bishop in a ward close to where the family had lived for so many years. It was such a small act of faith that prompted that prayer on that June morning, but such a tender voice that was gratefully heard to accomplish the will of the Lord for that good man.

As we continue with section 18, we find the following.

Section 18:
> Worship the Father in *my* name (v. 40)
> And by your hands, *I* will work a marvelous work (v. 44)
> That they may come unto the kingdom of *my* Father (v. 44)
> The blessings which *I* gave unto you are above all things (v. 45)

Section 18 gives profound testimony from the Savior about His Father. Over and over again, we understand the divine relationship between the Only Begotten Son and His Eternal Father. There is never an attempt to draw attention away from the Father. There is never a hint of self-serving interest. He gives the Father all honor and glory and respect for the work of salvation in the kingdom of the Father.

Finally, the spring of 1830 had arrived. Section 19 was given to Joseph Smith in March of that most significant year. We are taught yet again of the majestic Atonement and the promise of Christ to overcome all the works of Satan and provide the great judgment of all men. How is this to be done? "I, having accomplished and finished the will of him whose *I* am, even the Father, concerning *me*—having done this that *I* might subdue all things unto *myself*" (v. 2).

Section 19:
> *I* shall pass [judgment] upon the inhabitants (v. 3)
> *I* will explain unto you this mystery (v. 8)
> *I* speak unto you that are chosen in this thing (v. 9)
> That you may enter into *my* rest (v. 9)
> Endless is *my* name (v. 10)
> Keep the commandments which you have received by the hand of *my* servant Joseph (v. 13)
> It is by *my* almighty power that you have received them (v. 14)
> *I*, God, have suffered these things for all (v. 16)
> Would that *I* might not drink the bitter cup, and shrink (v. 18)
> Glory be to the Father, and *I* partook and finished *my* preparations (v. 19)
> *I* command you that you preach naught but repentance (v. 21)
> *I* am Jesus Christ (v. 24)
> *I* came by the will of the Father (v. 24)
> Pray always, and *I* will pour out *my* Spirit upon you (v. 38)

It is impossible to capture the magnitude of the teachings of the Savior in this section without a review of these few thoughts and phrases from His words. Suffice it to say, His ministry is exceedingly personal and powerful as depicted in these sections of the Doctrine and Covenants.

Joseph was assured by the Lord on the same day that the Church was organized that "Him have *I* inspired to move the cause of Zion in mighty power for good, and his diligence *I* know, and his prayers *I* have heard" (D&C 21:7). Over two hundred pages of sacred text would yet be received by the Prophet before his mortal ministry would conclude in 1844.

With this transition in the record, I will close my review of the personal ministry of Jesus Christ in the early sections of the Doctrine and Covenants.

The Savior said to Joseph Smith in March 1829, "But this generation shall have my word through you" (D&C 5:10). The theme of this symposium is likewise "You Shall Have My Word." I bear my testimony that the Lord Jesus Christ has indeed spoken to His servants in recent generations. I have heard His voice and know His words as His servant and as a member of His Church.

Some forty years ago, I was a young and new member of the stake presidency. At the conclusion of a Saturday evening session of stake conference, I was pondering upon subjects that I could speak about the next morning in the concluding session. As another member of the stake presidency announced the name and number of the closing hymn for the evening session, I heard, "'I Stand All Amazed,' hymn number 193." Imagine my surprise as the congregation began singing another hymn! I realized when driving home that evening that the Spirit had given me the topic and a three-verse outline of my talk for the Sunday conference session. I stand all amazed at the love Jesus offers me and thank Him with all my heart for the words He has shared with me through His power and His Spirit. I agree with Elder Oaks: "Revelation . . . should be a reality for every Latter-day Saint, because each has the gift of the Holy Ghost."[4]

I am one who can claim with Joseph Smith that the Book of Mormon is the keystone of my religion. I am one who can testify that a man can get closer to God by abiding by the precepts of that book than by any other book. But in addition, I testify that a man can get close to God by abiding by the additional words and personal witness of the Lord Jesus Christ in the Doctrine and Covenants. I bear testimony of these things as one of those who is a witness, ordained and sent forth to testify that God lives, that Jesus is the

Christ. The Holy Ghost will help us through this life. The Church of Jesus Christ of Latter-day Saints is the true Church on the earth today. We have a living prophet, President Thomas S. Monson, who follows in the footsteps of the first prophet of the Restoration, Joseph Smith. This Church holds the keys to salvation in the next life through authorized servants of God who walk the earth today. Many of you have taught the things Jesus has taught us in the Doctrine and Covenants as you have invited people to repent, and you have invited them to come unto Christ through the waters of baptism. You have bestowed upon them the gift of the Holy Ghost that they might walk with that consummate guide in their lives also. I thank God for sending His Holy Son to the earth in these latter days to teach as He taught: "*my* word, *my* rock, *my* church, and *my* gospel, that you [we] may know of a surety *my* doctrine" (D&C 11:16).

Notes

1. Dallin H. Oaks, *Life's Lessons Learned* (Salt Lake City: Deseret Book, 2011), 115.
2. Dieter F. Uchtdorf, "Waiting on the Road to Damascus," *Ensign*, May 2011, 70.
3. Quentin L. Cook, "The Doctrine of the Father," *Ensign*, February 2012, 36.
4. Oaks, *Life's Lessons Learned*, 115.

2

"That They Might Come to Understanding": Revelation as Process

Steven C. Harper

On a spring Sabbath in 1843, a gathering of Latter-day Saints opened their worship service with a hymn. Wilford Woodruff prayed, and "then Joseph the Seer arose & said It is not wisdom that we should have all knowledge at once presented before us but that we should have a little[. T]hen we can comprehend it."[1] Joseph had learned early in his prophetic ministry about the power of transcendent revelatory events, like his First Vision or his visits from Moroni. But he also learned that such events were part of the process by which revelation distilled over time. Like compound interest on investments, light and knowledge accumulate as revelatory events combine with insight from experience and thought.

In November 1831, as Joseph was preparing to publish his revelation texts, he sought and received a preface for them. In a revelatory event, he dictated the text that is now Doctrine and Covenants section 1. It sets forth the Lord's reason for revealing himself in process to Joseph as he did. "These commandments are of me," the Lord said, speaking of the revelation texts, "and were given unto my servants in their weakness, after the manner of their

---

Steven C. Harper is a professor of Church history and doctrine at Brigham Young University.

language, *that they might come to understanding*" (D&C 1:24; emphasis added). This passage is key in appreciating revelation as a process of communication between a divine being and mortal ones, a process that is not complete once the revelation text has been written or published or read, but rather once it has been internalized and acted upon. Revelation, in this sense, is best understood as a process that leads to understanding rather than an event in which knowledge is fully disclosed in an instant.

Elder David A. Bednar invited us to understand two patterns of the spirit of revelation. One is like turning on a light switch and dispelling darkness in an instant; this is what I mean by a revelatory event, like the First Vision or the reception of section 1. The other is like watching night turn into morning as the rising sun gradually and subtly replaces darkness.[2] This is what I mean by the process of revelation, which yields accumulated insight born of ongoing inspiration. Significantly, it was late in Joseph's life, not on his return from the Sacred Grove, when he articulated the idea that our wise Heavenly Father does not give us all knowledge at once, but in a process that we can understand. It was also late in his life that Joseph wrote reflectively about his remarkable, revelatory life. He reviewed his experiences with a veritable "who's who" of heavenly messengers—Moroni, Michael, Peter, James, John, Gabriel, and Raphael—"all declaring their dispensation . . . giving line upon line, precept upon precept; here a little, and there a little" (D&C 128:21). Joseph was remembering revelatory events in his past, but he had experienced enough to reflectively recognize that such events were part of the revelatory process.

"Revelation," according to Elder Bednar, "is communication from God to His children on the earth."[3] So a basic understanding of communication theory may help us understand the nature of revelation. In any communication there is an encoder that sends the signal, the decoder that receives it, and the noise between them that hinders perfect transmission and reception. In terms of communication, noise is not always audible. Sound can interrupt revelation, but other kinds of noise hinder communication too. One type, semantic noise, happens when the encoder sends signals that the decoder lacks the power to decipher. Imagine Joseph receiving revelation in Spanish or computer programming code; that would be an example of semantic noise. Another type, psychological noise, happens when a decoder's assumptions, prejudices, preconceived notions, or emotions prevent an accurate interpretation of the signal.

Revelation is communication in which God is a flawless, divine encoder, but mortals are the decoders. Various kinds of "noise" prevent perfect understanding. There is no evidence that Joseph Smith thought in technical terms of communication theory, but he understood these ideas well. He did not assume as we might that his revelation texts were faxed from heaven. He understood that the Lord could certainly send signals seamlessly, but he knew better than anyone else that he lacked the power to receive the messages immaculately or to recommunicate them perfectly. He considered it "an awful responsibility to write in the name of the Lord," as he put it, largely because he felt confined by what he called the "total darkness of paper pen and Ink and a crooked broken scattered and imperfect Language."[4]

Religion scholar David Carpenter described revelation as "a *process* mediated through language."[5] The very language whose communicative inadequacies Joseph lamented was the means by which God condescended to Joseph's level and condescends to ours. Remember the Lord's rationale in section 1: he gave the revelations "unto my servants in their weakness, after the manner of their language, [so] that they might come to understanding" (D&C 1:24). Joseph rightfully regarded his language as a deeply flawed medium for communication. Even so, the Lord consciously revealed the sections of the Doctrine and Covenants in Joseph's corrupt tongue, not his own "diction, dialect, or native language."[6] He revealed in the language Joseph could come to understand so that we too could come, by a process, to understand (see D&C 1:24). A divine encoder chose to communicate with his servants in their weakness in order to maximize their ability to comprehend. The communicative limits of Joseph's revelation texts are inherent not in the Lord who gave them but in the imperfect language spoken by his weak servants, who had to decode the divine messages with various kinds of noise inhibiting them. Brigham Young did not believe, as he put it, "that there is a single revelation, among the many God has given to the Church, that is perfect in its fulness. The revelations of God contain correct doctrine and principle, so far as they go; but it is impossible for the poor, weak, low, grovelling, sinful inhabitants of the earth to receive a revelation from the Almighty in all its perfections. He has to speak to us in a manner to meet the extent of our capacities."⁷ No wonder Joseph felt the weight of his calling and longed for a pure language.

Joseph also longed for friends who would sustain him and the imperfect texts he made of the revelations he received. In November 1831, he convened a council at the Johnson home in Hiram, Ohio, and said that "the Lord has bestowed a great blessing upon us in giving commandments and revelations." Joseph laid the manuscript revelations before his associates and asked for their help in getting them published. He testified that the contents of such a book should "be prized by this Conference to be worth to the Church the riches of the whole Earth."⁸ During the discussion Oliver Cowdery asked "how many copies of the Book of commandments it was the will of the Lord should be published in the first edition of that work?"⁹ The council eventually voted for ten thousand. It was in these council meetings, which went on for more than a week, that the Lord revealed the preface for the book, Doctrine and Covenants section 1. In it he essentially said that though he was a divine being, he communicated to mortals in their language so that they could come to understand (see D&C 1:24).¹⁰

Joseph's history tells us that the council engaged in a discussion "concerning revelations and language."¹¹ The discussion may well have raised the same issues discussed here about the kind of writing that can be considered scripture. Everyone in the room must have recognized that they were being asked to support a nearly twenty-six-year-old poorly educated farmer who was planning to publish ten thousand copies of revelations that were unequivocally declared to be the words of Jesus Christ, revelations that called their neighbors idolatrous, referred to Missourians as their enemies, commanded them all to repent, and foretold calamities upon those who continued in wickedness. Moreover, the revelation texts were not always properly punctuated, the spelling was not standardized, and the grammar was inconsistent.

Though lacking confidence in his own language, or perhaps even because of his limitations, Joseph was sure that his revelation texts were divine, if imperfect, productions. He promised the brethren present that they could know for themselves as well. Just a few days earlier, Joseph had prophesied that if the Saints could "all come together with one heart and one mind in perfect faith the vail [sic] might as well be rent to day as next week or any other time."¹² Seeking confirmation of the revelations, the brethren tried to rend the veil like the brother of Jared in the Book of Mormon. They failed.

Joseph asked the Lord why, and he received the answer in Doctrine and Covenants section 67.

In that text the Lord assured the Church leaders that he had heard their prayers and knew all the desires in their hearts. "There were fears in your hearts," he told them, and "this is the reason that ye did not receive" (D&C 67:3). He then testified of the truthfulness of the Book of Commandments and Revelations lying before them. They had been watching Joseph, listening to him talk, observing his imperfections, and wishing secretly, or perhaps even assuming, that they could do a better job than he; the Lord offered them the opportunity. He told them to have the wisest man in the council (or any of them who cared to) duplicate the simplest revelation in the manuscript revelation book before them. The Lord told the elders that if they succeeded in composing a pseudo-revelation text equal to the least of Joseph's, then they could justifiably say that they did not know the revelations were true. But if they failed, the Lord said he would hold them guilty unless they testified to the veracity of the revelations (see D&C 67). The Lord's words led the men to recognize that whatever imperfections the revelation texts showed—communicated as they were in "their language" (D&C 1:24), not God's—they conformed to divine laws, were full of holy principles, and were just, virtuous, and good. They could conclude on those criteria that even communicated with a "crooked broken scattered and imperfect Language," such revelations came from God.[13]

Joseph's history and other sources tell us how the brethren acted out the instructions in section 67 and became willing to testify before the world that the revelations were true, but not flawless literary productions. William McLellin, who had acted as scribe the preceding week as Joseph dictated section 66, now "endeavored to write a commandment like unto one of the least of the Lord's, but failed."[14] Joseph had asked the men present "what testimony they were willing to attach to these commandments which should shortly be sent to the world. A number of the brethren arose and said that they were willing to testify to the world that they knew that they were of the Lord," and Joseph revealed a statement for them to sign as witnesses.[15] The resulting "Testimony of the witnesses to the Book of the Lords commandments which he gave to his church through Joseph Smith Jr" reads, "We the undersigners feel willing to bear testimony to all the world of mankind to every creature upon all the face of all the Earth <&> upon the Islands of the Sea that god hath ~~bor~~ born record to our souls through the Holy Ghost shed forth upon us that these commandments are given by inspiration of God & are profitable for all men & are verily true we give this testimony unto the world the Lord being ~~my~~ <our> helper." William McLellin signed this statement, along with four others. Then other elders signed the statement in Missouri when the book arrived there for printing.[16]

The discussion about revelations and language concluded as "the brethren arose in turn and bore witness to the truth of the Book of Commandments. After which br. Joseph Smith jr arose & expressed his feelings and gratitude."[17] With a clear sense that the revelation texts were both human and divine, the November 1831 conference resolved that Joseph "correct those errors or mistakes which he may discover by the holy Spirit."[18] Joseph, and to some extent others (including Oliver Cowdery, Sidney Rigdon, and the printer William Phelps), thus edited his revelation texts repeatedly based on the same premise that informed their original receipt, namely that Joseph Smith represented the voice of God as he condescended to communicate in Joseph's broken language.[19] Joseph only admonished his associates that they "be careful not to alter the sense" of the revelation manuscripts.[20]

Editing the revelation texts was no simple matter, even without textual variants and other complexities. For example, Joseph Smith dictated a revelation on December 6, 1832, as Sidney Rigdon wrote it (D&C 86). Frederick Williams then transcribed the text. Orson Hyde copied this transcription. John Whitmer then recorded Hyde's copy in the Book of Commandments and Revelations, from which it was finally edited for publication. Few of Joseph's revelations made their textual journeys so arduously, but none of them is an urtext, meaning a pristine original. By a process imbued both with God's power and with faltering human mediation, Joseph somehow received the words of these texts and transmitted them to his scribe, who committed them to paper, then into manuscript books, and finally into published volumes of scripture. Not only were there both intentional and erroneous changes made at every step, but also, as a mortal decoder imprisoned by a broken language, Joseph originally received the revelations imperfectly. "He never considered the wording infallible" and he continued to revise and amend his revelation texts throughout his life to reflect his latest understanding and to increase their ability to communicate the mind of God.[21]

Revising, amending, and expanding earlier revelation texts is the prerogative of prophets, and Joseph Smith considered such revisions one of his major responsibilities. He revised the Bible, making hundreds of changes in the process that were designed not to restore lost or ancient text (as some of his revisions were) but rather to improve communication for a modern English-speaking audience. He edited the Book of Mormon after it was published in 1830, adding a clarifying clause to 1 Nephi 20:1 and revising numerous Hebraisms to communicate better with English readers, for example.

Similarly, Joseph edited his own revelation texts. He added information on priesthood offices or quorums to revelations that were originally received before such knowledge had been revealed to him. The current version of section 20 includes information about priesthood offices that was not known when that text was originally written on April 10, 1830. Section 42 now says that the bishop and his counselors should administer the law of consecration, but the Church's lone bishop did not yet have counselors when that text was originally written. Section 68, originally revealed in 1831, said that bishops should be chosen by a council of high priests; it now puts that responsibility in the hands of the First Presidency, which was organized in 1832.

In addition to incorporating more material as it became clear to him, Joseph and other "stewards over the revelations" (D&C 70:3) edited his revelation texts in order to make them communicate more clearly. The revelation in section 20, for example, originally said that one duty of an apostle was "to administer the flesh and blood of Christ," meaning the sacrament. Before publishing it in the Doctrine and Covenants, Joseph amended this clause to its current reading, namely, "to administer bread and wine—the emblems of the flesh and blood of Christ" (D&C 20:40). Section 7 is another text whose original wording may have been clear to Joseph but whose meaning would be ambiguous to us at best if Joseph had not clarified it. Given to answer the question of whether the Apostle John lived or died, the text originally had John asking the Lord, "Give unto me power that I may bring souls unto thee." Joseph amended it for publication in the Doctrine and Covenants so that it clarifies what John asked for and received: "Give unto me power over death, that I may live and bring souls unto thee" (D&C 7:2).

Joseph not only added newly revealed or clarifying text but also deleted some passages from his revelation texts that were no longer relevant, as in section 51's original instruction to Bishop Edward Partridge to obtain a deed for Leman Copley's land if Copley was willing, which he was not. Joseph apparently amended the law of consecration to reconcile its wording with changing legal dynamics. Moreover, he, Sidney Rigdon, and others made hundreds of simple changes for clarity of communication. For instance, they added surnames to given names mentioned in the texts so that readers who were not intimate with the situation and the subject of the revelation could make more sense of it. Oliver Cowdery reported to the Saints on the progress of this process, saying that the revelation texts "are now correct," adding, "if not in every word, at least in principle."[22]

Critics prey on the ignorance and assumptions of some Saints by writing about this process with clever titles like *Doctored Covenants*.[23] Why all the changes? they ask, but they are not on a quest for answers as much as they are trying to insinuate that the Church tries to keep its members ignorant of its sinister manipulations of scripture. Joseph, his associates, and their successors did not alter the revelation texts conspiratorially. Joseph revised his revelation texts with the sustaining vote of Church leaders and openly before the Saints. Noting that some critics present the many editorial changes made to the revelations as evidence that they are not true, President Boyd K. Packer observed, "They cite these changes, of which there are many examples, as though they themselves were announcing revelation, as though they were the only ones that knew of them. Of course there have been changes and corrections. Anyone who has done even limited research knows that. When properly reviewed, such corrections become a testimony for, not against, the truth of the books."[24]

William McLellin originally had that understanding, but he lost it. A week before he tried unsuccessfully to compose a pseudorevelation text, McLellin wrote the original dictation manuscript of section 66 as Joseph rendered the Lord's communication in the best words he had at his disposal. McLellin later testified that in this revelation the Lord answered every one of his intimate questions, which were unknown to Joseph. McLellin subsequently reported to his relatives that he had spent about three weeks with Joseph, "and from my acquaintance then and until now I can truely say I believe him to be a man of God. A Prophet, a Seer and Revelater to the church of christ." Later in the same letter, McLellin related, "We believe that Joseph Smith is a true Prophet or Seer of the Lord and that he <u>has</u> power and <u>does</u> receive revelations from

God, and that these revelations when received are of divine Authority in the church of Christ."[25]

William McLellin knew as well as anyone that Joseph received revelations, that they were both divine and human products, and that Joseph had been appointed by the Church to prepare them for publication, including revising "by the holy Spirit."[26] But in 1871, McLellin asserted that Joseph Smith had lost power to act for God in 1834 after Joseph and others edited the revelation texts for publication. "Now if the Lord gave those revelations," McLellin reasoned, "he said what he meant, and meant what he said."[27] Though he was present—a participant who knew better and who testified repeatedly with good evidence that Joseph's revelations were true—William McLellin later assumed, as many Latter-day Saints do, that Joseph "simply repeated word-for-word to his scribe what he heard God say to him." Grant Underwood, a careful analyst of Joseph's revelation texts, wrote that "Joseph seems to have had a healthy awareness of the inadequacy of finite, human language, including his own, to perfectly communicate an infinite, divine revelation."[28] McLellin, however, concluded that Joseph could receive revelation flawlessly and communicate it perfectly, and that everyone would understand the full import and meaning of his revelations in an instant, in a single event, as if by turning on a light switch.

Those who, like William McLellin, argue for perfect scriptures (which, notice, is not a scriptural doctrine) assume that divine communication is complete and perfect, that mortals can decode the divine without corruption. They do not recognize that it takes revelation to understand a revelation. Consider some examples. Six times in the Doctrine and Covenants the Lord says, "I come quickly" (33:18; 35:27; 39:24; 41:4; 49:28; 68:35). What does he mean? Does the adverb *quickly* mean "speedily" or does it mean "soon"? Both possibilities existed in Joseph's language.[29] All six instances of that prophecy were revealed by 1832. Because it has been so long since then, at least by our sense of time, should we conclude that the Lord meant not that he comes soon but that when he comes, it will be speedy? Or should we consider that our interpretation of *soon* is not the intended one? Of course, we need not conclude that it is either soon or speedy. It may be both. But if so, how should *soon* be understood?

Some passages of Joseph's revelations could not be understood well at the time they were received, not even by Joseph. The Lord, for example, told the earliest Saints who were called to settle Jackson County, Missouri, that Zion would be built there, but not yet. Rather, it would "follow after much tribulation" (D&C 58:2–4). How much, they could not have imagined, as the Lord explained: "Ye cannot behold with your natural eyes, for the present time, the design of your God concerning those things which shall come hereafter" (D&C 58:3). Again the Lord prophesied "much tribulation" in anticipation of Zion, but the depth, breadth, and length of that tribulation would be finally understood only in the process of time and experience (D&C 58:4).

After the bewildered Saints were driven from Jackson County, the Lord reminded Joseph of this tribulation clause, which had much more meaning in that context (see D&C 103:12). Then the Lord told Joseph that Zion in Missouri would "come by power," and he called for an army to march to Missouri to reclaim the Saints' land (D&C 103:15). Every man who subsequently marched thought that he would provide the military power the Lord must have meant. But when they arrived, the Lord taught them more as part of his process of revelation. He taught them that Zion would not yet be redeemed, that the Saints must "wait for a little season" (D&C 105:9). He taught that the power he intended was an endowment waiting for them in the temple back in Kirtland, Ohio, and that they should return there. Why had the Lord not spared them the trouble? Perhaps the Lord let them make the journey because they became sanctified in the process and were better positioned to understand the Lord's purposes after their tribulation than they were before. Joseph wrote, after several months of unjust imprisonment at Liberty, Missouri, "It seems to me that my heart will always be more tender after this than ever it was before." He recognized that experiences "give us that knowledge to understand the minds of the Ancients," like Abraham. "For my part," Joseph wrote, "I think I never could have felt as I now do if I had not suffered the wrongs that I have suffered."[30] Even though Joseph had been in the presence of God and Christ, and had entertained ministering angels and learned from them the mysteries of godliness, he still needed time and experience in order to process the revelations he had received and internalize their implications. Joseph processed much revelation in that stinking dungeon cell, where he learned that what had seemed like purposeless, interminable suffering to him was a small moment of exalting experience to God. He wrote, as a result of his revelations and reflections, that "the things of God Are of deep import, and time and expeariance and carful and pondurous and solom though[ts] can only find them out."³¹

In addition to time, experience, careful pondering, and solemn thought, the Holy Ghost is vital to the process of revelation. When elders were bewildered by strange, counterfeit spiritual gifts in the spring of 1831, the Lord invited them to come and reason with him, "that ye may understand" (D&C 50:10). The Lord asked the elders questions that caused them to think carefully and solemnly about their recent experiences, and to compare their experiences with the Holy Spirit with the manifestations they had observed but not understood. Having done such careful thinking, they were ready to understand that unless the Spirit of God mediated communication, that communication was not coming from God. "Why is it that ye cannot understand and know," the Lord asked the elders, "that he that receiveth the word by the Spirit of truth receiveth it as it is preached by the Spirit of truth?" Only communication mediated by the Holy Ghost enables the encoder ("he that preacheth") and the decoder ("he that receiveth") to "understand one another." Communication by the power of the Holy Ghost is edifying. It builds and grows and illuminates line upon line until understanding is full and complete and "perfect" (D&C 50:22–25; see also D&C 93:26–28). Without the Holy Ghost, communication can be a dark, confusing process. The Holy Ghost is the perfect mediator of otherwise imperfect communication; revelation is communication that is mediated by the power of the Holy Ghost. Reading a revelation text by the power of the Holy Ghost and thinking about it carefully over time and in light of experience will enable us to "come to understanding" (D&C 1:24).

In this way of thinking about revelation as a process by which we come to understand, the question is not whether the Lord said what he meant and meant what he said. The question, rather, is whether we have understood what he meant and acted obediently on what he said. The question is not whether words were accurately written "with ink" or "on tablets of stone," but whether they were written "with the Spirit of the living God . . . on tablets of human hearts" (NRSV 2 Corinthians 3:3).

It seems likely that the Lord will continue to reveal to us in our language so that we might come to understand by experience and careful thought in light of the Holy Ghost. Such language is not stagnant. Unless enlivened by the Holy Ghost, ink on a page arranged into words will not communicate with us all that the Lord intends, even if it was originally perfect. Prophets will continue to guide us as we continue to receive revelation actively in an ongoing quest for light and knowledge. They may amend the scriptures "by the holy Spirit," as Joseph did, when they discern ways to communicate with today's global congregation more clearly.[32]

The prophets have made changes to the scriptures throughout history, including in this dispensation. I remember how as a missionary I ignorantly tried to refute charges that there had been hundreds of textual changes made to the Book of Mormon. Today, thanks to the work of devoted, faithful Latter-day Saint scholars, it is clear that there have been thousands of such changes, including many by Joseph Smith and others by prophets since.[33] Similarly, the recent publication of a critical edition of Joseph Smith's New Translation of the Bible shows that he made thousands of changes to the biblical text as well.[34] We can choose to recoil in ignorance and disbelief from such facts, or we can rejoice that we live in a time of wonderful discovery of our scriptural texts.

Perhaps we can learn from history about how to approach this moment of enlightenment. European scholars in the early modern period (1500–1800) began to study the Bible critically, using historical, textual, and linguistic analyses to assess the composition of biblical texts. They discovered that the oldest source materials for the Bible show the influence of several writers of what we casually call the books of Moses, all written from different periods and perspectives. It became obvious that the biblical texts had been revised and redacted again and again. As evidence and arguments mounted that biblical texts had been composed in a more complicated process than many believers had assumed, some concluded that mortal influence on scripture making precluded the possibility that the Bible was divinely inspired. Other people retrenched behind fundamentalism, the idea set forth by a group of American Protestants in the late nineteenth and early twentieth centuries that the Bible is inerrant. These two camps created a false dilemma, unnecessarily concluding that the scriptures must be either divine or human texts.

Latter-day Saints are now faced with a similar situation regarding Restoration scripture. In 2009, the Church Historian's Press published the *Joseph Smith Papers: Manuscript Revelation Books*, a massive eight-pound volume that includes painstaking transcriptions and high-resolution images of the earliest extant manuscripts of Joseph Smith's revelation texts. As with the oldest biblical manuscripts, these texts are full of evidence that the revelations were revised and redacted. Studying them leads to "a richer, more nuanced view, one that sees Joseph as more than a mere human fax machine through whom God communicated revelation texts composed in heaven."[35] This is not a problem for believers who think of revelation as a process of communication between God and mortals whereby we come to understand the revelations. It is not a problem for Saints who believe the eighth and ninth articles of faith and the title page of the Book of Mormon. The definition of scripture set forth in the Doctrine and Covenants does not envision a pristine, unchangeable set of marks on a page but rather describes scripture as "the mind of the Lord" communicated "by the Holy Ghost" through fallible servants in their imperfect languages (D&C 68:3–4; see also D&C 1:24). However, the reality of these revelation texts and the process of revelation they evidence can be a problem for those who make fundamentalist assumptions about scripture—assumptions that are not doctrinal, scriptural, or consistent with the teachings of Joseph Smith.

The doctrine of The Church of Jesus Christ of Latter-day Saints is that God has revealed himself in the past, does so now, and will yet, but that the records of such revelations are not the revelations themselves; they are but representations captured in our language so that we might come to understand them if we consider the words carefully and solemnly, in light of experience and the Holy Spirit. We make no claim that any scripture is inerrant or infallible. In fact, the title page of the Book of Mormon asserts that even that most correct book is a combination of "the things of God" and "the mistakes of men." Such was Joseph Smith's understanding of scripture, including the scriptures based on his revelation texts. Joseph knew better than anyone else that the words he dictated were both human and divine, the voice of God clothed in the words of his own limited, early American English vocabulary. He regarded himself as a revelator whose understanding accumulated over time. Joseph recognized as a result of the revelatory process that the texts of his revelations were not set in stone. Rather, he felt responsible to revise and redact them to reflect his latest understanding. He was always open, in other words, to receive more revelation. He knew, too, especially as he reflected with the aid of much experience, that a loving God sometimes turns on the lights in an instant, but even then it takes time for our eyes to adjust and then it requires experience for us to make sense of what we see.

Notes

1. Wilford Woodruff Journal, May 14, 1843, Yelrome, Hancock County, Illinois, in Joseph Smith, *The Words of Joseph Smith*, ed. Andrew F. Ehat and Lyndon W. Cook (Provo, UT: Religious Studies Center, Brigham Young University, 1980), 200–202.

2. David A. Bednar, "The Spirit of Revelation," *Ensign*, May 2011, 87.

3. Bednar, "Spirit of Revelation," 87.

4. Manuscript History, Book A-1, Church History Library, The Church of Jesus Christ of Latter-day Saints, Salt Lake City, handwriting of Willard Richards, 161–62. Joseph Smith to William W. Phelps, November 27, 1832, in Dean C. Jessee, comp. and ed., *Personal Writings of Joseph Smith*, rev. ed. (Salt Lake City: Deseret Book; Provo, UT: Brigham Young University Press, 2002), 284–87.

5. David Carpenter, "Revelation in Comparative Perspective: Lessons for Interreligious Dialogue," Journal of Ecumenical Studies 29, no. 2 (Spring 1992): 185–86; emphasis in original.

6. Richard Lyman Bushman, *Joseph Smith: Rough Stone Rolling* (New York: Knopf, 2005), 174.

7. Brigham Young, in *Journal of Discourses* (Liverpool: F. D. Richards; London: Latter-day Saints' Book Depot, 1855), 2:314.

8. Far West Record, November 1, 1831, Church History Library.

9. Far West Record, November 12–13, 1831.

10. Far West Record, November 1, 1831.

11. Manuscript History, Book A-1, 161–62, Church History Library; also in *History of the Church of Jesus Christ of Latter-day Saints*, ed. B. H. Roberts, 2nd ed. rev. (Salt Lake City: Deseret Book, 1980), 1:224. See also Jan Shipps and John W. Welch, eds., *The Journals of William E. McLellin, 1831–1836* (Urbana: University of Illinois Press; Provo, UT: BYU Studies, 1994), 251.

12. Far West Record, October 15, 1831.

13. Manuscript History, Book A-1, 161–62, Church History Library, handwriting of Willard Richards. Joseph Smith to William W. Phelps, November 27, 1832, in *Personal Writings of Joseph Smith*, 284–87.

14. Manuscript History, Book A-1, Church History Library, 161–62.

15. Far West Record, November 1, 1831.

16. Robin L. Jensen, Robert J. Woodford, Steven C. Harper, eds., *Manuscript Revelation Books*, vol. 1 in the Revelations and Translations series of *The Joseph Smith Papers*, eds. Dean C. Jessee, Ronald K. Esplin, and Richard Lyman Bushman (Salt Lake City: Church Historian's Press, 2009), 214–15.

17. Far West Record, November 1–2, 1831.

18. Kirtland Council Minutes, November 8, 1831, Church History Library.

19. Joseph's journal entry for December 1, 1832, for instance, says that he "wrote and corrected revelations &c." Dean C. Jessee, Mark Ashurst-McGee, and Richard L. Jensen, eds., *Journals, Volume 1: 1832–1839*, vol. 1 of the Journals series of *The Joseph Smith Papers*, eds. Dean C. Jessee, Ronald K. Esplin, and Richard Lyman Bushman (Salt Lake City: Church Historian's Press, 2008), 10.

20. Joseph Smith to William W. Phelps, July 31, 1832, in *Personal Writings of Joseph Smith*, 284–87.

21. Bushman, *Rough Stone Rolling*, 174.

22. Oliver Cowdery, *The Evening and the Morning Star* (1835; repr., Burlington, WI: n.p., 1992), 16. Grant Underwood elaborates more examples of revisions in Grant Underwood, "Revelation, Text, and Revision: Insight from the Book of Commandments and Revelations," *BYU Studies* 48, no. 3 (2009): 77.

23. Greg Anderson, *Doctored Covenants* (Salt Lake City: Modern Microfilm, 1963).

24. Boyd K. Packer, in Conference Report, April 1974, 137.

25. *Journals of William E. McLellin*, 79–84.

26. Minute Book 2, November 8, 1831, Church History Library.

27. Stan Larson and Samuel J. Passey, eds., *The William E. McLellin Papers, 1854–1880* (Salt Lake City: Signature Books, 2007), 474–75; *Joseph Smith Papers, Revelations and Translations, Vol. 1: Manuscript Revelation Books*, xxix.

28. Underwood, "Revelation, Text, and Revision,"78.

29. *Noah Webster's First Edition of an American Dictionary of the English Language* (San Francisco: Foundation for American Christian Education, 1967), s.v. "quickly."

30. Joseph Smith to Presendia Huntington Buell, March 15, 1839, Liberty, Missouri, in *Personal Writings of Joseph Smith*, 386–87.

31. Joseph Smith, Hyrum Smith, Lyman Wight, Caleb Baldwin, and Alexander McRae to Edward Partridge and the Church, March 20, 1839, Liberty, Missouri, Church History Library; *Personal Writings of Joseph Smith*, 388–407.

32. Minute Book 2, November 8, 1831, Church History Library.

33. For example, see "The Book of Mormon Critical Text Project," *Journal of Book of Mormon Studies* 7, no. 1 (1998): 30.

34. Scott H. Faulring, Kent P. Jackson, and Robert J. Matthews, eds., *Joseph Smith's New Translation of the Bible: Original Manuscripts* (Provo, UT: Brigham Young University Religious Studies Center, 2004), *passim*.

35. Underwood, "Revelation, Text, and Revision," 78.

3

"I Will Send You Elijah the Prophet"

Kenneth L. Alford

During the night of Sunday, September 21, 1823, at the dawn of the gospel's restoration, the angel Moroni visited the teenager Joseph Smith Jr. and announced "that he was a messenger sent from the presence of God" (Joseph Smith—History 1:33). After telling young Joseph about the Book of Mormon plates, Moroni "commenced quoting the prophecies of the Old Testament," including Malachi 4:5–6, but he did so "with a little variation from the way it reads in our Bibles" (Joseph Smith—History 1:36). Echoing the prophet Malachi, Moroni prophesied that Elijah would return "before the coming of the great and dreadful day of the Lord" to "plant in the hearts of the children the promises made to the fathers, and the hearts of the children shall turn to their fathers" (D&C 2:1–2). Of all the scriptural passages Moroni taught Joseph Smith that night, only one has been included in the Doctrine and Covenants (D&C 2). The prophecy of Elijah's return was also included in the Nephite record (see 3 Nephi 25:5–6) by the Savior during his ministry in the Americas and in Joseph Smith—History 1:38–39, making it available in all four of the Latter-day Saint standard works. President

---

Kenneth L. Alford is an associate professor of Church history and doctrine at Brigham Young University.

Joseph Fielding Smith called this prophecy "perhaps the most direct promise recorded in the scriptures."[1]

Elijah did return, as prophesied. On Easter Sunday, April 3, 1836, in the newly dedicated Kirtland Temple, he appeared—with other heavenly messengers—to Joseph Smith Jr. and Oliver Cowdery in order to restore essential priesthood "keys of this dispensation" (D&C 110:16). The Savior appeared first and accepted the recently completed temple built in his name. Moses appeared next and "committed unto us the keys of the gathering of Israel from the four parts of the earth," and then Elias, who "committed the dispensation of the gospel of Abraham" (D&C 110:11–12).[2] Elijah was the final visitor, and he restored the all-important keys of the sealing power as "spoken of by the mouth of Malachi" (D&C 110:14). Prior to his departure, Elijah proclaimed to Joseph that "the keys of this dispensation are committed into your hands" (D&C 110:16).[3]

Christian and Jewish theologians had worked for centuries to unlock the meaning of Malachi's prophecy. A British scholar in 1832, for example, noted that this prophecy "is peculiarly worthy of our closest attention."[4] Another Christian writer, in 1835, recognized that the prophecy of Elijah's return was "the last words, of the last of the prophets, under the Mosaic dispensation; and [that] circumstance, alone, [was] sufficient to give them interest in our eyes."[5]

Latter-day Saint doctrine regarding the mission of Elijah is unique. By reviewing what other Christian theologians taught on this subject prior to 1836 and then comparing it with Latter-day Saint scriptures and prophetic commentary, we can better understand the differences. This essay investigates how early nineteenth-century Christian theologians answered three key questions regarding Malachi's prophecy. First, *how* would Elijah return? Second, *when* would Elijah return? And finally, *why* would Elijah return?

How Would Elijah Return?

Questions surrounding Elijah's return and the fulfillment of Malachi's prophecy have consumed a surprising amount of spoken and printed words. In focusing on *how* Elijah would return, Christian scholars have attempted to answer the following: (1) was John the Baptist the "Elijah" promised by Malachi, and (2) would Elijah the prophet himself return to the earth?

Was John the Baptist the promised Elijah? There is a good deal of evidence within the verses of the New Testament to support the belief that John the

Baptist fulfilled Malachi's promise, and many Christian scholars argue exactly that. When the angel Gabriel visited Zacharias to announce the birth of his son, John (the Baptist), he clearly echoed Malachi's prophecy stating that "he [John] shall go before him [Christ] in the spirit and power of Elias, to turn the hearts of the fathers to the children" (Luke 1:17). Later, when John began his ministry, his first conversation recorded in scripture also involves Malachi's prophecy. Jewish priests and Levites sent from Jerusalem asked John, "Who art thou?" and he responded, "I am not the Christ." Unsatisfied, the Jewish leaders then asked John, "What then? Art thou Elias? And he saith, I am not. Art thou that prophet? And he answered, No" (John 1:19–21).

Part of the confusion surrounding whether or not John the Baptist was "Elias" derived from the fact, as noted in the LDS Bible Dictionary, that the name Elias has multiple meanings. Two relevant definitions are that Elias is the Greek (New Testament) form of the Hebrew (Old Testament) name Elijah. Elias is also "a title for one who is a forerunner."[6] The Jewish leaders were asking John if he was Elijah returning as prophesied by Malachi.

In the book of Matthew, the Savior is quoted as saying, "For all the prophets and the law prophesied until John. And if ye will receive it, this is Elias, which was for to come" (Matthew 11:13–14). Elias is also mentioned prominently in the Gospel accounts of the Savior's Transfiguration. In the Gospel of Mark, the following dialogue with the Savior is recorded following his transfiguration: "And they asked him, saying, Why say the scribes that Elias must first come? And he answered and told them, Elias verily cometh first, and restoreth all things. . . . But I say unto you, That Elias is indeed come, and they have done unto him whatsoever they listed" (Mark 9:11–13).

Based on the previously listed Gospel verses, many Christian theologians identified the fulfillment of Malachi's prophecy with the person and mission of John the Baptist. Here are representative statements from early nineteenth-century theologians and religious scholars:

> 1814: "For our Saviour does not say simply that John was Elias. . . . [This] is the Elias who, according to the prediction [in Malachi], was to come."[7]
>
> 1822: "Elijah could be no other than John the Baptist. . . . John the Baptist was the Elias promised . . . whence it doth plainly follow,

that they who do not think John the Baptist, and he only, was the Elias mentioned by the prophet [Malachi], must [be] mistake[n]."[8]

1826: "Christ identifies John with Elias, as the predicted forerunner."[9]

1827: "Jesus Christ has instructed to consider it [Malachi 4:5–6] as accomplished in the person of John Baptist."[10]

1832: "If Jesus Christ is to be believed Elijah had already come even in his day. He was no other than John Baptist."[11]

1835: "With good reason, then, does Malachi apply to the son of Zacharias, the title of Elijah the Tishbite; and in very truth, we may believe, that, in him the prophecy has been fulfilled ... [Matthew xi. 14]."[12]

Other scholars of that period, though, expressed the view that Malachi's prophecy applied instead to both Christ "as well as his forerunner John the Baptist, who should come in the spirit and power of Elijah."[13] Some theologians did not accept that John the Baptist was "that Elias" (meaning Elijah), noting that "the Elias mentioned by Malachi was to turn the hearts of the fathers to the children, and was, according to our Saviour's acknowledgement, to restore or set all things in order; which seemeth not to have been done by the ministry of the Baptist, who continued but a short time, and did no such things as these words seem to imply; it remains, therefore, that these words should be fulfilled by an Elias, who should be the forerunner of Christ's second advent."[14]

To those who argued that John the Baptist did not fulfill Malachi's prophecy because he was not actually Elijah the prophet returned from the dead (as the Jews expected), the Reverend Charles Simeon, an influential English cleric, reminded his readers in 1832 that the Jews called their Messiah "David," not because they expected him to actually be King David returned but because "he was typified by David." By analogy he then asked, "Why may not John [the Baptist], who came *in the spirit and power of Elias*, bear *his* name?"[15]

Still other Christian writers decided that "with respect to the meaning of the prophecy, it makes no difference whether Jesus was right in the person to whom he applied it."[16] They believed Jesus made a mistake by identifying John as Elias. "The question of the disciples [Mark 9:11] was put to him [Christ] before he had time to reflect upon the event, or deduce the obvious conclusions, which a short consideration would not have failed to suggest."[17] Other Christian scholars went further, questioning "this imagination of the appearance of the Tishbite [Elijah]" and wondering also if "the doctrine of the millennium . . . must be true."[18]

What a blessing it is to have latter-day prophets who can speak authoritatively to answer questions like this. Joseph Smith Jr. received the answer in 1831 as he worked with Sidney Rigdon on the new translation of the Bible. According to the Joseph Smith Translation of Matthew 11:15, the Lord clearly stated that John "was the Elias, who was for to come and prepare all things." The Lord inspired the Prophet to add an additional verse after Matthew 17:12, which reads as follows: "But I say unto you, *Who is Elias? Behold, this is Elias, whom I send to prepare the way before me*" (Joseph Smith Translation, Matthew 17:13; emphasis added). Joseph Smith also corrected the following verse to read: "Then the disciples understood that he spake unto them of John the Baptist, *and also of another who should come and restore all things, as it is written by the prophets*" (Joseph Smith Translation, Matthew 17:14; emphasis added). John the Baptist, serving as the forerunner of the Messiah, most certainly served as an Elias—in partial, but not complete, fulfillment of Malachi's prophecy. With an understanding that Elijah's return could apply to more than one circumstance, one nineteenth-century theologian correctly suggested that this prophecy possessed "like many of the prophecies, a double sense,—a sense applicable, on the one hand, to the Baptist, and which has been fulfilled in him;—and, on the other, to Elijah himself, and which remains yet to be fulfilled." He observed that "many of the prophecies of Scripture have a double sense, and are to be interpreted accordingly."[19]

Would Elijah personally return? Some Christian clerics left open the possibility that it was possible that while John the Baptist could certainly be considered an Elias, in fulfillment of Malachi's prophecy, it did not preclude additional and later fulfillment of the same prophecy. The Protestant theologian James Anderson argued in 1835 that no "calm inquirer after the truth, [should] be perplexed or offended, at this double meaning of the sacred prophecies; on the contrary, he will recognize, in this very circumstance, a fresh evidence of their divine original. For he will perceive, that, this double meaning does not arise . . . from any doubt 'as to their fulfillment in *either* sense, but from a foreknowledge of their accomplishment in *both*.'" He asked why the possibility of a double prophetic meaning should "not apply to the words of Malachi" and allow us to "believe that Elijah will again personally appear upon earth, to prepare the way for the second coming of the Lord?" Realizing he may have overreached, he backtracked a little, stating,

> I am not prepared to say, that this opinion is *not* correct; because it is difficult to prove a negative in any instance;—and much more difficult must it be, of course, with regard to the future counsels of the unseen God. To deny, therefore, the possibility of such an interpretation being correct, would be as absurd as if mariners, upon a voyage of discovery, were to determine that there could be no land, because they can discern nothing but sea. Still, it may be doubted, whether the truth of this opinion can be ever satisfactorily established, in our present state of knowledge; and, whether, in seeking to establish it, we may not be in danger of wasting our time, our strength, and the best energies of our nature, in the prosecution of a vain pursuit.[20]

Subsequent prophetic pronouncements have answered those questions.

Christian traditions regarding Elijah's return have often seemed to intermix with longstanding Jewish traditions. An 1827 Protestant writer noted that it was "a standing tradition among the Jews, that their Shiloh, or Messiah, their avenger and king, is not to appear till the coming of Elijah; and they are persuaded that they have had one Elijah, who is to appear again at the renewing of the world. Elijah, according to them, is to introduce the great sabbath, the great Messiah, and the general revolution of all things. This notion has been received among Christians. Elijah is to come to declare the dissolution of this world, and a new order of things," and he then declared his personal belief that "almost all the fanatics expect an Elijah."[21]

Antoine Augustin Calmet, a French Catholic theologian, taught that the "fathers and commentators have generally explained this passage (Mal. Iv, 5,) as relating to the final judgment and the second coming of the Savior; It has been the constant tradition of both the Synagogue and the Church, that the Prophet Elias will appear really, and in person, previous to the end of the world."[22] Several Protestant theologians took a similar view. Nathaniel Homes wrote in 1833 that "an Elijah [is] yet to come . . . either (as we said) *personally*,— that is, he himself *individually* in his own person; or else personatedly,—that is, (if I may so speak) *specifically*, being represented by one of the like kind and degree of parts exactly like unto him; viz. mighty in spirit and action . . . when he shall *'restore all things.'*"²³

Homes and others argued correctly that John the Baptist's mission as an Elias did not represent complete fulfillment of Malachi's prophecy—"the *all* of Elijah's coming" as Homes phrased it.²⁴ Adherents to this point of view noted that when the Savior spoke of Elijah's coming (see Matthew 17:12) he spoke in the present tense "intimating that he [Elijah] is still coming. . . . Therefore as Christ comes twice, so with the proportionable decorum, his harbinger comes twice, both times to usher in his master. The one is past in John Baptist; the other is to *come*, in him that is still called and expected by the name of Elijah."²⁵ Another Protestant theologian, writing in 1834, argued that the angel Gabriel's declaration to Zacharias that his son, John, "shall go before him [the Messiah] in . . . [the] spirit and power [of Elias]" (Luke 1:17) actually implies an additional "appearance of Elijah in person."²⁶

Protestant thinking on this subject was not consistent. One 1801 article went so far as to suggest that "the name Elijah (Malachi iv. 5) is a corrupt reading for Enoch. . . . It was very natural for Malachi to announce the coming of another Enoch before the second judgment, before the other great and dreadful day of the Lord. Whereas the name of Elijah is strangely unsuitable."²⁷ Taking an alternate view, the Reverend John Fry concluded in 1822 that "John's ministry was not what was ultimately intended . . . by Elijah in Malachi; but that these symbols must have a more remote and fuller accomplishment hereafter. . . . John, in no sense, 'restored all things;' but Elijah, or whatever be intended by Elijah's coming, will."²⁸

Writing in rebuttal to Calmet and fellow Protestants with similar views, the 1832 *Christian Messenger* suggested that it was nothing more than "Jewish superstition" to look "for the return of the old prophet Elijah in person."²⁹ In an overreaching attempt to speak on behalf of all Protestants, the writers stated that Protestants reject this "groundless tradition" and "unite in rejecting . . . the *traditions* of the Synagogue and the mother Church. This opinion, therefore, that Elias or Elijah will personally re-appear previous to the end of the world, and the great day of final judgment is abandoned."³⁰ In 1835, a few months prior to Elijah's actual visit in Kirtland, the Reverend Edward Johnstone wrote that those who looked forward to Elijah's actual return "erroneously expect him" and misunderstood "the prediction of Malachi which foretold the coming of the Lord . . . supposing that He was to come in power and majesty . . . and make Jerusalem the metropolis of the world." Elijah the Tishbite would not, he wrote, "in his own person, return from heaven, as the Lord's messenger and forerunner."[31] Yet that is what occurred in Ohio a few months later.

In 1835 Anderson noted that "however plausible may be the arguments, and however ingenious the hypothesis, which are framed in support of this, or of any other interpretation of unfulfilled prophecies, we cannot . . . take them to our bosoms, with the same unreserved and implicit confidence. . . . For, in the absence of any specific revelation explaining it, a prophecy can only be interpreted by the event; and if the prophecy be unfulfilled, i.e. if the event have not yet come to pass,—how can we possibly take upon ourselves, to determine the precise mode, in which it shall come to pass?"[32] Indeed! Latter-day Saints should recognize that without the declarations of modern prophets stating that Elijah the prophet had returned, they would also be left to ponder when, where, and how Malachi's prophecy might be fulfilled.

Nineteenth-century Christian theologians could not adequately explain or interpret Malachi's prophecy. As Elder Matthias F. Cowley, a Latter-day Saint Apostle, pointed out:

> When we ask Catholic and Protestant ministers if an angel has come to any of them with the everlasting Gospel, they answer in the negative, and deride the idea of new revelation. Ask them if Elijah the Prophet has come to them, to plant in the hearts of the children the promise made to the fathers. They say no. . . . The very question itself is treated with utter astonishment, and the man who asks it is regarded as being erratic. We must therefore turn from sects having forms of godliness "but denying the power thereof," to other sources to find some one who has received, or shall receive, the revelations of the Almighty in the last days.[33]

Elder Howard W. Hunter, a Latter-day Saint Apostle and later Church President, suggested that "no passage in scripture gives students of the Old Testament greater problems of interpretation than this one in the Book of Malachi. . . . Without further revelation we would be left in darkness as to his [Elijah's] mission and the meaning of the promise stated by Malachi."[34] Church President Joseph Fielding Smith explained that the "reason for this stumbling is due largely to the failure of *Bible* commentators to comprehend that it is both possible and reasonable for an ancient prophet, who lived nearly 1,000 years before the time of Christ, to be sent in these days."[35] Joseph Smith had been expecting Elijah's return since Moroni's 1823 instruction to him that the Lord "will reveal *unto you* the *Priesthood*, by the hand of Elijah" (D&C 2:1; emphasis added).[36] Doctrine and Covenants 110 declares unequivocally that the Old Testament Prophet Elijah personally returned on April 3, 1836, in Kirtland, Ohio, in fulfillment of Malachi 4:5–6.

When Would Elijah Return?

The scriptures state that if Elijah did not return, the Lord would "smite the earth with a curse" (Malachi 4:6) and "the whole earth would be utterly wasted at his [Christ's] coming" (D&C 2:3). Malachi prophesied that Elijah would return "before the coming of the great and dreadful day of the Lord" (Malachi 4:5 and D&C 2:1). For devout Jews throughout the centuries, it has been almost as though Elijah never really left. They believe Elijah is an unseen witness at every circumcision ceremony, and during Passover each year Jewish families invite Elijah to enter their home and sit in a seat reserved for him.[37]

Christian ministers and writers have vigorously debated the exact meaning of "the great and dreadful day of the Lord." Some scholars argued that it meant "the consummation of all earthly things"; other intellectuals claimed that it referred to "the subversion of the Jewish state and polity" or "the final destruction of the Jews."[38] Some scholars were so certain that their understanding was correct, they proclaimed that "no Protestant will question [this doctrine] unless he is prepared to go back to the traditions and fooleries of the dark ages."[39] Some theologians believed that the great and dreadful day referred to "the destruction of Jerusalem." Others believed that it was "the day of final retribution; and that Elijah, the real and personal Elijah, shall proclaim the coming of that day."[40] Still others admitted that they did not know what the great and dreadful day meant, only that it was not fulfilled during the Savior's life—"the gospel day was not the great and terrible day of the Lord, but the visitation of mercy."[41]

Latter-day scripture and modern prophets, seers, and revelators have given us a better understanding of the great and dreadful day. D&C 110 reminds us that Elijah was "sent, before the great and dreadful day of the Lord come" (D&C 110:14), which eliminates all speculation that the announced day had occurred before 1836. Two verses later, Elijah told Joseph Smith and

Oliver Cowdery that "by this [his coming and bestowing priesthood keys] ye may know that the great and dreadful day of the Lord is near, even at the doors" (D&C 110:16). D&C 128:17 and 138:46 also reference "the great and dreadful day of the Lord" which modern prophets and Apostles have defined as "Christ's second coming" which will be "the end of the world" when "Jehovah, the Messiah, will come in glory. The wicked will all be destroyed."[42]

Why Would Elijah Return?

As Elder Henry B. Eyring noted, "It is important to know why the Lord promised to send Elijah."[43] It is on this question that early nineteenth-century scholars proposed the fewest number of possible answers. Jewish scholars have generally been more forthright and declarative than their Christian counterparts on this subject—teaching that Elijah's return was necessary so that he could, among other things, anoint the Messiah prior to his appearance. The Qahal Qadosh Gadol (Great Congregation) Synagogue in Jerusalem actually has a chair mounted near the ceiling in one of its worship rooms for Elijah to use when he shall anoint the Messiah. For centuries this congregation "cherished an old *shofar* (ram's horn trumpet) and oil jug in a niche in one of the synagogue walls. Tradition whispered from generation to generation that with this very shofar the prophet Elijah would announce the coming of the Messiah and with oil poured from this ancient juglet the Messiah would be anointed."[44]

More important than asking *whether* Elijah would return is asking and understanding *why* Elijah would return. Malachi stated there was something connected to Elijah's return that would "turn the heart of the fathers to the children, and the heart of the children to their fathers" (Malachi 4:6). In September 1823, Moroni slightly modified that wording, stating that Elijah's visit "shall *plant* in the hearts of the *children* the *promises made* to the fathers, and the hearts of the children shall turn to their fathers" (D&C 2:2; emphasis added).

Christian scholars prior to Elijah's 1836 return speculated about Malachi's meaning. An 1823 scriptural commentary suggested that turning the hearts of the fathers to the children meant only that Elijah "should preach to young and old, conversion and repentance."[45] An 1832 book of religious discourses proposed that turning the hearts meant the "*harmonious* expectation of the Messiah; 'fathers *with* their children, and children *with* their fathers.'"[46] And in 1835, Anderson suggested that Malachi's words "might be rendered, with equal correctness, and perhaps with greater force of meaning, 'to turn the hearts of the fathers *with* the children;' to bring all, i.e. of every age and rank, to the work of repentance, and the prayer of faith."[47]

With knowledge provided by the Restoration of the gospel, President Joseph Fielding Smith explained that the fathers mentioned by Malachi are "our dead ancestors who died without the privilege of receiving the gospel, but who received the promise that the time would come when that privilege would be granted them." The children referred to "are those now living who are preparing genealogical data and who are performing the vicarious ordinances in the temples." He further explained that the "turning of the hearts of the children to the fathers is placing or planting in the hearts of the children that feeling and desire which will inspire them to search out the records of the dead."[48] Temple ordinances and the sealing of families eternally together became possible because of Elijah's return.

Joseph Smith also stressed the importance of receiving the keys of the sealing power. He explained in September 1842 that "the great and grand secret of the whole matter . . . consists in obtaining the powers of the Holy Priesthood. For him to whom these keys are given there is no difficulty in obtaining a knowledge of facts in relation to the salvation of the children of men, both as well for the dead as for the living" (D&C 128:11). Elijah's visit enables us to be prepared when Christ returns (see D&C 38:30).

Blessings of the Restoration

Elijah's return was a mission of eternal significance. Temple ordinances are able to bind families eternally together because the sealing keys are once again in the hands of the Lord's authorized servants. Latter-day Saints understand the significance of the priesthood keys that Elijah restored at Kirtland, Ohio. As Elder LeGrand Richards observed, "Nobody in this world, I am sure, outside of this church, could tell you what the message of Elijah was. We wouldn't know either, except that Elijah came and appeared to Joseph Smith and Oliver Cowdery on the third day of April 1836."[49]

Joseph Smith spoke of the sweeping reach of the doctrines related to priesthood sealing keys and the mission and spirit of Elijah. "The spirit, power, and calling of Elijah," he said, "is, that ye have power to hold the key of the revelations, ordinances, oracles, powers and endowments of the fullness of the Melchizedek Priesthood and of the kingdom of God on the earth; and to receive, obtain, and perform all the ordinances belonging to the kingdom of God, even unto the turning of the hearts of the fathers unto the children, and the hearts of the children unto their fathers, even those who are in heaven."[50] He noted that "the greatest responsibility in this world that God has laid upon us is to seek after our dead."[51] The Prophet further asked, "What is the object of this important mission? . . . The keys are to be delivered, the spirit of Elijah is to come, the Gospel to be established, the Saints of God gathered, Zion built up, and the Saints to come up as saviors on Mount Zion."[52] It is the sealing power that enables us not only to seek but to provide saving ordinances for the dead.

Summary

Anderson noted in 1835 that "every attentive reader of Scripture must have observed the manner in which the pencil of inspired prophets has continually shadowed out the grand events of futurity."[53] Malachi certainly "shadowed out" one of the grandest events of our dispensation when he prophesied Elijah's future return. Essential priesthood keys were restored in the Kirtland Temple in 1836, but "none of more far reaching or greater significance than the keys of authority bestowed by Elijah."[54] The importance of the restored doctrines regarding the sealing power and the blessings that flow from them cannot be overstated. Writing to the Church members in 1842, Joseph Smith called this work the "most glorious of all subjects belonging to the everlasting gospel" (D&C 128:17).

Christian and Jewish writers had struggled for centuries to explain and understand Malachi's prophecy, but it was through Joseph Smith and temple-building Latter-day Saints that the world learned how the ancient prophecy was fulfilled. "No one else," explained President Joseph Fielding Smith, "knew what was meant by this passage of scripture."[55] The Church of Jesus Christ of Latter-day Saints bears enthusiastic testimony to the world that Elijah came and restored necessary priesthood keys that can bless all the families of the earth.

Notes

1. Joseph Fielding Smith, "The Promises Made to the Fathers," *Improvement Era*, July 1922, 830; see also Joseph Fielding Smith, *Doctrines of Salvation*, comp. Bruce R. McConkie (Salt Lake City: Bookcraft, 1956), 2:157.

2. Joseph Fielding Smith noted that there may also have been additional, unrecorded visitors that spring day: "It was in the Kirtland Temple, April 3, 1836, that the Lord sent to the Prophet Joseph Smith and Oliver Cowdery some of the ancient prophets with their keys. How many came we do not know." Smith, *Doctrines of Salvation*, 3:126.

3. The vision (in D&C 110) was recorded in Joseph Smith's journal (by his scribe Warren Cowdery, Oliver's older brother), and Joseph made reference to Elijah's return in D&C 128:17. The vision itself was first printed on November 6, 1852 (in the Salt Lake City *Deseret News*). Joseph Smith and other Church leaders made references to Elijah's return and mission after April 1836, but section 110 did not appear in the Doctrine and Covenants until the 1876 edition. See Trever R. Anderson, "Doctrine and Covenants Section 110: From Vision to Canonization" (master's thesis, Brigham Young University, 2010).

4. Reverend Charles Simeon, *Horae Homileticae: or Discourses*, (London: Holdsworth and Ball, 1832), 10:627. Charles Simeon (1759–1836) was an English clergyman. A 1902 review of important nineteenth-century religious leaders noted that "among the great religious leaders of the first half of the nineteenth century in England and America there is surely to be reckoned Charles Simeon. . . . He was an indefatigable preacher, a great Bible student, a born son of consolation, a man of most thorough consecration to his church, a man to whom religion was not a part of life but the whole of life—the great subject of conversation and of private thinking. He also had the true missionary instinct to impart these views to others, and so by means of his university lectures, unpublished and published sermons, innumerable letters, and by means of weekly gatherings in his rooms . . . he moulded [sic] the university life and educated large numbers of ministers in his way of thinking." Samuel Macauley Jackson, "Charles Simeon," in *Christendom Anno Domini MDCCCCI*, ed. Reverend William D. Grant (New York: Chauncey Holt, 1902), 2:115–16.

5. James S. M. Anderson, *Discourses on Elijah, and John the Baptist* (London: Gilbert & Rivington, 1835), 1. Anderson was an influential English theologian whose formal title was "Chaplain in Ordinary to the Queen, Perpetual Curate of St. George's Chapel, Brighton, and Chaplain to the Sussex County Hospital." The discourses quoted in this essay were delivered in St. George's Chapel—several of them while the queen was in attendance.

6. Bible Dictionary, "Elias," 663.

7. Edward Everett, *A Defence of Christianity, against the Work of George B. English* (Boston: Cummings and Hilliard, 1814), 183. At the time he made this statement, Edward Everett (1794–1865) was pastor of the Brattle Street Congregational and Unitarian Church in Boston. After leaving the ministry to become a professor of Greek literature at Harvard, he served ten years (1825–35) in the US House of Representatives,

representing Massachusetts's Fourth Congressional District. He also served as the governor of Massachusetts (1836–39), ambassador to Great Britain (1840–45), president of Harvard University (1846–49), US secretary of state (1852), and US senator from Massachusetts (elected in 1853; he resigned in 1854). In 1860 he ran for vice president on the Constitutional Union Party ticket, which received nearly 13 percent of the vote. At the time of his death, it was suggested that he was "the most mellifluous, winning, accomplished public speaker the country has ever produced, and it must be a long time before the nation will behold and hear his equal." As the main speaker during the November 1853 ceremony to dedicate the cemetery at Gettysburg, Edward Everett spoke for over two hours prior to President Abraham Lincoln giving his Gettysburg Address. See Reverend A. P. Putnam, *A Sermon Occasioned by the Death of Edward Everett, Preached at the Church of the Saviour, Brooklyn, N.Y. January 22, 1865* (New York: George F. Nesbitt, 1865), 5.

8. Simon Patrick, William Lowth, Richard Arnald, Daniel Whitby, Moses Lowman, and John Pitman, *A Critical Commentary and Paraphrase on the Old and New Testament and the Apocrypha*, (London: J. F. Dove, 1822), 5:121.

9. Reverend Daniel Guildford Wait, *A Course of Sermons Preached before the University of Cambridge, in the Year M.DCCC.XXV.* (London: C. & J. Rivington, 1826), 134. Reverend Wait (1789–1850) was an English clergyman, scholar, and author. According to the title page of this publication, Reverend Wait was a "member of St. John's College, Rector of Blagdon, Somersetshire, and member of the Royal Asiatic Society of Great Britain." He also translated numerous religious works into English.

10. The Reverend Samuel Burder, *Sermons of The Rev. James Saurin*, trans. Robert Robinson, Henry Hunter, and Joseph Sutcliffe (Princeton: D. A. Borrenstein, 1827). Reverend Burder was associated with Clare Hall (advanced studies) at Cambridge University. He was the author of several books, including a four-volume revision of *The Genuine Works of Flavius Josephus* (1824). He also served as a Lecturer of the United Parishes of Christ Church, Newgate Street, and St. Leonard Foster Lane in London and was Chaplain to his Royal Highness the Duke of Kent.

11. T. J. Sawyer and P. Price, eds., *The Christian Messenger, Devoted to the Doctrine of Universal Benevolence*, (New York: P. Price, 1832), 1:334.

12. Anderson, *Discourses on Elijah*, 163–64.

13. *The New and Complete American Encyclopaedia: or, Universal Dictionary of Arts and Sciences*, vol. 5 (New York: John Low, 1808), 212.

14. Patrick et al., *Critical Commentary*, 5:122.

15. Simeon, *Horae Homileticae*, 628–29; emphasis in original.

16. *The Theological Repository; Consisting of Original Essays, Hints, Queries, etc. Calculated to Promote Religious Knowledge*, (Birmingham: Pearson and Rollason, 1788), 6:168.

17. *Theological Repository*, 173.

18. Patrick et al., *Critical Commentary*, 121.

19. Anderson, *Discourses on Elijah*, 163–64.

20. Anderson, *Discourses on Elijah*, 167–69; emphasis in original.

21. *The Literary Gazette, and American Athenaeum*, (New York: Dixon & Sickels, 1827), 3:247.

22. Quoted in Sawyer and Price, *Christian Messenger*, 334. Calmet (1672–1757) was a Benedictine monk.

23. Nathaniel Homes, *The Resurrection Revealed, or the Dawning of the Day-Star* (London: Simpkin and Marshall, 1833), 224; emphasis in original.

24. Homes, *Resurrection Revealed*, 224; emphasis in original.

25. Homes, *Resurrection Revealed*, 224; emphasis in original.

26. Edward Greswell, *An Exposition of the Parables and of other Parts of the Gospels* (Oxford: J. G. & F. Rivington, 1834), 1:157–58. The son of a clergyman, Edward Greswell (1797–1869) was a fellow of Corpus Christi College at Oxford University and a chronologist. See Leslie Stephen and Sidney Lee, eds., *Dictionary of National Biography* (New York: Macmillan; London: Smith, Elder & Co., 1890), 23:156.

27. "Remarks on the Book of Enoch," *The Monthly Magazine; or, British Register*, May 1, 1801, 300.

28. Reverend John Fry, *The Second Advent; or, the Glorious Epiphany of our Lord Jesus Christ*, vol. 1 (London: Ogle, Duncan, and Co., 1822), 275–76. Reverend Fry was quite interested in the mission and ministry of Elijah; he wrote and published, for example, an extended poem (over one hundred printed pages) entitled *The History of Elijah and Elisha, in Two Parts: A Poem*. See John Fry, *Select Poems, Containing Religious Epistles, etc. Occasionally Written on Various Subjects* (Stanford, England: Daniel Lawrence, 1805), 95–224.

29. Sawyer and Price, *Christian Messenger*, 334.

30. Sawyer and Price, *Christian Messenger*, 334; emphasis in original.

31. Reverend Edward Johnstone, *The Life of Christ: A Manual of Elementary Religious Knowledge* (London: Longman, Rees, Orme, Brown, Green, and Longman, 1835), xlvii–xlix. According to the title page, Reverend Johnstone was "Chaplain of the Incorporated General Cemetery, Harrow Road: and Evening Preacher at Eaton Chapel, Eaton Square" in London.

32. Anderson, *Discourses on Elijah*, 168.

33. Matthias F. Cowley, *Cowley's Talks on Doctrine* (Chattanooga: Ben E. Rich, 1902), 26–27.

34. Howard W. Hunter, "Elijah the Prophet," *Ensign*, December 1971, 70–71.

35. Smith, *Doctrines of Salvation*, 1:171; emphasis in original.

36. See "The Prophetic Value of Section Two," *Improvement Era*, July 1906, 668.

37. Boyd K. Packer, *The Holy Temple* (Salt Lake City: Bookcraft, 1991), 113.

38. Sawyer and Price, *Christian Messenger*, 334. Edward Chandler, *A Defence of Christianity from the Prophecies of the Old Testament; Wherein are Considered All the Objections against this Kind of Proof* (London: James and John Knapton, 1728), 68. Edward Chandler (1668?–1750) was an English bishop (serving in both Lichfield and Durham, England). See *Alumni cantabrigienses; a biographical list of all known students, graduates and holders of office at the University of Cambridge, from the earliest times to 1900* (Cambridge: The University Press, 1922–54).

39. Sawyer and Price, *Christian Messenger*, 83.

40. Anderson, *Discourses on Elijah*, 163–64.
41. Fry, *Second Advent*, 276.
42. Gordon B. Hinckley, "His Latter-day Kingdom Has Been Established," *Ensign*, May 1991, 92; Henry B. Eyring, "Hearts Bound Together," *Ensign*, May 2005, 78.
43. Eyring, "Hearts Bound Together," 78.
44. Danie Haim, *Four Ancient Synagogues—The Beating Heart of the Sephardi Community in Jerusalem* (unpublished handout distributed to synagogue visitors, n.d.), 3; emphasis in original. I am grateful to Dr. Craig Ostler, who brought this handout to my attention.
45. Reverend Charles Swan, *Sermons on Several Subjects; with Notes, Critical, Historical, and Explanatory and an Appendix* (London: C. and I. Rivington, 1823), 43. Reverend Swan was a British cleric associated with St. Catharine's College at the University of Cambridge.
46. Simeon, *Horae Homileticae*, 630; emphasis in original.
47. Anderson, *Discourses on Elijah*, 171; emphasis in original.
48. Smith, *Doctrines of Salvation*, 2:127.
49. LeGrand Richards, "The Second Coming of Christ," *Ensign*, May 1978, 74.
50. Joseph Smith, *History of the Church of Jesus Christ of Latter-day Saints*, ed. B. H. Roberts, 2nd ed. rev. (Salt Lake City: Deseret Book, 1978), 6:251.
51. *Teachings of Presidents of the Church: Joseph Smith* (Salt Lake City: The Church of Jesus Christ of Latter-day Saints, 2007), 475.
52. Smith, *History of the Church*, 6:184.
53. Anderson, *Discourses on Elijah*, 166.
54. Smith, *Doctrines of Salvation*, 3:126.
55. Joseph Fielding Smith, in Conference Report, April 1920, 108.

4

"Commissioned of Jesus Christ": Oliver Cowdery and D&C 13

Mark L. Staker

When Joseph Smith and his associates prepared to publish the Doctrine and Covenants in 1835, they rearranged the order of revelations from their original placement in the Book of Commandments, adding greater emphasis to priesthood. This change in formatting included the addition of boldface headings to introduce the subject of three of the earliest sections as priesthood, and it included a similar heading more than halfway through the book to introduce a number of sections collectively as addressing priesthood and callings. Joseph also added revelatory material to some of these sections, including information on priesthood and its role in the Church of Jesus Christ. We expect this. We know that revelation is given precept upon precept, line upon line, here a little and there a little (see Isaiah 28:10) and that the canon of revelation is still open.

During 1875 and into 1876, Orson Pratt, acting under the direction of Brigham Young, rearranged the sections in the Doctrine and Covenants into a generally chronological order and added a significant number of additional revelations to the volume, including Moroni's words promising priesthood

---

Mark L. Staker is lead curator of the LDS Church Historic Sites Division.

restoration (see section 2) and John the Baptist's words restoring priesthood authority and keys (see section 13). John the Baptist's words were already available to members in two different accounts published by Franklin D. Richards in the 1851 Pearl of Great Price, where he included not only Joseph Smith's history but also a footnote with Oliver Cowdery's retelling of the same event.[1] But those accounts were not yet considered scripture, and the inclusion of section 13 elevated Joseph's recitation of John the Baptist's words, making them more widely available as part of the official canon.

While the Pearl of Great Price gave two alternate renditions of John the Baptist's words for readers to draw on, both viewed by many members today as scripture,[2] the inclusion of Joseph's account in the Doctrine and Covenants elevated its status and gave it primacy. When Franklin D. Richards and James A. Little compiled their *Compendium of the Doctrines of the Gospel* in 1882, one of the first detailed expositions of Latter-day Saint doctrine, they cited the account published six years earlier in Doctrine and Covenants 13 as representing the testimony of both Joseph and Oliver to the restoration of the Aaronic Priesthood.[3]

Even though many members of the Church consider both recitations of John the Baptist's words as scripture, a few scholars have noted there are subtle differences in Joseph's and Oliver's accounts, with one concluding that Oliver's account is "a bit more precise."[4] But they have not addressed all of the differences or attempted to explain why, if Oliver's account is more precise, Joseph's account deserves a place in our scriptural canon.[5]

I believe that Oliver Cowdery cited John the Baptist's words exactly as they were spoken but that Joseph Smith drew on revelation he received afterward and used his mantle as a prophet of God to add inspired commentary to those words. Oliver's account focuses on the fulfillment of revelation in Malachi, while Joseph's account focuses on the role of priesthood in the Church until that revelation is fulfilled. As a result, D&C 13 is not only more complete doctrinally but more useful to the restored Church of Jesus Christ.

Original Text

Both Joseph's and Oliver's accounts of John the Baptist ordaining them to priesthood were given as part of longer recitations of their experiences in Harmony, Pennsylvania. Joseph recalled being forced to keep secret the circumstances of both his ordination and his baptism because of local persecution (see Joseph Smith—History 1:74), and there is no evidence he shared oral accounts of his experience early in his history. Some of his associates even recalled not being told initially about priesthood restoration. Although Joseph mentioned receiving authority from angels in an 1832 account,[6] the first documented time he shared the circumstances surrounding receiving priesthood authority with others was on April 21, 1834, when he, Oliver Cowdery, Sidney Rigdon, and others gathered fifty-one miles south of Kirtland in Norton, Ohio, at the home of local gristmill operator and member Benjamin Carpenter. Joseph elected to share his experiences with the priesthood in the context of discussions about building a temple in Kirtland. When Sidney Rigdon addressed the congregation after Joseph, he discussed, among other things, "the Endowment of the Elders with power from on High according to former promises." After this, both Joseph and Sidney spoke to the congregation on the endowment of power and shared revelations about the proposed Kirtland Temple.[7] Joseph delivered these sermons after he "gave a relation of obtaining and translating the Book of Mormon, the revelation of the priesthood of Aaron . . . [and] the revelation of the high priesthood."[8] Unfortunately, Oliver, who kept minutes in that meeting, did not record the content of Joseph's account of priesthood restoration. When Oliver returned to Norton five months later, however, he sat down on September 7, 1834, in the evening after Sunday meetings, and wrote a letter describing what happened. His account was intended for readers of the Church-owned Missouri newspaper *Evening and Morning Star* who did not have regular access to Joseph's sermons, but "owing to a press of other matter" it was held over and published in the first issue of the Kirtland newspaper *Messenger and Advocate*.[9]

Joseph was aware of Oliver's effort to describe John the Baptist's visit, and he offered to "assist" Oliver in producing his history, although the extent of Joseph's involvement in the effort is not known. This letter turned out to be the first of a series of letters Oliver published outlining the early history of the Church, and it was reprinted in the Nauvoo Church newspaper *Times and Seasons* in November 1840 as Joseph was preparing his own history of the same events for publication.[10]

Joseph Smith began dictating his history in 1838, but the portion that included his account of John the Baptist's restoration of priesthood authority was lost, and the earliest surviving document dates to 1839 when he prepared a copy for publication.[11] In October 1840, Joseph dictated a "Treatise on Priesthood" to his scribe as though it were revelation, touching on John the Baptist's visit. This sermon was read in general conference the day after Joseph announced plans for the construction of the Nauvoo Temple.[12] Joseph's 1839 account of John the Baptist's visit was eventually published in the August 1842 *Times and Seasons*.[13] This newspaper account later served as the source for the Pearl of Great Price version and ultimately D&C 13.

D&C 2 and the Context of John the Baptist's Visit

Ancient prophets anticipated John the Baptist's visit with Joseph and Oliver. Many early Latter-day Saints viewed his appearance as a fulfillment of the prophecy found in the book of Revelation describing an angel "fly[ing] in the midst of heaven" who would come with the everlasting gospel (Revelation 14:6–7).[14] Joseph's religious contemporaries understood that Elijah in the Old Testament was referenced in the New Testament using the Greek form of his name, Elias, and that this name was sometimes applied to John the Baptist, such as when the angel in the temple promised Zacharias his son would go before the Lord "in the spirit and power of Elias, to turn the hearts of the fathers to the children, and the disobedient to the wisdom of the just; to make ready a people prepared for the Lord" (Luke 1:17).

When Orson Pratt selected part of Moroni's instructions to Joseph in 1876 for inclusion in the Doctrine and Covenants as section 2, he recognized this reference to Old Testament prophecy (see Malachi 4:5–6) was at least partially fulfilled in the coming of John the Baptist. A few years earlier, Orson preached a lengthy sermon on the subject and argued that Isaiah and Malachi both foresaw John the Baptist's role in priesthood restoration. Most nineteenth-century readers of the New Testament already understood that Elias would "make a people prepared for the Lord" during his sojourn on earth, but Orson argued Elias was also called "not only to prepare the way for the first coming but prepare for His second coming" as well.[15] He also explained that Malachi knew a messenger would be sent "that the sons of Levi might be prepared to offer an offering in righteousness," and he asked, "Who was that messenger? John the Baptist. . . . Did John accomplish all things predicted by the prophet Malachi during his first mission upon the earth? No."[16] He went on to argue that the Lord did not come suddenly to his temple during the first visit but to a manger, and the wicked were able to abide the day of his first coming. Orson Pratt argued that Malachi foresaw John the Baptist's second mission as well, a mission when John would come to prepare the sons of Levi to make an offering in righteousness for the Lord when he came suddenly to his temple.[17]

Joseph Smith later specifically addressed the topic of the spirit of Elias in his recounting the restoration of the Aaronic Priesthood. In order to fully appreciate his comments, however, we need to consider Joseph's and Oliver's recitations of John the Baptist's words when they were ordained.

Quoting John the Baptist?

Joseph's and Oliver's wording. When Joseph Smith recounted what took place in the Harmony woods on May 15, 1829, he had access to Oliver Cowdery's narrative of the same events and even had Oliver's account reprinted as he prepared his own. He could easily have corrected Oliver's letter before it was reprinted if he felt it was inaccurate, or he could have drawn from Oliver's words if he felt they represented what he wanted to say. Instead, he let Oliver's account stand but provided his own as well.

Oliver Cowdery's 1834 citation of John the Baptist's words during the priesthood ordination reads as follows:

> Upon you my fellow-servants, in the name of Messiah I confer this Priesthood and this authority, which shall remain upon earth, that the Sons of Levi may yet offer an offering unto the Lord in righteousness!

Joseph Smith's 1839 rendition is somewhat longer, and I have emphasized here in italics the places where he differs from Oliver.

> Upon you my fellow servants in the name of Messiah I confer *the Priesthood of Aaron, which holds the keys of the ministering of angels and of the gospel of repentance, and of baptism by immersion for the remission of sins, and this shall never be taken again from the earth, untill* the sons of Levi *do* offer *again* an offering unto the Lord in righteousness.[18]

The name of Messiah. If we ignore differences in punctuation, since they were obviously not part of John the Baptist's original dialog, it is noteworthy that Oliver and Joseph used identical language when citing John the Baptist's introduction to the ordination: "Upon you my fellow servants, in the name of Messiah." To our ears the lack of a definite article before Messiah is noticeable and we want to hear "in the name of *the* Messiah." Joseph and Oliver's contemporaries would have longed to hear the same definite article. While using "the name of Messiah" is acceptable English, and it appeared in some publications during the early nineteenth century, a digital search of word usage in more than twenty million books suggests the phrase was extremely rare during that period and readers were much more likely to come across "name of *the* Messiah."[19] This is exactly the word choice Oliver and Joseph consistently used in their other writings.[20] Oliver even used "*the* Messiah" twice elsewhere in the same letter where he cited John the Baptist. The lack of a definite article with the word *Messiah* in both Joseph's and Oliver's citations of John the Baptist was clearly intentional.

The reference to priesthood. Oliver and Joseph differ slightly in their phrasing of the messenger's next statement, with Oliver quoting John the Baptist saying, "I confer *this* Priesthood and *this* authority," while Joseph reports him saying, "I confer the Priesthood of Aaron" (D&C 13:1). Since the word *this* as used by Oliver clearly referred to a statement that was not included, he implied that John the Baptist addressed the priesthood before beginning the ordination. Joseph confirmed this in his Nauvoo account of priesthood restoration discussed below.

Joseph Smith's use of "the Priesthood of Aaron" appears to have been added for clarification. Surviving sources indicate that the terms *Aaronic* and *Melchizedek* were not initially associated with the restored priesthood. Religious writers in early nineteenth-century America sometimes wrote about priesthood in the Old Testament as Aaronic Priesthood, the Priesthood of Aaron, or, taking their cue from the New Testament, the order of Aaron (see Hebrews 7:11), and some even talked about a continuation of Aaronic Priesthood after the crucifixion.[21] Although these terms were familiar to nineteenth-century speakers, they were not initially used in the restored Church. The earliest sources consistently referred to authority restored by John the Baptist as "lesser priesthood," a term unique to Mormonism that implied that all priesthood was not equivalent but could be divided into distinct spheres of influence.[22]

As late as September 1832, when Joseph Smith received a major revelation on priesthood now published as D&C 84, authority was described as the "greater priesthood" (v. 19) and "the lesser priesthood" (v. 26). The revelation indicated that the greater, also known as "*the* priesthood," was "received . . . from Melchizedek" (v. 14) while the lesser, known as "*a* priesthood" (v. 18), had been conferred on Aaron. This reference to the two individuals usually associated with authority placed them in a more familiar nineteenth-century context, but it did not tie them to the names of these authorities, and a year later when Joseph ordained his father as patriarch, he still referenced the two distinct authorities as "the lesser priesthood, and . . . the holy priesthood."[23]

The September 1832 revelation indicated that priesthood was connected to Melchizedek and Aaron (and it emphasized this "lesser priesthood" had passed through generations to John the Baptist), but it did not specifically give a name for these two spheres of authority other than referring to them as "lesser" and "greater." By the time Joseph gave his sermon in Norton, Ohio, on April 21, 1834, however, he was speaking about "the revelation of the priesthood of Aaron."[24] On March 28, 1835, Joseph dictated a revelation which specifically named the two priesthoods Melchizedek and Aaronic and explained why they each received their designated name (see D&C 107:1–6, 13–14, 18–20). Oliver then began to make a transition in terminology but was still more comfortable with the "lesser" and "greater" usage that appears in earlier documents. He recalled a few months after Joseph's revelation receiving "the lesser or Aaronic priesthood. . . . After this we received the high and holy priesthood."[25]

By 1839, when Joseph Smith wrote his account of John the Baptist's visit, the terms *Aaronic* and *Melchizedek* were fully entrenched in Latter-day Saint discourse, and he used them both in his account of John the Baptist's visit.[26] After Joseph published his account of priesthood restoration, however, he summarized the same events in 1844, using different terminology in a lengthy account. Joseph said, "I must go back to the time at Susquehannah river when I retired in the woods pouring out my soul in prayer to Almighty God. An Angel came down from heaven and laid his hands upon me and ordained me to the power of Elias and that authorised me to babtise with water unto repentance. It is a power or a preparatory work for something greater . . . that is the power of the Aronick preisthood."[27] Joseph said the angel gave him instructions on the nature of the "power of Elias" when he explained, "This said the Angel is the <u>Spirit of Elias.</u>"[28] He expounded, "The spirit of Elias is to prepare the way for a greater revelation of God which is the [purpose of the] priesthood of Elias *or* the Priesthood that Aaron was ordained unto."[29] Joseph added that John the Baptist had ordained him to "be a priest after the order of Aaron," which connected this authority to the ancient patriarch Aaron in terms familiar to the Saints since their days in Kirtland.[30]

Priesthood keys. Joseph Smith's account continued by including a phrase not used by Oliver Cowdery: "which holds the keys of the ministering of angels, and of the gospel of repentance, and of baptism by immersion for the remission of sins" (D&C 13:1). This definition of "keys" associated with the Priesthood of Aaron reflects revelations Joseph received in Kirtland.

In Joseph's September 1832 revelation on priesthood, he learned that the keys of the mysteries of the kingdom belonged to the "greater priesthood" (D&C 84:19) while the "lesser priesthood" held "the key of the ministering of angels and the preparatory gospel; which gospel is the gospel of repentance and of baptism, and the remission of sins, and the law of carnal commandments" (D&C 84:26–27). The revelation then noted that this priesthood had been passed on through a direct lineage from Aaron to John the Baptist, who used it to prepare people for the first coming of the Lord. Since the Book of Mormon addressed the role of ministering angels as "to call men unto repentance, and to fulfil and to do the work of the covenants of the Father" (Moroni 7:29–31), the September 1832 revelation's reference to ministering angels emphasized the role of Aaronic Priesthood as centered on repentance and on its preparatory role for something greater.

The 1832 revelation went on to declare that those faithful in obtaining both the lesser and greater priesthood would become these sons of Moses and Aaron that would offer an acceptable offering and sacrifice in the house of the Lord (see D&C 84:27–37). Less than three years later, the Apostles in the restored Church asked for a written revelation to express the mind and will of the Lord concerning their duty.[31] They received through Joseph Smith a revelation which defined, among other things, the lesser priesthood as the priesthood of Aaron and addressed its keys as "the keys of the ministering of angels, and to administer in outward ordinances" such as baptism (D&C 107:20).

Aaronic Priesthood to "remain" or be "taken." Joseph and Oliver concluded their accounts by returning to identical words spoken by John the Baptist, but these were preceded by some subtle, yet significant, differences. Oliver Cowdery cited John as saying this authority would "remain upon earth, *that the Sons of Levi may yet offer an offering unto the Lord in righteousness*" while Joseph Smith related that the authority would "never be taken again from the earth, *until* the sons of Levi do offer again an offering unto the Lord in righteousness." The statements are not contradictory, since authority can "remain" on the earth so the sons of Levi "may yet" make an offering while not being "taken . . . until" the offering is made "again," but the emphasis in the two accounts differs.

Oliver Cowdery's narrative emphasized the Second Coming of Jesus Christ and the role of the lesser priesthood in that event. This is consistent with doctrine Joseph taught. In October 1840, Joseph prepared one of his few formal written sermons, a "Treatise on Priesthood," that he had his scribe, Robert B. Thompson, read on his behalf in general conference the day after he announced plans for construction of the Nauvoo Temple. In his sermon, Joseph noted, "All things had under the Authority of the Priesthood at any former period shall be had again—bringing to pass the restoration spoken of by the mouth of all the Holy Prophets. Then shall the sons of Levi offer an acceptable sacrifice to the Lord."[32] Joseph indicated that this would fulfill the prophecy in Malachi 3:3–4 that this sacrifice would be made at the Second Coming of Jesus Christ. Oliver's account emphasized the importance of this event—John the Baptist restored the priesthood that was essential to carrying out this sacrifice. Oliver even used wording consistent with Malachi, which emphasized the enabling aspect of authority that the sons of Levi "may" offer an offering in righteousness in the temple (Malachi 3:3).

While Oliver Cowdery's account emphasized the sacrifice and thus the Second Coming, Joseph Smith's account emphasized the preparatory role of the lesser priesthood and the important interim period "until" the acceptable sacrifice would be made. Joseph's account was more useful to Latter-day Saints since it emphasized the period in which we currently live and, in conjunction with his insertion of an identification of specific keys connected to that authority, outlined the purpose of that priesthood until the prophesied sacrifice was made. Joseph's use of *until* emphasized the role of priesthood up to that point in time; it did not attempt to address the role of Aaronic Priesthood after the sacrifice would be made.

Orson Pratt recognized the preparatory nature of Aaronic Priesthood and that its role in bringing about repentance would lead to something greater. He argued, "The authority of the priesthood will continue until the end shall come, the end of the wicked . . . until the sons of Levi shall be purified."[33] Joseph had taught this idea in Nauvoo when he preached that "the power of Elias" restored through John the Baptist was "a preparatory work for something greater."[34] Even though there was overlap between the New Testament Elias and the Old Testament Elijah in terms of John the Baptist, Joseph recognized that the "lesser" and "greater" priesthoods also divided the roles of an Elias and an Elijah to an extent, with the "lesser" priesthood fulfilling the preparatory role. The "person who holds the keys of Elias hath a preparitory work" that leads to the "spirit power & calling of Elijah," he explained, which includes "the keys of the revelations ordinances, oricles powers & endowments of the fullness of the Melchezedek Priesthood."[35]

Joseph considered that the role of Elias would fold into that of Elijah and argued, "The Melchisadeck Priesthood comprehends the Aaronic or Levitical Priesthood and is the Grand head, and holds the highest Authority which pertains to the Priesthood the keys of the Kingdom of God in all ages of the world to the latest posterity on the earth and is the channel through which all knowledge, doctrine, the plan of salvation and every important matter is revealed from heaven."[36] He used the word *comprehend* as a synonym for *include* to suggest the Melchizedek Priesthood is all encompassing.

Within this context, Joseph's use of the word *until* in relation to the Aaronic Priesthood becomes clearer. After the Aaronic Priesthood accomplishes its preparatory role to lead us to what Joseph Smith called the spirit, ordinances, powers, and endowment of Elijah, it becomes subsumed into the Melchizedek Priesthood of which it is a part. Recognizing that the Melchizedek Priesthood both includes and supersedes the Aaronic Priesthood helps explain Joseph's emphasis in his citation of John the Baptist's words on the preparatory role the Aaronic Priesthood plays in divine communication, repentance, and baptism. Its purpose is to lead us to something greater.

In addition to the role of priesthood in preparing individuals for the coming of Jesus Christ, Joseph's account of the offering to be made by the sons of Levi included the word *again* to emphasize the role of this sacrifice as part of the restoration of all things foretold in scripture. Brigham Young understood that this sacrifice would be made by literal descendants of Levi through Aaron. During a discussion on the Levitical Priesthood, he lamented "that no son of Levi has yet been found in these last days to minister at the altar."[37] More than twenty years later he still expected that eventually these Levites would be available to perform ordinances, saying, "By and by the descendents of Aaron come along and they officiate in lesser priesthood but they will receive their endowments," as if to emphasize that they would still be subsumed within what Joseph Smith called the spirit, power, and calling of Elijah.[38] Brigham Young never saw that long-prophesied day of sacrifice fulfilled.

Conclusion

Both Oliver Cowdery's and Joseph Smith's accounts of priesthood restoration are significant. Oliver's account was written closer to the actual event and appears to represent John the Baptist's ordination as it was delivered. Any historical account of that important event would want to pay close attention to Oliver's recollections. On the other hand, Joseph's account provides an accurate summary of the event as it occurred but includes important doctrinal refinements building on Joseph's later revelations that make it a significant revelation for Latter-day Saints in its own right and an important contribution to the Doctrine and Covenants.

God promised us in revelation that we would have his word through Joseph Smith (D&C 5:10) in order to become "born of [Him]." When this promise was republished in the Doctrine and Covenants, Joseph Smith included the inspired clarification that he and Oliver would not immediately be reborn through baptism, but "you must wait yet a little while, for ye are not yet ordained" (D&C 5:16–17), highlighting the role of proper authority. Even though they were already baptized when this clarification was added, it emphasized the importance to readers of proper authority in performing ordinances as later taught by Joseph when he said, "Being born again comes by the Spirit of God through ordinances."[39] He also drew on inspiration to expand the words of John the Baptist in his account of priesthood restoration to emphasize the role priesthood would continue to play not just in eventually performing an important sacrifice by the sons of Levi but also in preparing us for that moment.

Notes

1. Oliver Cowdery, "The following communication . . . ," *Messenger and Advocate*, October 1834, 13–16.

2. An informal sample of Church History Department employees conducted in October 2011 suggests that about half of those asked consider the Cowdery Pearl of

Great Price account as scripture and half consider it equivalent to a section heading or other contextual material but not scripture. An informal sample of Church-service missionaries serving in the same department suggested that almost all of them considered Oliver Cowdery's account as scripture.

    3. Franklin D. Richards and James A. Little, *A Compendium of the Doctrines of the Gospel* (Salt Lake City: George Q. Cannon and Sons, 1882), 71.

    4. Charles R. Harrell, "The Restoration of the Priesthood," *Studies in Scripture, Vol. 1: The Doctrine and Covenants*, ed. Robert L. Millet and Kent P. Jackson (Salt Lake City: Deseret Book, 1989), 90.

    5. This perspective is supported fully or in part by Hyrum M. Smith and Janne M. Sjodahl, *The Doctrine and Covenants Commentary*, rev. ed. (Salt Lake City: Deseret Book, 1967), 70; Daniel H. Ludlow, *A Companion to Your Study of the Doctrine and Covenants* (Salt Lake City: Deseret Book, 1978), 1:115; Richard O. Cowan, *Doctrine and Covenants: Our Modern Scripture*, rev. ed. (Provo, UT: Brigham Young University Press, 1978), 36; and Monte S. Nyman, *More Precious Than Gold: Commentary on The Doctrine and Covenants* (Orem, UT: Granite, 2008), 1:135.

    6. Dean C. Jessee, ed., *The Papers of Joseph Smith*, vol. 1, *Autobiographical and Historical Writings* (Salt Lake City: Deseret Book, 1989), 3.

    7. Minute Book 1, April 21, 1834, 44–51, The Joseph Smith Papers, http://josephsmithpapers.org/paperSummary/minute-book-1#48.

    8. Minute Book 1, 44.

    9. Cowdery, "The following communication . . . ," 13.

    10. Oliver Cowdery, "Copy of a Letter . . . ," *Times and Seasons*, November 1, 1840, 200–202.

    11. Jessee, *Papers of Joseph Smith*, 230–31, 265–67, 290.

    12. Andrew F. Ehat and Lyndon W. Cook, *The Words of Joseph Smith: The Contemporary Accounts of the Nauvoo Discourses of the Prophet Joseph* (Provo, UT: Religious Studies Center, 1980), 38–44, 50–51.

    13. Joseph Smith, "History of Joseph Smith," *Times and Seasons*, August 1, 1842, 865–67.

    14. Ronald O. Barney, "Priesthood Restoration Narratives in the Early LDS Church," unpublished manuscript in author's possession, cited with permission.

    15. The original shorthand version of Orson Pratt's sermon can be found in Orson Pratt, June 5, 1859, Papers of George D. Watt, Church History Library, The Church of Jesus Christ of Latter-day Saints, Salt Lake City, MS 4534 box 3 disk 1, images 299–306. LaJean Carruth has transcribed this sermon, and I have confirmed and edited the transcription and punctuated the portion included here. Space limitations only allow for the reproduction of a small selection from the sermon. The entire sermon is in the author's files. Pratt preached in part: "The authority of the [Aaronic] priesthood will continue until the end shall come—the end of the wicked. That was the promise of the angel when the angel came and conferred first authority of priesthood upon Joseph Smith and Oliver Cowdery [in] 1829. What was the promise of that angel before this church took its rise when he laid his hands on those two individuals? What did he say? 'In the name of Messiah I confer this priesthood, which is the priesthood of Aaron, upon you,

and it shall continue upon you, and it shall never be taken from the earth while it shall stand. It shall continue upon you until the sons of Levi shall be purified and shall offer unto the Lord an offering in righteousness.' . . . Isaiah predicted that the messenger should be sent forth to prepare the way of [the] Lord not only to prepare the way for [his] first coming but prepare for his second coming. Read the 40 chapter of Isaiah. The same thing is quoted by the evangelist applying to John where he should be sent as messenger before his face and he should be as one crying in the wilderness make straight in the desert highway for our God, every valley exalted, and rough places made straight, etc. [See Mark 1:3, Matthew 3:3, Luke 3:4; John 1:23, and Isaiah 40:3–5]. Did John do all that as Isaiah predicted in forepart of 40 chapter? No. Yet he was the very person mentioned. . . . Why then not John come in last dispensation of fullness of times and confer that everlasting priesthood upon the heads of other chosen vessels, that they might act therein and be an instrument in hands of God by restoring authority that should prepare the way for the Savior's second advent? The same thing is predicted in 3 chapter prophecy of Malachi. 'Behold,' says he that prophet, or the Lord by his mouth, 'I will send my messenger before my face, and he shall prepare the way before me, and the Lord whom ye seek shall suddenly come to his temple. The messenger of the covenant whom I delight in, behold he shall come. But who may abide the day of his coming, and who shall stand when he appeareth? For he is like devouring fire, and he shall sit upon the sons of Levi, and purify them as gold and silver, that they may offer to the Lord an offering in righteousness. And the offering of Judah and Jerusalem shall be pleasant unto the Lord as in former years.' Who was that messenger? John the Baptist. And applied to him by the evangelist. Did John accomplish all things predicted by the prophet Malachi during his first mission upon the earth? No."

16. Orson Pratt, June 5, 1859, Papers of George D. Watt, Church History Library, MS 4534 box 3 disk 1, image 304.

17. Orson Pratt, June 5, 1859, images 303–5.

18. *Papers of Joseph Smith*, 290.

19. This evaluation was carried out using the Google Ngram feature.

20. Joseph Smith consistently used "*the* Messiah" in his own speech (see D&C 109:67 and Patriarchal Blessing Book, October 2, 1835, recording a blessing given December 18, 1833, as cited in Joseph Fielding Smith, "Restoration of the Melchizedek Priesthood," *Improvement Era*, October 1904, 943), and, although we don't know to what extent Joseph Smith's language patterns influenced his translation efforts, the definite article appears consistently throughout the Book of Mormon. See 1 Nephi 1:19; 10:4, 7, 9–10; 15:13; 2 Nephi 2:6, 8, 26; 3:5; 6:13–14; 25:14, 19; 26:3; Jarom 1:11; Mosiah 13:33; Helaman 8:13; and in references Joseph inserted into the Bible, see the Joseph Smith Translation of Genesis 50:24–25; Matthew 3:6; Mark 14:36. Other than his citation of John the Baptist's ordination, the only instance where Joseph Smith did not include a definite article with "Messiah" was when he cited words spoken directly by the Lord to Enoch (see Moses 7:53).

21. Joseph Smith related an anecdote of an Episcopal priest who claimed to hold the priesthood of Aaron. *Words of Joseph Smith*, 244.

22. Adam Clarke noted in his commentary on Hebrews 7:5 that "Melchisedec... therefore must be considered as having a more honourable priesthood than even Aaron himself" and thus implied that Melchizedek's priesthood was greater, but he never used the terms "lesser" or "greater" in his commentary. Adam Clarke, *The Holy Bible... with a Commentary and Critical Notes* (New York: Daniel Hitt and Abraham Paul, 1817), chap. 7.

23. Joseph Smith, December 18, 1833, as cited in John W. Welch, ed., *Opening the Heavens: Accounts of Divine Manifestations, 1820–1844* (Provo, UT: Brigham Young University Press, 2005), 236. See Richard Lyman Bushman, *Joseph Smith: Rough Stone Rolling* (New York: Alfred A. Knopf, 2005), 614n48 for an argument that this account may date to December 18, 1834.

24. Minute Book 1, April 21, 1834, 48.

25. Welch, *Opening the Heavens*, 243.

26. Oliver Cowdery would also later use Aaronic and Melchizedek for the lesser and higher priesthoods but continued to occasionally refer to "the Lesser Priesthood—and... the Greater," see Welch, *Opening the Heavens*, 244–45. Joseph also remained flexible in his use of terminology, distinguishing the authorities on one occasion as "a priest after the order of Aaron & ... a greater work." *Words of Joseph Smith*, 327. Joseph also spoke of three distinct priesthoods using interchangeable names, Levitical or Aaronic, Patriarchal or Abrahamic, and Melchizedek. See *Words of Joseph Smith*, 243–47.

27. *Words of Joseph Smith*, 332–33.

28. *Words of Joseph Smith*, 334.

29. *Words of Joseph Smith*, 328; emphasis added.

30. *Words of Joseph Smith*, 327.

31. Minute Book 1, March 28, 1835. This revelation was combined with an earlier revelation received November 11, 1831, before it was published as D&C 107. See Robert J. Woodford, "The Historical Development of the Doctrine and Covenants" (PhD diss., Brigham Young University, 1974), 3:1398–1403; Revelation Book 1:122–23; and Revelation Book 2:84–86, in Robin Scott Jensen, Robert J. Woodford, and Steven C. Harper, *The Joseph Smith Papers: Revelations and Translations* (Salt Lake City: Church Historian's Press, 2009), 1:217–19, 585–91.

32. *Words of Joseph Smith*, 42; struck-out words omitted.

33. Orson Pratt, June 5, 1859, Papers of George D. Watt, Church History Library, MS 4534 box 3 disk 1, image 304.

34. *Words of Joseph Smith*, 328, 332–34.

35. *Words of Joseph Smith*, 328–29.

36. *Words of Joseph Smith*, 38.

37. *Manuscript History of Brigham Young, 1846–1847*, ed. Elden J. Watson (Salt Lake City: Elden J. Watson, 1971), 503.

38. Brigham Young, School of the Prophets, January 27, 1868, Papers of George D. Watt, Church History Library, MS 45 34 box 5 disk 4, images 71–74, transcribed from shorthand by LaJean Carruth.

39. *Words of Joseph Smith*, 12.

5

The Lord's Supper in Early Mormonism

Justin R. Bray

On June 22, 1836, Joseph Smith escorted his mother, Lucy Mack Smith, and aunt Clarissa to Painesville, Ohio, where these sisters would await their husbands' return from a mission to the eastern states. Upon arrival, Joseph "broke bread" and administered the Lord's Supper "after the ancient order."[1] The company then ate and drank until "they satisfied their appetites." According to George Q. Cannon, former member of the First Presidency, in the early years of the Church between 1830 and 1844, the "bread and the wine were not passed as is the custom now among us. It was an actual supper." He believed that "this would be the proper manner to administer this ordinance now if circumstances permitted"; however, congregations apparently outgrew this approach.[2]

Other aspects of the ordinance also underwent significant refinement since the first formal and official instructions in the Articles and Covenants of the Church, now section 20 of the Doctrine and Covenants. This early revelation did not outline the Lord's Supper in great detail, leaving most of the procedural aspects and understanding of the ordinance open to influences

---

Justin R. Bray is an archivist at the Church History Department in Salt Lake City.

from Joseph Smith's and other early leaders' religious backgrounds and cultural surroundings. As a result, the sacrament was irregularly and inconsistently administered during the first years of The Church of Jesus Christ of Latter-day Saints.

This paper is an effort to understand what the Lord's Supper meant to early members as well as an attempt to piece together—from the Doctrine and Covenants and other early records—the order and sequence of distributing the bread and wine in the LDS Church between 1830 and 1844.[3]

Background

The sacrament of the Lord's Supper was a ceremonial meal, instituted and celebrated by early members of the LDS Church in accordance with Jesus' instructions at the Last Supper as documented in the New Testament. With the disciples gathered, Jesus broke pieces of bread, pleading with his brethren to eat "in remembrance of [him]" (Luke 22:19). He then similarly distributed the wine. As instructed, the Apostles and early Christians sought to observe the Lord's Supper following Jesus' death (see 1 Corinthians 11:26–30).

However, the meaning and sequence of the ordinance underwent significant alterations following the death of the early Apostles. For example, Cyril, a bishop in Jerusalem around AD 350, believed the Holy Ghost descended "upon the bread and wine at the prayer of the celebrant, and change[d] them into the body and blood" of Jesus. Another early theologian, Irenaeus, was convinced the bread and wine literally transformed each communicant, making their bodies "no longer corruptible."[4] Other ideas regarding the physical performance of the ordinance surfaced over the centuries and created diverse methods of administering the emblems. During Joseph Smith's youth, for example, religions differed in their interpretation and procedure of the ordinance. The Catholic Church taught transubstantiation, a belief that communicants "miraculously ingest the literal body and blood of Christ, although the outward appearance of the emblems . . . remain the same."[5] Some faiths, like the Methodist Church, had unique procedures during the "commemorative ordinance," and its members physically "approached the communion-table" rather than receiving the emblems in the pews.[6] Some feasted on bread and wine, while others shared small servings. Several faiths honored the sacred rite only once a month, some even less frequently.

With the vast amount of interpretations of the Lord's Supper, as well as limited instructions on the ordinance in Joseph Smith's revelations, early leaders in the LDS Church seemed to incorporate aspects from their previous faith into the administration of the sacrament. These Latter-day Saints, for example, referred to the ordinance by several names, including the Lord's Supper, the sacrament of the Lord's Supper, "breaking bread," Communion, and the Eucharist. It took many years for all members to universally term the ordinance "the sacrament," which was what the Lord called it in Joseph Smith's revelations (D&C 20:46). Likewise, even after the Lord taught Joseph that "it mattereth not what ye shall eat or what ye shall drink when ye partake of the sacrament" (D&C 27:2), wine was still regularly used until the early 1900s.[7] Thus it was not until second or third generational members of the Church when the ordinance evolved into what it is today. Perhaps the most significant differences in the sacrament during Joseph Smith's lifetime from how we now administer it were in the procedure, frequency, and meaning of the ordinance.

Procedure

Only some of the pattern for performing the ordinance was outlined in section 20 of the Doctrine and Covenants, but members filled in where there were gaps. For example, verse 46 called on priests to "administer the sacrament," which was a broad term for overseeing and directing the preparation, blessing, and distribution of the bread and wine. However, who exactly carried out these duties was open to question.

Preparation. It is unclear who regularly prepared the sacrament during Joseph Smith's time. Even women could have been involved, since they helped prepare the emblems and care for the linens on sacrament tables after the migration to Utah.[8] However, without formal instructions in Joseph Smith's revelations, the duty likely rested on more spiritually mature members of the Church who held the ordinance in high regard, such as members of the Quorum of the Twelve or the First Presidency, including Joseph Smith himself.

Blessing. According to the Doctrine and Covenants, elders or priests were responsible for blessing the sacramental emblems (see D&C 20:46), yet higher ranking officials, usually members of the Quorum of the Twelve or traveling missionaries, officiated at "the sacred desk" and offered the blessings on the bread and wine.[9] They were "mouth" for the rest of the congregation, and they kneeled (see D&C 20:76).[10] However, there's reason to believe the prayers given in section 20 to bless the bread and wine were not initially recited verbatim.

This idea of an unscripted sacrament prayer was reflected in one of Brigham Young's sermons after the migration to Utah. In his address, President Young stressed the importance of using the prescribed blessings in the Doctrine and Covenants, saying, "Take this book and read this prayer." He continued, "The people have various ideas with regard to this prayer. They sometimes cannot hear six feet from the one who is praying, and in whose prayer, perhaps, there are not three words of the prayer that is in this book, that the Lord tells us that we should use."[11]

This was further evidenced in missionary reports printed in the *Times and Seasons*, an early Church periodical. Some of these accounts sounded as though there were no set sacrament prayers.[12] Interestingly, however, according to Richard Bushman, perhaps the most notable scholar in Mormon history, Joseph Smith's revelations were printed so that they were "carried around by Church members." In fact, Joseph even said that members "snatched" his revelations "as soon as given."[13] Thus the instructions on the sacrament in section 20 of the Doctrine and Covenants, then chapter 24 of the Book of Commandments, were apparently available and circulating among members despite the destruction of their printing press, persecution, and continuous uprooting. Still, it seemed priesthood holders officiating at the sacrament table incorporated aspects of the Lord's Supper from their previous faiths, in which there was sometimes no prescribed prayer for blessing the bread and wine.

Methodist preachers and circuit riders at the time, for example, "laid aside" their books and prayed extempore when blessing the emblems of the Lord's Supper. Even though Methodists themselves had prescribed blessings on the bread and wine, they believed "they could pray better, and with more devotion while their eyes were shut, than they could with their eyes open."[14] Moreover, many of the early Latter-day Saints who would have likely assisted in the sacrament had been converted from Methodism, such as Brigham Young, John Taylor, Oliver Cowdery, David W. Patten, Thomas B. Marsh, Orson Hyde, and George Q. Cannon, among others. It wasn't until the early

1900s—when young men began officiating at the sacrament table—that the prayers were read "just as the Lord has given them."[15]

Passing. As with the preparation of the sacrament, it is uncertain who regularly distributed the bread and wine throughout the congregation. Probably more than anyone else, "the twelve apostles passed the emblems of the Lord's Supper" in large meetings.[16] However, in some accounts, the sacrament was passed by "Presidents," referring to the First Presidency and Aaronic Priesthood leaders, such as Newel K. Whitney.[17] Even Joseph Smith sometimes "assisted" in "distributing the Lord's Supper to the Church."[18]

Though the bread would have required multiple men to pass it among those in attendance, the wine was poured in a "common cup" from which every member and nonmember of the Church sipped, regardless of age, health, gender, or social standing. This goblet was taken from the sacrament table to the pews, where the communicants themselves passed it "along the row to others."[19] Thus it seems those distributing the emblems only carried the cup from the communion table to the first row.[20]

Years later, Heber J. Grant, then President of the Church, explained that there was "no rule in the Church" that only priesthood holders could distribute the emblems among the pews. It had become only "custom" for men to perform this duty, which practice developed during Joseph Smith's lifetime. Apparently Grant had "no objection" to "brethren lacking priesthood" to participate in the ordinance if there were no ordained men available.[21] Not only was the sacrament administered varyingly as such, but it was infrequent as well.

Frequency

The Lord's Supper was administered for the first time in the Church of Christ on the day the Church was organized—April 6, 1830—when about thirty men and women gathered "to partake of bread and wine in the remembrance of the Lord Jesus" (D&C 20:75). It was on a Tuesday. The next best reference to the sacrament came three months later at the first general conference of the Church, held on June 9, 1830, a Wednesday. Moreover, Sunday was not designated as the day to meet and administer the sacrament until August 1831, a year and four months after the organization of the Church (see D&C 59:9). In the meantime, members were counseled to "meet together often" and administer the ordinance (D&C 20:75). However, because of persecution and continuous uprooting, the sacrament was only distributed when occasion permitted, which was apparently sporadic, according to early records.

Even after the Lord commanded members to "offer up [their] sacraments upon [his] holy day" (D&C 59:9) in 1831, the ordinance was not regularly administered until the completion of the Kirtland Temple in 1833. Before the construction of temples, according to Hyrum Smith, there was "a great deal of difficulty" with distributing the bread and wine.[22] Members had been meeting in either inadequately small homes, one-room schoolhouses, or outdoors, where weather concerns often caused setbacks in the sacrament. Wintertime was especially challenging due to inclement conditions. However, the temple in Kirtland and later Nauvoo provided members sufficient shelter and space to administer the ordinance to large numbers "on every Sabbath."[23]

In places besides Kirtland and Nauvoo, however, members and missionaries continued to administer the Lord's Supper only when conditions were right. For example, members of the Church in Iowa upheld the ordinance "every second Sabbath."[24] This pattern of performing the sacrament more frequently at the Church's headquarters than outlying areas continued after the migration to Utah, when the emblems were distributed in community-wide meetings at the Salt Lake Tabernacle until the "country wards" finally constructed their own meetinghouses and leaders emphasized the sacrament in individual units.

Also unique to the early years of the Church, the sacrament was customarily the last item of business in each meeting. Leaders often spoke either leading up to or during the ordinance, with the distribution of the bread and wine as the climax and conclusion of the meeting. Wilford Woodruff, then member of the Quorum of the Twelve, said it "closed the labor of the day."[25]

Meaning

The sacrament held a slightly less prominent position in Latter-day Saint worship during the early years of the Church. Not only was it administered infrequently, as explained above, but the ordinance apparently took a backseat to sermonizing and establishing Church government, which were the focus of worship services during Joseph Smith's lifetime. This idea was symbolically reflected through the communion table in the Kirtland Temple, which was a drop-leaf extension on one of the pulpits—not a standing fixture of its own. C. Mark Hamilton, an architectural historian, even pointed out that "the sacrament table was typically not a major physical feature [in early Mormon architecture]" and that "the pulpit was the main focus of the interior."[26] This layout suggests, at least early on, that preaching held more honor in the Church than formal liturgy. However, members still considered the sacrament an important institution, and its meaning in early Mormonism was expressed in Emma Smith's 1835 hymnbook.

This first Latter-day Saint hymnal certainly "represent[s] the doctrines taught by Joseph Smith" and includes five songs under the heading "On Sacrament."[27] William W. Phelps, an early member of the Church, wrote one of the sacrament hymns, while Emma borrowed the remaining four from other faiths, particularly the Methodist Church. Although these hymns could be considered a sung sacramental prayer, three of the five did not mention bread or wine but rather "taught and exemplified the sufferings of Christ."[28] Thus the Lord's Supper was a "token of . . . fellowship" with Jesus Christ and held "covenantal obligations" for communicants to remember him. By so doing, according to Brigham Young, one could receive "fresh strength" to thwart Satan's temptations.[29]

Furthermore, early members heavily emphasized the importance of partaking of the emblems worthily. In fact, according to available records, the most Joseph Smith ever spoke on the sacrament was after the funeral of Seth Johnson in February 1835, when he warned against dishonoring the ordinance: "Previous to the [sacrament] administration, I spoke of the propriety of this institution in the Church, and urged the importance of doing it with acceptance before the Lord, and asked, How long do you suppose a man may partake of this ordinance unworthily, and the Lord not withdraw His Spirit from him? How long will he thus trifle with sacred things, and the Lord not give him over to the buffetings of Satan until the day of redemption! The Church should know if they are unworthy from time to time to partake, lest the servants of God be forbidden to administer it."[30] And they did. On at least one occasion, members "did not break bread because there was such a general division in the Church."[31] This idea of withholding the sacrament because of disunion among members became more common after the migration to Utah.

Early leaders also accepted a literal interpretation of the Apostle Paul's teachings in the New Testament (see 1 Corinthians 11:26–30) and preached that partaking of the sacrament unworthily resulted in severe penalties, including "sickness and even death."[32] For example, Wilford Woodruff later remembered how Lyman E. Johnson stood in the aisles of the Kirtland Temple and cursed Joseph Smith prior to the blessing of the emblems. When the bread was passed throughout the congregation, Johnson partook of it and turned completely "black in the face."[33] Woodruff, among other early leaders, taught that anyone who defamed the sacrament immediately and literally "ate and drank damnation to himself."[34] There was no way to "escape condemnation," George Q. Cannon warned.[35]

Perhaps members were so cautious in partaking of the sacrament worthily because the ordinance not only provided a moment to reflect on the life and sacrifice of Jesus but also precluded great spiritual outpourings. For example, when the sacrament was distributed at the Kirtland Temple dedication, the "sacred ritual thrilled the congregation" and was followed by a "sensation very elevating to the soul."[36] Some of the attendees attested to seeing "great manifestations of power," including the administration of angels.[37] On another occasion, immediately after Joseph Smith helped administer the sacrament, a "vision was opened" unto him and Oliver Cowdery.[38] Occasionally, the sacrament meeting even included "confessions and rejoicings," but more often than not, it resulted in a "refreshing time" or "solemn meeting."[39]

Conclusion

Within the last half century, Latter-day Saints have witnessed the standardization of the sacrament from an inconsistent and infrequent procedure in the 1830s to one of the most regular and important forms of worship in the LDS Church. This all stemmed from Joseph Smith's revelations, found in the Doctrine and Covenants, which did not bring with them extensive instructions regarding the meaning and method of administering the ordinance. Instead, early members were left to incorporate aspects of the Lord's Supper from their various religious backgrounds.

Over time, however, leaders of the LDS Church clarified the meaning of the Lord's Supper and improved its procedure. Now the sacrament is regarded by some—even Presidents of the Church—as the most sacred ordinance administered in The Church of Jesus Christ of Latter-day Saints.[40]

Notes

1. Joseph Smith, *History of the Church of Jesus Christ of Latter-day Saints*, ed. B. H. Roberts, 2nd ed. rev. (Salt Lake City: Deseret Book, 1957), 2:447.

2. George Q. Cannon, "Editorial Thoughts," *Juvenile Instructor*, January 15, 1897, 52–53.

3. The closest research on the Lord's Supper in early Mormonism comes from William G. Hartley, who chronicles the history of the priesthood. He touches on different aspects of the sacrament, but only to briefly illustrate the refinements in Church government and priesthood organization.

4. Cited in Milton R. Hunter, "The Common Source of Religious Truth," *Improvement Era*, March 1940, 149.

5. Paul B. Pixton, "Sacrament," in *Encyclopedia of Mormonism*, ed. Daniel H. Ludlow (New York: Macmillan, 1992), 1244.

6. J. H., *A Wesleyan Methodist's Thoughts about Prayer, the Bible, the House of God, Baptism, the Lord's Supper, the Covenant, My Ministers, My Class, Home, My Master, My Servant, My Country, Giving, Sorrow, Sickness, and Death* (Toronto: Wesleyan Book Room, 1839), 10–11.

7. *Church, State, and Politics: The Diaries of John Henry Smith*, ed. Jean Bickmore White (Salt Lake City: Signature Books, 1990), 570.

8. William G. Hartley, *My Fellow Servants: Essays on the History of the Priesthood* (Provo, UT: Brigham Young University Press, 2010), 70.

9. *History of the Church*, 2:435. It was also common for "traveling elders" in the Methodist church to "preside at the Lord's Supper." Sarah D. Brooks, "Reforming Methodism, 1800–1820" (PhD diss., Drew University, 2008), 97.

10. It was not uncommon for those officiating at the sacrament table to "kneel with the church" (D&C 20:76). In fact, some entire LDS congregations kneeled during the sacrament prayers until the late 1800s.

11. Brigham Young, in *Journal of Discourses* (London: Latter-day Saints' Book Depot, 1854–86), 16:161.

12. In several accounts in the *Times and Seasons*, missionaries wrote that a blessing on the sacrament was offered, whereas in later records such as the *Journal of Discourses*, scribes generally wrote that *the* blessing on the sacrament was offered.

13. As cited in Richard Lyman Bushman, *Joseph Smith: Rough Stone Rolling* (New York: Alfred A. Knopf, 2005), 130.

14. As cited in Fred Hood, "Community and the Rhetoric of 'Freedom': Early American Methodist Worship," *Methodist History* 9, no. 1 (October 1970): 13; see also Karen B. Westerfield Tucker, *American Methodist Worship* (New York: Oxford University Press, 2001), 119–20.

15. Even in the 1890s, "deviations were sometimes permitted." See George Q. Cannon, "The Sacrament of the Lord's Supper," *Juvenile Instructor*, August 15, 1897, 53; see also Charles W. Penrose, "The Sacrament of the Lord's Supper," Journal History of The Church of Jesus Christ of Latter-day Saints, December 3, 1908.

16. As cited in Thomas G. Alexander, *Things in Heaven and Earth: The Life and Times of Wilford Woodruff, A Mormon Prophet* (Salt Lake City: Signature Books, 1993), 50.

17. *History of the Church*, 2:435; see also *Doctrine and Covenants Student Manual* (Salt Lake City: The Church of Jesus Christ of Latter-day Saints, 2001), 274.

18. *History of the Church*, 2:435.

19. David L. McDonald, "The Individual Sacrament Cup," *Young Woman's Journal*, April 1912, 217.

20. This chalice, which was a symbolic representation of union among believers in Jesus Christ, lasted about eighty years until the early 1910s, when individual cups became standardized. James R. Clark, *Messages of the First Presidency* (Salt Lake City: Deseret Book, 170), 4:269.

21. Quoted in William G. Hartley, *My Fellow Servants: Essays on the History of the Priesthood* (Provo, Utah: Brigham Young University Press, 2010), 64.

22. *Times and Seasons*, August 1, 1844, 596–97.

23. *History of the Church*, 2:408

24. *Times and Seasons*, December 1, 1844, 725.

25. As cited in Susan Staker, *Waiting For World's End: The Diaries of Wilford Woodruff* (Salt Lake City: Signature Books, 1993), 362.

26. C. Mark Hamilton, *Nineteenth-Century Mormon Architecture and City Planning* (New York: Oxford University Press, 1995), 164.

27. Mary D. Poulter, "Doctrines of Faith and Hope Found in Emma Smith's 1835 Hymnbook," *BYU Studies* 37, no. 2 (1997–98): 34, 45.

28. *Times and Seasons*, April 15, 1844, 500; see Kaimi Wenger, "Women and the Sacrament," *The Times and Seasons Blog*, July 9, 2007, http://timesandseasons.org/index.php/2007/07/women-and-sacrament/.

29. See also John S. Tanner, "Sacrament Prayers," in *Encyclopedia of Mormonism*, 1245; Brigham Young, in *Journal of Discourses*, 2:2–3.

30. *History of the Church*, 2:204.

31. *The Journals of William E. McLellin, 1831–1836*, ed. Jan Shipps and John W. Welch (Provo, UT: Brigham Young University Press, 1994), 141.

32. Joseph F. Smith, "Partaking of the Sacrament," in *Collected Discourses*, vol. 2, *1890–1892*, ed. Brian H. Stuy (Burbank, CA: B. H. S., 1988), 367; see also *Gospel Truth: Discourses and Writings of President George Q. Cannon*, vol. 2, ed. Jerreld L. Newquist (Salt Lake City: Deseret Book, 1974), 155.

33. Wilford Woodruff, "The Power of Evil," in *Collected Discourses*, vol. 4, *1894–1896*, ed. Brian H. Stuy (Burbank, CA: B. H. S., 1991), 290. Lyman E. Johnson later drowned himself in a river, which Woodruff attributed to his partaking of the sacrament unworthily.

34. Woodruff, "Power of Evil," 290.

35. As cited in *Gospel Truth: Discourses and Writings of President George Q. Cannon*, ed. Jerreld L. Newquist (Salt Lake City: Deseret Book, 1957), 2:155.

36. As cited in Richard S. Van Wagoner, *Sidney Rigdon: A Portrait of Religious Excess* (Salt Lake City: Signature Books, 1994), 172; "Autobiography of Truman O.

Angell," in *Our Pioneer Heritage*, comp. Kate B. Carter (Salt Lake City: Daughters of Utah Pioneers, 1967), 10:198.

37. George A. Smith, in *Journal of Discourses*, 11:10.
38. *History of the Church*, 2:435.
39. *Journals of William E. McLellin*, 99, 117.
40. *Teachings of Presidents of the Church: David O. McKay* (Salt Lake City: The Church of Jesus Christ of Latter-day Saints, 2003), 34.

6

Sacramental Connections: Deliverance, Redemption, and Safety (D&C 27)

Matthew O. Richardson

The Restoration of The Church of Jesus Christ of Latter-day Saints included the authoritative reinstitution of the ordinance of the sacrament. The Lord instructed the Saints that it is "expedient that the church meet together often" to participate in this ordinance (D&C 20:75). Most references dealing with the sacrament in the Doctrine and Covenants address the administrative aspects of this ordinance. For example, the scriptures address the authority required to perform the ordinance (see D&C 20:46, 58, 76), sacramental emblems (see D&C 20:75–79; 27:1–5), prayers (see D&C 20:77, 79), the frequency of partaking of the sacrament (see D&C 20:75), and personal preparation for participation therein (see D&C 20:68; 46:4). Such instruction is vital in maintaining the veracity of this sacred ordinance, but if we are not careful, we may focus too much on scriptural texts dealing with administering the ordinance alone and thus overshadow the possibilities of recognizing additional insights, understanding broader purposes, and receiving additional blessings of the sacrament.

Matthew O. Richardson is a professor of Church history and doctrine at Brigham Young University.

When considering how the sacrament is represented in the scriptural text of the Restoration, we can see that section 27 of the Doctrine and Covenants makes a unique contribution. It connects other textual concepts and administrative aspects of the sacrament by constructing a framework for understanding and applying the sacrament. The power of this revelatory text, however, is accessed only when its various parts are viewed as being connected and integrated one with the other. This chapter examines how the text of section 27 uniquely connects three purposes of the sacrament, namely, directing our attention to remembering the genesis of our deliverance (see vv. 1–4), inviting us to look forward to our future redemption (see vv. 5–14), and showing us how the sacrament provides safety and protection in how we live our lives presently (see vv. 15–18).

Textual Connections

The presentation and eventual publication of the revelatory text now known as section 27 are an instructive example of how scriptural principles and practices are revealed and how they are connected "line upon line, precept upon precept, here a little and there a little" (2 Nephi 28:30). Keeping this in mind helps us understand the powerful connections of the three different "lines" or "precepts" found in this revelation.

According to Joseph Smith's account, this revelation was received when Newel Knight and his wife, Sally, visited Joseph and Emma Smith in Harmony, Pennsylvania, in August 1830. During the course of their visit, it was proposed that Sally and Emma, who were previously baptized, be confirmed members of the Church and then afterwards, the group would partake of the sacrament together. Joseph left his home to find wine for the sacrament service and was met by a heavenly messenger. Joseph recounted that he recorded the "first paragraph" of the revelation with the remainder of the revelation being recorded the following September.[1]

The "first paragraph" described by Joseph first appeared in the *Evening and Morning Star* in March 1833.[2] That very same paragraph was also included in the 1833 Book of Commandments as section 28.[3] While the majority of that text deals with safely procuring and using acceptable sacramental emblems, this text outlines, albeit briefly, the three sacramental concepts necessary for us to better understand and apply the sacrament: remembering the past, looking to the future, and protecting the present.

The remainder of Joseph's revelation, not recorded in the earlier publications, was finally published as part of the original text by 1835 as section 50 in the first edition of the Doctrine and Covenants.[4] It is possible that this publication may have included additions to the original revelation received in 1830, for as Elder B. H. Roberts explained, some changes to the earlier revelations were made by "the Prophet himself" to correct errors and "throw increased light upon the subjects treated in the revelations."[5]

That first paragraph published in 1833 was expanded by 457 words in the 1835 edition of the Doctrine and Covenants and is nearly identical to the current text found in section 27 of the Doctrine and Covenants today.[6] Rather than adding new concepts or purposes to the original publication, the text added considerable detail to the purposes of looking forward to our future redemption and providing safety and protection in how we live our lives presently. This detail will be considered in later sections of this chapter.

Remembering the Past: The Genesis of Our Deliverance

The Doctrine and Covenants emphasizes that the sacrament is a ritual for remembering the genesis of our deliverance—the Atonement and Resurrection of Jesus Christ. In April 1830, for example, it was revealed to Joseph that partaking of the bread was to be "in remembrance of the body of [the] Son" (D&C 20:77) and drinking of the wine was to be "in remembrance of the blood of [the] Son" (D&C 20:79). With this sacred ritual, we are to direct our thoughts partly to an upper room in ancient Jerusalem, to the nearby grove of olive trees known as the Garden of Gethsemane, and to a garden tomb near Golgotha as we remember associated events.

Remembering is a powerful and necessary experience. President Spencer W. Kimball once said that the most important word in the dictionary could be the word *remember*.[7] He explained the power of this word as he said, "I suppose there would never be an apostate, there would never be a crime, if people remembered, really remembered, the things they had covenanted at the water's edge or at the sacrament table and in the temple. I suppose that is the reason the Lord asked Adam to offer sacrifices, for no other reason than that he and his posterity would remember—remember the basic things that they had been taught."[8]

While the sacrament prayers revealed in Doctrine and Covenants section 20 instruct us to remember the Atonement and Resurrection, section 27 provides an additional witness that the sacrament is a time for "remembering unto the Father [Christ's] body which was laid down for you, and [Christ's] blood which was shed for the remission of your sins" (D&C 27:2). As important as the additional witness of this point is, the text in section 27 provides vital instruction about the importance and value of tokens or emblems in sharpening the focus of our remembrance.

It was revealed to Joseph Smith that "it mattereth not what ye shall eat or what ye shall drink when ye partake of the sacrament" (D&C 27:2). While this may appear to be a simple administrative detail, it actually underscores the vital purpose of the sacrament itself—to completely focus our thoughts on the events of our deliverance. This textual passage actually underscores that the emblems used for sacramental worship are just that—emblems. As such, their purpose is nothing more and nothing less than turning our attention to a greater event, to focus our thoughts and feelings, and to remember the past in such a way as to make it not only relevant but very real. Some delight in discovering that it "mattereth not" what emblems are used during the sacrament. Their delight is tempered when they realize that sacramental emblems are not symbols of palatable pleasure or amusement but symbols meant to help us focus on the Atonement and Resurrection of Jesus Christ. "For behold," verse 2 teaches, "it mattereth not what ye shall eat or what ye shall drink when ye partake of the sacrament, *if*"—and this is a very important transition—"*if* it so be that ye do it with an *eye single* to my glory—*remembering* unto the Father my body which was laid down for you, and my blood which was shed for the remission of your sins" (v. 2; emphasis added). In truth, the value of the emblem—whatever it may be—is determined only by how well it helps us remember and focus on the Atonement and Resurrection of Jesus Christ. This means that any emblem, including the bread or the water, which distracts from the singular purpose of reminding us of the Savior's Atonement, is ineffective or, in other words, it is used in vain. As such, those who prepare and pass the emblems of sacrament must be vigilant in their duty, for they may unwittingly distract from the sacrament ritual in the way they prepare, bless, and present the sacramental emblems.

President Kimball taught, "I guess we as humans are prone to forget. It is easy to forget. Our sorrows, our joys, our concerns, our great problems seem to wane to some extent as time goes on, and there are many lessons that we learn which have a tendency to slip from us."[9] Tokens or emblems sharpen our focus and through tangible connectors help us remember events and concepts we hope to never forget. For example, many married couples exchange and wear rings as an emblem or symbol of their marriage. This particular emblem shows others that a person is married, but even more importantly, it reminds the married person of his or her spouse and of what is expected of a married person. Thus, when glancing at a wedding band, vivid memories and feelings return to the day when covenants were made. Remembering that event may actually inspire married individuals to renew their efforts and act accordingly. In this way, tokens or emblems that symbolize something from the past reconnect those events with the present in tangible and meaningful ways.

The sacrament is a consecrated event. Therefore, we must remember and focus on the past just as covenant Israel did during Passover. They intentionally looked to their past and remembered how they were miraculously delivered from captivity, oppression, angst, and despair. Likewise, Latter-day Saints also look to the past and remember the events that miraculously delivered them from captivity, oppression, angst, and despair, in any form. The Atonement is the genesis of our redemption, and if the present and the future do not connect with it, they hold very little prospect.

Looking to the Future: Our Redemption

Remembering the past is only effectual if it informs future events. Covenant Israel, for example, used the Passover to remember their great day of deliverance but perhaps failed to use the Passover's lessons of the past to inform and direct their view for future redemption. As a result, they did not recognize the Savior and crucified him instead of receiving him wholeheartedly. Likewise, Latter-day Saints may use the sacrament to remember the Atonement but then fail to use the sacrament to inform and direct their attention to a time when they might be with the Savior when he comes again. President John Taylor pointed out this crucial relationship between the past and the future as he said, "For in partaking of the sacrament we not only commemorate the death and sufferings of our Lord and Savior Jesus Christ, but we also shadow forth the time when he will come again and when we shall meet and eat bread with him in the kingdom of God."[10]

Directing our minds to the future has always been a key component of the sacrament.[11] For example, as Christ first instituted the sacramental wine during his mortal ministry, he said to his Apostles, "But I say unto you, I will not drink henceforth of this fruit of the vine, until that day when I drink it new with you in my Father's kingdom" (Matthew 26:29). Even at that first sacrament meeting, the Savior was encouraging his disciples to look forward with anticipation to a *future* meeting—when Jesus and disciples would gather together again to partake of the sacrament.

Nearly 1,800 years later, the Savior provided almost the same type of instruction to his latter-day disciples. After teaching about the emblems of the sacrament and the importance of remembering the Savior's Atonement, the 1833 text of section 50 (now section 27) immediately turns our attention to the future. "Behold this is wisdom in me, wherefore marvel not, for the hour cometh that I will drink of the fruit of the vine with you, on the earth, and with all those whom my Father hath given me out of the world."[12] Here the Lord speaks of his eventual return and a time when he will partake of the sacrament again. Just like the first sacrament in Jerusalem, Jesus is still urging disciples to remember the past *and* look to the future.

In the later published versions of this revelation, 70 percent of the words added were details pertaining to this future sacramental meeting.[13] The principle of looking forward to partaking of the sacrament with the Savior is still the focal point, but now the revelation gave more detail concerning who would be at this event. Joseph Smith was informed that he would be present at the meeting along with other recognizable individuals. Section 27 specifically names other participants such as Moroni, Elisha, John the Baptist, Elijah, Joseph, Jacob, Isaac, Abraham, Michael (Adam), Peter, James, and John.[14] We would assume from Matthew's account of the first sacrament meeting that those then present would also be in attendance to "drink [the sacrament] new" with the Savior. Elder Bruce R. McConkie also included at this gathering "those who have held keys and powers and authorities in all ages from Adam to the present [meaning when the future meeting is held]." [15]

Among all those listed in the later publication, we must not forget that group mentioned in both the 1833 and 1835 publications of this revelation. This is the group known as "all those whom my Father hath given me out of the world" (D&C 27:14). The wording here is reminiscent of Christ's great discourse and Intercessory Prayer given just prior to the Atonement in Gethsemane. At that time, Christ said, "I pray for them: I pray not for the world, but for them *which thou hast given me*; for they are thine. And all mine are thine, and thine are mine; and I am glorified in them" (John 17:9–10;

emphasis added). These individuals are the very same group that Christ specifically called "the men which thou gavest me out of the world" just three verses earlier in John 17:6.

In his discourse and prayer, Christ described these individuals as those who "bear witness" of him (John 15:27); "remember" him (John 16:4); and allow the Comforter, or Holy Ghost, to come upon them to "guide [them] into all truth" and "shew [them] things to come" (John 16:13). Christ said that these are they who received the name of God and kept God's word (see John 17:6). The wording and phrases used here to describe those "given out of the world" neatly align with all those who worthily and properly partake of sacramental covenants.

As such, we find wonderful connections with the sacrament prayers revealed to Joseph Smith in April 1830. These prayers also contain words and phrases like "witness unto thee," "in remembrance," "do always remember him," "willing to take upon them the name of thy Son," "keep his commandments which he has given them," and "that they may always have his Spirit to be with them" (D&C 20:77–78). When considering the future meeting where prophets of all ages and those "given out of the world" will partake of the sacrament with the Savior once again, it appears that this meeting will include those who have entered into covenants and who worthily participate in the sacramental ordinance. In fact, Elder Bruce R. McConkie asserted those described in section 27 as "given out of the world" to be "all the faithful members of the Church then living [at the time of the meeting] and all the faithful saints of all the ages past." No wonder Elder McConkie described this future sacramental gathering with the Savior as "the greatest congregation of faithful saints ever assembled on planet earth."[16]

For some, it may be difficult to pinpoint when this future sacrament meeting spoken of in section 27 will actually take place. Elder Bruce R. McConkie, when speaking on the subject, taught, "Before the Lord Jesus descends openly and publicly in the clouds of glory, attended by all the hosts of heaven; before the great and dreadful day of the Lord sends terror and destruction from one end of the earth to the other; before he stands on Mount Zion, or sets his feet on Olivet, or utters his voice from an American Zion or a Jewish Jerusalem; before all flesh shall see him together; before any of his appearances, which taken together comprise the second coming of the Son of God—before all these, there is to be a secret appearance to selected members of his Church."

He then said of this "secret appearance" that "it will be a sacrament meeting. It will be a day of judgment for the faithful of all the ages. And it will take place in Daviess County, Missouri, at a place called Adam-ondi-Ahman."[17]

The Present Day: Seeking Protection and Safety

After directing our attention to the past and then to the future, this revelation teaches that the sacrament should also cause us to consider the present day and our current conduct. This should not be surprising, as it has been said that the Doctrine and Covenants was "meant in part as a current guide to how Latter-day Saints should live their religion."[18] In the 1833 publications of this revelation, the final verse reads, "Wherefore lift up your hearts and rejoice, and gird up your loins and be faithful until I come."[19] The later publications of this revelation added 136 words (nearly 30 percent of the additions) to this final theme, giving it a more robust approach to using the sacrament as a means for real-time protection and safety (see D&C 27:15–18). When considering the additions, we now read the original 1833 sentence as, "Wherefore, lift up your hearts and rejoice, and gird up your loins, *and take upon you my whole armor, that ye may be able to withstand the evil day, having done all, that ye may be able to stand*" (D&C 27:15; 1835 wording italicized).[20] Several additional verses are then included that deal directly with the armor of God. Some may interpret this passage merely as an additional witness of Paul's writings about the importance of the armor of God (see Ephesians 6:10–17). However, if this segment is directly connected with the sacrament and the other purposes thereof, these additional verses provide deeper insights on how the sacrament protects us now and prepares us for the future.

The connection of this final purpose of the sacrament with the two other purposes outlined in this revelation may be found in the textual wording of the revelation itself. For example, this final section begins with the word "wherefore" (D&C 27:15). In 1828, the word *wherefore* was commonly defined as "for which reason," which means "because of this."[21] After the section describes a future meeting with Jesus Christ to partake of the sacrament (see vv. 5–14), the next verse could be read as, *"For which reason"* or *"Because of this* [meaning vv. 5–14], lift up your hearts and rejoice, and gird up your loins, and take upon you my whole armor, that ye may be able to withstand the evil day, having done all, that ye may be able to stand." In this way, verses 5–14 are directly connected to verses 15–18. This pattern was also used earlier in the revelation to connect the first two purposes of the sacrament together. Consider how the text outlines the sacramental purpose of using emblems to remember the past events of our deliverance (see vv. 1–4), and then recall that the very next verse states, "Behold, this is wisdom in me; *wherefore,* [or *because of this purpose we must*] marvel not, for the hour cometh that I will drink of the fruit of the vine with you on the earth" (D&C 27:5; emphasis added).

These direct connections are important because rather than considering this revelation as three independent purposes, principles, precepts, or practices, we can see that each purpose is textually connected to the other. In other words, the only way to be worthy of and qualify for the future sacramental meeting or redemption is for individuals to remember the past events of the Atonement and Resurrection *and* to lift their hearts, rejoice, gird up their loins, and put on the armor of God today. Richard Lloyd Anderson pointed out, "For through remembering Jesus' past sacrifice, we promise to transform our own lives in preparation for an eternal future with him."[22]

With an established connection between the sacrament and the armor of God, we can see in vivid ways how the sacrament protects us. It is important to remember that Christ described those "given out of the world" with attributes directly tied to the sacramental covenants (bear witness of him, remember him, have the Holy Ghost with them, bear the name of God, and keep God's commandments) and that he then said that such individuals were "not of the world" as he was "not of the world" (John 17:16). In his intercessory prayer, Christ prayed that the Father would not "take them out of the world" but instead "keep them from the evil" and "sanctify them through thy truth" (John 17:15, 17). Obviously, the sanctifying power spoken of here can come only through Jesus Christ's Atonement and Resurrection. As for keeping the Saints from evil, consider President Howard W. Hunter's reference to the Passover as "an ancient covenant of protection" and his statement that, in similar manner, the sacrament is "the new covenant of safety."[23] According to section 27, the armor of God is intended to protect the Saints so they might withstand the evil day and ultimately stand with Christ in the end (see D&C 27:15). Making additional connections between the sacrament and the armor of God provides unique insights to the protecting power of this sacred covenant and is worthy of further examination.

Armor of God

While the Apostle Paul used the imagery of physical armor, he was clear that he wasn't speaking about physical protection as much as spiritual protection. "For we wrestle not against flesh and blood," Paul wrote, "but against . . . the darkness of this world . . . against spiritual wickedness" (Ephesians 6:12). Elder Harold B. Lee offered a more detailed explanation regarding the symbolism of the armor of God which lays a foundation for making sacramental connections as well. Elder Lee explained, "We have the four parts of the body that . . . [are] the most vulnerable to the powers of darkness. The loins, typifying virtue, chastity. The heart, typifying our conduct. Our feet, our goals or objectives in life and finally our head, our thoughts."[24] With this important symbolism in mind, we are now in a position to see the powerful connection between the armor of God and the sacrament.

Helmet of salvation. The helmet is designed to protect the head or brain during physical combat. Without such protection, a serious wound is deadly. According to Elder Lee, in *spiritual warfare*, the helmet is to protect one's thoughts. Obviously if unprotected, our thoughts can likewise be spiritually fatal. According to section 27, the best way to protect our thoughts is with salvation (see D&C 27:18). To understand how salvation can protect our thoughts, consider how King Benjamin taught that salvation comes by no other name or means save Jesus Christ (see Mosiah 3:17).

As we partake of the sacrament, we don a helmet of salvation by covenanting to remember Christ. Jesus encouraged us to "look unto [him] in every thought; doubt not, fear not" (D&C 6:36). The sacrament helps us with this protection, as our thoughts are first turned to his Atonement and Resurrection. This makes it possible for us to consider our future redemption in Christ. This in turn provides opportunity for candid evaluation of our present condition. The sacrament firmly places the "helmet of salvation" upon those entering into this covenant as they covenant they will "always remember him [Jesus Christ]" (D&C 20:77, 79). Think how differently our actions would be if they were always preceded by thoughts of the Savior, how he lived, and what he would have us do. With our eye single to him in our remembrance of the past and by remembering him in all we do every day, our thoughts are protected in such a way as to secure a glorious future.

Breastplate of righteousness. A physical breastplate is designed to protect the heart and lungs—both life-sustaining organs. According to Elder Lee, the spiritual breastplate, or our righteousness, protects our conduct. It is critical to point out that it is not our conduct that protects our righteousness but our righteousness that protects our conduct. This may appear to be a matter of semantics to some, but it is much more than merely haggling over words. Elder David A. Bednar points out that "it is possible for us to have clean hands but not have a pure heart."[25] A person without a righteous character might engage in appropriate activities, but that in and of itself may not afford the protection needed to withstand the evil day. Of course, righteous character cannot be obtained or even sustained without righteous conduct. Elder Bednar reasoned, "Both clean hands and a pure heart are required to ascend into the hill of the Lord and to stand in His holy place."[26] As such, the way to obtaining the character of righteousness is, as Elder Bednar pointed out, "through the process of putting off the natural man and by overcoming sin and the evil influences in our lives through the Savior's Atonement." He clarified that "hearts are purified as we receive His strengthening power to do good and become better. All of our worthy desires and good works, as necessary as they are, can never produce clean hands and a pure heart. It is the Atonement of Jesus Christ that provides both a *cleansing and redeeming power* that helps us to overcome sin and a *sanctifying and strengthening power* that helps us to become better than we ever could by relying only upon our own strength. The infinite Atonement is for both the sinner and for the saint in each of us."[27]

Doctrine and Covenants 27:15 instructs every person to "take upon you [the Lord's] whole armor" so that "ye may be able to *withstand* the evil day, having done all, that you may be able to *stand*" (emphasis added). It then reads, "Stand, therefore, . . . having on the breastplate of righteousness" (D&C 27:16). It is hard to think of anything more foundational in forging and securing the breastplate of righteousness than the sacrament. Paul taught that obedience yields righteousness (see Romans 6:16). As such, all who worthily partake of the sacrament covenant to "keep his commandments which he [God] has given them" (D&C 20:77). Thus we pledge to become righteous through obeying the commandments that God has given. Obviously, this requires an omission from wrongdoing. But the commandments of God are not limited to proscriptions alone. As we avoid things of the world, we must also seek for the "things of a better" (D&C 25:10). Elder Bednar described this process as "the dual requirements of (1) avoiding and overcoming bad and (2) doing good and becoming better."[28] These "dual requirements" are at the core—or at the very heart—of establishing and maintaining the character of our righteousness. But it is not enough to have only clean hands, for our hearts must also be pure—a condition made possible, as Elder Bednar pointed out, only by accepting and applying the atoning sacrifice of Jesus Christ. Once again, it is the sacrament that empowers us to embrace the altering powers of the Atonement that focus our obedience and change our disposition as well. Elder Bednar also taught that "this mighty change is not simply the result of working harder or developing greater individual discipline. Rather, it is the consequence of a fundamental change in our desires, our motives, and our natures made possible through the Atonement of Christ the Lord."[29] More than mere determination, it is our righteous character that quite literally protects our conduct. Consider young Joseph while a prisoner in Egypt as an example. Undoubtedly, he was an obedient disciple and diligently kept the commandments of God. It is clear that his character aligned with his devoted obedience. When Potiphar's wife tempted him to act in ways contrary to the commands of God, Joseph did not respond with "I am not allowed" or "This type activity is against my religion" or "I am not supposed to participate in those types of things." Instead he outright refused and with incredulity queried, "How then can I do this great wickedness, and sin against God?" (Genesis 39:9). Joseph's reaction wasn't so much a product of determined obedience as much as it was a reflection of his integrity—his very being, who he was. His refusal meant something like "I, meaning the type of person that I am, cannot do this type of thing!" It was against his nature—his character—to do such things. It was Joseph's righteousness that protected his conduct. A sacramental covenant to keep the commandments protects the choices made by a willing disciple.

Girdle of truth. God's armor also includes a girdle protecting the loins—another part of the body that has mortal implications. Spiritually speaking, the loins represent our virtue or chastity, which, according to section 27, is best protected by the truth (see D&C 27:16). In a world that condones promiscuity, openness, and indulgence, one may suppose that the best way to protect virtue and chastity would be with abstinence, abhorrence, or maybe even strict seclusion. Yet in his infinite wisdom, the Lord revealed that the best way to protect our virtue and chastity is with the truth.

In a world awash with an "everything goes" attitude, Elder Henry B. Eyring said that sin is "presented incessantly and attractively." He added that sin "doesn't even look like a sea of filth to the young people swimming in it. In fact, they may not even be swimming, because the presentation is so incessant and so attractive that they may not notice that there is a need to swim."[30] In reality, Satan's presentation is alluring to those who are unaware or unsure of the truth. This is why temptation is especially effective with those who have not yet entrenched themselves on the Lord's side and who are teetering in their allegiance. President Kimball reminded us that "the Savior said that the very elect would be deceived by Lucifer if it were possible. He will use his logic to confuse and his rationalizations to destroy. He will shade meanings, open doors an inch at a time, and lead from purest white through all the shades of gray to the darkest black. Young people are confused by the arch deceiver, who uses every device to deceive them."[31]

It isn't surprising that the "father of all lies" (2 Nephi 2:18) uses biology, psychology, and sociology to justify immoral behavior. Satan's despicable portrayal of a "tolerant virtue" and a "new chastity" seems to be of tidal-wave proportions and on the brink of consuming everything and everyone in its path. Thus leaders, parents, and disciples wonder if anything can protect their children, congregations, and friends from the impending moral doom and deception. President Ezra Taft Benson taught, "The law of chastity is a principle of eternal significance. We must not be swayed by the many voices of the world. We must listen to the voice of the Lord and then determine that we will set our feet irrevocably upon the path he has marked."[32] Long ago, during his mortal ministry, Christ taught his disciples that "ye shall know the truth, and the truth shall make you free" (John 8:32).

In a world filled with deception and lies on every side, wouldn't a guide to point out the truth in every circumstance be most effective and gratefully received? The sacrament serves to secure such a personal guide. Those who make worthy sacramental covenants actually pledge to live their lives in such a way that "they may always have his Spirit to be with them" (D&C 20:77). Whether through the scriptures, the living prophets, or personal revelation, the voice of the Lord is manifest in our mind and heart by the Holy Ghost, which was "sent forth to teach the truth" (D&C 50:14). Nephi taught that in addition to telling and teaching truth, the Holy Ghost "will *show* unto you all things what ye should do" (2 Nephi 32:5; emphasis added). Once again, it is the sacrament that can add yet another piece of God's armor to protect and sanctify the Saints in all things, places, and times.

Feet shod with preparation. It may be surprising to many that a soldier whose feet are not shod may be in mortal peril. Many do not place shoes in the same category as a helmet, a breastplate, or even a girdle. Yet shoes are just as vital in warfare as any other piece of armor. This particular piece of armor is protective in a very different way, however. Rather than protecting the foot itself, it is actually protecting the function of the foot. A soldier's mobility in battle is crucial to his success. If a warrior is unable to advance, adjust to the terrain of the battle, or even retreat, his chances of survival are slim. In Roman times, soldiers were issued hobnailed sandals. These sandals had nails driven through the soles and could be the ancient equivalent to what we call cleats today. Hobnailed shoes gave a soldier an advantage of sure traction and increased mobility.

The armor of God also includes having our feet, or, as Elder Lee pointed out, our goals and our objectives, shod with the "preparation of the gospel of peace" that was sent by angels (D&C 27:16). This means that our goals, our plans for the future, and the objectives of our life and how we plan to live it are directed and given traction by the preparation of the gospel sent by an angel, or, in other words, by the restored gospel of Jesus Christ.

Once again, it is difficult to find a platform that helps us develop such preparation derived from the restored gospel of Jesus Christ better than does the sacrament. Those who worthily partake of the sacrament actually covenant to be "willing to take upon them the name of [the] Son" (D&C 20:77). Taking the name of Christ upon us is more than merely accepting a label or a brand of worship. This is much more than saying "I am a Christian" or "I am a Latter-day Saint." In the very beginning, Adam was commanded, "Thou shalt do all that thou doest in the name of the Son" (Moses 5:8). Thus those who are willing to take upon them the name of Christ are willing to do more than just receive a namesake; they are willing do whatever Christ does. Like Christ, they too begin to wrestle with ultimate discipleship, as experienced in Gethsemane when Christ perfectly aligned his will with the Father's will. "Father," Christ prayed, "if thou be willing, remove this cup from me." We then see the demonstration of ultimate discipleship as Christ said, "Nevertheless not my will, but thine, be done" (Luke 22:42). All disciples of Christ pass through similar challenges in submitting their will to God's and in unifying their will with his.

Those willing to act as Christ did find that their desires, hopes, and plans take on a greater—even broader—context. Their preparation in his gospel influences every thought, motive, feeling, and perception. C. S. Lewis said, "I believe in Christianity as I believe that the Sun has risen, not only because I see it, but because by it I see everything else."[33] This type of preparation is directly connected with our sacramental covenant to take Christ's name upon us. Elder Dallin H. Oaks taught that "our willingness to take upon us the name of Jesus Christ affirms our commitment to do all that we can to be counted among those whom he will choose to stand at his right hand and be called by his name at the last day. In this sacred sense, our witness that we are willing to take upon us the name of Jesus Christ constitutes our declaration of candidacy for exaltation in the celestial kingdom."[34] Thus we must be vigilant that we never neglect our baptismal and sacramental covenants of taking Christ's name upon us, or else we risk taking Christ's name in vain.

Conclusion

Section 27 of the Doctrine and Covenant provides illuminating instruction concerning the sacrament. It helps us remember the past, look to the future, and focus on how we are presently living. The sacrament protects us and preserves us by helping us don the armor of God and evaluate our standing each week through specific covenants. Thus through the sacrament, the transforming power of the Atonement changes our very character. When we do more than just go through the motions, the sacrament can infuse the power and protection of the Atonement into our character. "At that ultimate stage," Elder Bruce C. Hafen explained, "we will exhibit divine characteristics not just because we think we should but because that is the way we are."[35]

As we embrace the sacrament as a ritual that is sacred and holy, we find peace, power, and contentment as it connects us with the past, present, and the future. Elder Dallin H. Oaks writes, "Any who may have thought it a small thing to partake of the sacrament should remember the Lord's declaration that the foundation of a great work is laid by small things." He then concluded, "Out of the seemingly small act of consciously and reverently renewing our baptismal covenants comes a renewal of the blessings of baptism by water and by the Spirit, that we may always have His Spirit to be with us. In this way all of us will be guided, and in this way all of us can be cleansed."[36]

Notes

1. *The Papers of Joseph Smith*, ed. Dean C. Jesse, vol. 1, *Autobiographical and Historical Writings* (Salt Lake City: Deseret Book, 1989), 321; see also *History of the Church of Jesus Christ of Latter-day Saints*, ed. B. H. Roberts, 2nd ed. rev. (Salt Lake City: Desert Book, 1980), 1:106. Newel Knight's journal account of this experience was slightly different in that he stated the second portion of the revelation was actually *revealed* to Joseph a few weeks after their August meeting in September. "Newell Knight's Journal," in *Scraps of Biography* (Salt Lake City: Juvenile Instructor's Office, 1883), 62.

2. *Evening and Morning Star*, March 1833, 78.

3. Robin Scott Jensen, Richard E. Turley Jr., and Riley M. Lorimer, eds., *Revelations and Translations, Volume 2: Published Revelations*, vol. 2 of the Revelations and Translations series of *The Joseph Smith Papers*, ed. Dean C. Jessee, Ronald K. Esplin, and Richard Lyman Bushman (Salt Lake City: Church Historian's Press, 2011), 72.

4. Jensen, Turley, and Lorimer, eds., *Revelations and Translations, Volume 2: Published Revelations*, 489–91.

5. *History of the Church*, 1:173.

6. The phrase "or the restorer of all things" in verse 6 was deleted after 1891. See Robert J. Woodford, "The Historical Development of the Doctrine and Covenants" (PhD diss., Brigham Young University, 1974), 1:398.

7. Spencer W. Kimball, "Circles of Exaltation," in *Charge to Religious Educators*, 2nd ed. (Salt Lake City: The Church of Jesus Christ of Latter-day Saints, 1982), 12.

8. *Teachings of Spencer W. Kimball*, ed. Edward L. Kimball (Salt Lake City: Bookcraft, 1982), 112.

9. *Teachings of Spencer W. Kimball*, 112–13.

10. John Taylor, *The Gospel Kingdom*, comp. G. Homer Durham (Salt Lake City: Bookcraft, 1964), 227.

11. Elder Charles Penrose taught, "We take this sacrament this afternoon not only in remembrance of the past but to direct our mind to the future." See Charles W. Penrose, in *Journal of Discourses* (London: Latter-day Saints' Book Depot, 1854–86), 22:83.

12. *Evening and Morning Star*, March 1833, 78; Jensen, Turley, and Lorimer, eds., *Revelations and Translations, Volume 2: Published Revelations*, 72.

13. In the current edition of the Doctrine and Covenants, 457 words were added to the published texts from 1833. Of these, 321 words deal directly with the future meeting where Jesus Christ will partake of the sacrament again on the earth.

14. This text also confirms that Joseph Smith received priesthood keys directly from Peter, James, and John and was ordained as an Apostle. We also learn that the archangel Michael and the "ancient of days" is Adam (see D&C 27:11–12).

15. Bruce R. McConkie, *The Millennial Messiah: The Second Coming of the Son of Man* (Salt Lake City: Deseret Book, 1982), 579.

16. McConkie, *Millennial Messiah*, 579.

17. McConkie, *Millennial Messiah*, 578–79.

18. Jensen, Turley, and Lorimer, eds., *Revelations and Translations, Volume 2: Published Revelations,* xxx.

19. *Evening and Morning Star,* March 1833, 78.

20. The final words of the original 1883 sentence, "and be faithful until I come," appear three verses later in the last sentence of the revelation (D&C 27:18).

21. Noah Webster, *American Dictionary of the English Language* (New York: S. Converse, 1829), "wherefore."

22. Richard Lloyd Anderson, "I Have a Question," *Ensign,* June 1975, 21.

23. Howard W. Hunter, "His Final Hours," *Ensign,* May 1974, 18.

24. Harold B. Lee, "Feet Shod with the Preparation of the Gospel of Peace" (address, Brigham Young University, Provo, UT, November 9, 1954), 2.

25. David A. Bednar, "Clean Hands and a Pure Heart," *Ensign,* November 2007, 82.

26. Bednar, "Clean Hands and a Pure Heart," 82.

27. Bednar, "Clean Hands and a Pure Heart," 82; emphasis in original.

28. Bednar, "Clean Hands and a Pure Heart," 82.

29. Bednar, "Clean Hands and a Pure Heart," 82.

30. Henry B. Eyring, "Eyes to See, Ears to Hear" (address, CES Symposium on the New Testament, August 16, 1984), 3.

31. Spencer W. Kimball, *Faith Precedes the Miracle* (Salt Lake City: Deseret Book, 1972), 152.

32. Ezra Taft Benson, "The Law of Chastity," *New Era,* January 1988, 4.

33. C. S. Lewis, "Is Theology Poetry?" in *The Weight of Glory and Other Addresses* (New York: Touchstone, 1980), 106.

34. Dallin H. Oaks, "Taking upon Us the Name of Jesus Christ," *Ensign,* May 1985, 83.

35. Bruce C. Hafen, *The Broken Heart: Applying the Atonement to Life's Experiences* (Salt Lake City: Deseret Book, 1989), 18.

36. Dallin H. Oaks, *With Full Purpose of Heart* (Salt Lake City: Deseret Book, 2002), 102.

7

Gathering the Lord's Words into One: Biblical Intertextuality in the Doctrine and Covenants

Lisa Olsen Tait

In February 1829, Joseph Smith Sr. was visiting in Harmony, Pennsylvania, with his son Joseph Jr. and his daughter-in-law Emma. Having long sought for religious truth while resisting organized religion, Father Smith was thrilled to see the potential for his desires to be answered through the work of his son, and in the course of the visit, Joseph received the revelation now known as section 4 on his behalf.[1] It is a short and beautiful passage of encouragement and counsel. "Now behold, a marvelous work is about to come forth among the children of men," the voice of the Lord begins. "Therefore, O ye that embark in the service of God, see that ye serve him with all your heart, might, mind and strength, that ye may stand blameless before God at the last day" (D&C 4:1–2).

We can only imagine how these words came as solace to the soul of Joseph Smith Sr. after a lifetime of anguish and searching. They must also have been a great comfort to his wife, Lucy Mack Smith, who had long hoped her husband would find the spiritual truths he sought and take his place as the spiritual leader of the family. And for the young prophet Joseph, this revelation

---

Lisa Olsen Tait is an adjunct professor of Church history and doctrine at Brigham Young University.

and others to follow would assure him repeatedly that he was not alone in the momentous responsibilities that rested so heavily on his shoulders.

Section 4 has become a classic in the Latter-day Saint canon. President Joseph Fielding Smith wrote that this revelation, short though it is, "contains sufficient counsel and instruction for a lifetime of study. . . . It is as broad, as high and as deep as eternity."[2] Missionaries are expected to memorize this section as part of their preparation to serve, and its counsel is readily applicable to all who serve in the Church.

Part of what makes section 4 so memorable is the beautiful language in which it is expressed, language that we readily recognize as echoing well-known passages in the Bible. This language would have been very familiar to Joseph Smith and his family in early 1829. They would have known the prophecy about a "marvelous work" from Isaiah 29:14, while the injunction to serve God "with all your heart, might, mind and strength" was familiar from several similar passages in both the Old and New Testaments (Deuteronomy 6:5; Mark 12:30; Luke 10:27).

The rest of the revelation continues to interweave biblical verses into an impressive collage: "For behold the field is white already to harvest [John 4:35]; and lo, he that thrusteth in his sickle [Revelation 14:15–19, alluding to Joel 3:13] with his might, the same layeth up in store [1 Timothy 6:19] that he perisheth not, but bringeth salvation to his soul" (D&C 4:4). Continuing on, we recognize "faith, hope, charity" from 1 Corinthians 13:13, an "eye single" to the glory of God from Matthew 6:22 and Luke 11:34, and the list of virtues enumerated in verse 6 from 2 Peter 1:5–7. The verse even begins with "remember," assuming the hearer has heard this list before. Finally, the closing injunction to "ask" and "knock" is repeated throughout the New Testament (see Matthew 7:7, for example).

Undoubtedly, the words of this revelation—many of which are repeated in subsequent revelations to other early believers (see, for example, D&C 6:1–5, 11; 12; 14; 15; 16)—would have resonated deeply with these people, farmers and tradesmen of the early American republic for whom the language of the Bible was thoroughly familiar and laden with meaning and authority. Indeed, the revelations of the Restoration would not have made sense, in many cases, unless the hearers already knew the Bible—and because they did know that book, the revelations reverberated with both familiar authority and new, enabling power.

The Doctrine and Covenants, then, is thoroughly interconnected with the Bible, not just in terms of doctrine and ideas but in terms of the very language in which those doctrines and ideas are expressed. This seems like an obvious point when it is stated outright, but it is one that we might easily overlook in our reading and discussion of the revelations. In our modern world, the Bible (especially the King James Version) has faded as a central and ubiquitous presence in the culture; even Latter-day Saints may be more familiar with modern revelation than with the Old or New Testaments. Therefore, we may not fully appreciate the extent to which the Doctrine and Covenants relies on the Bible.[3]

Literary scholars use the term *intertextuality* to describe the complex relationships of language, both written and spoken. Anything we write or say will be influenced by our previous experiences with language, and that experience comes primarily from our exposure to the spoken language of other people and to previously written texts. When something new is written, then, it will necessarily draw on language that has already been written (or spoken). Sometimes this occurs very consciously through direct quotes or comments on another text; sometimes it happens quite unconsciously through echoes of the words or ideas of familiar expressions. Intertextual references can be a single word or phrase, or they can consist of extended passages of shared language.

To illustrate briefly, some expressions that may be very familiar to us from the Doctrine and Covenants actually have their origin in the Bible. For example, the closing verses of section 89 outlining the Word of Wisdom are often quoted: "And all saints who remember to keep and do these sayings, walking in obedience to the commandments, shall receive health in their navel and marrow to their bones." This verse repeats Proverbs 3:8, in which we are told that fearing the Lord and departing from evil will be "health to thy navel, and marrow to thy bones." Continuing on, verse 20 of section 89 gives the well-known promise that we shall "run and not be weary, and shall walk and not faint"—a quotation of Isaiah 40:31. Another often-repeated expression found in the Doctrine and Covenants is found in both D&C 98:12 and D&C 128:21: "line upon line, precept upon precept." This phrase is also found in Isaiah 28, in verses 10 and 13.

Theorists have spilled much ink exploring the idea of intertextuality and its implications,[4] but at base, the concept of intertextuality affords a very simple insight and provides a useful term for use in discussion of texts. In short, when applied to the Doctrine and Covenants, that insight is this: the Doctrine and Covenants is a thoroughly intertextual book. That is, in almost every revelation, the text itself draws on the language of other scripture and functions to bring the dispensations into dialogue with each other. In the very language of the texts, the Doctrine and Covenants melds dispensations. This insight can powerfully reorient our study and teaching of the scriptures. It can help us to better appreciate the richness and complexity of the revelations in the Doctrine and Covenants, and it can help us realize the great power and meaning these revelations had for Joseph Smith and the early Saints. It can also help us come to see more fully the beauty and unity of the Lord's communications with his children throughout history.[5]

In this article, I offer a broad overview of the purposes, meanings, and function of biblical intertextuality in the Doctrine and Covenants. I will first consider three possible reasons for the presence of this feature in the text of the revelations. Then I will discuss several ways in which this intertextuality functions. Of necessity, this is a brief and suggestive treatment of a vast and complex subject, offered by way of making visible a feature of the Doctrine and Covenants that, for some, may be easily overlooked. In my experience, it is something that, once we have been alerted to its presence, can become a new and illuminating addition to our awareness when studying the scriptures.[6]

Reasons for Biblical Intertextuality

Why would there be so much intertextuality in the Doctrine and Covenants? We will consider three related answers to this question. The first reason relates to the nature of God and his perspective on revealing the gospel throughout time. The second reason is related to the complexities of "translating" revelation into language. The third reason, which is related to the second, grows out of the historical and cultural setting in which the revelations were given, a time in which biblical language was widely familiar and recognized as authoritative. These reasons are ultimately interrelated and are not mutually exclusive.

The Lord himself has declared one reason for the intertextuality of the scriptures: "I speak the same words unto one nation like unto another" (2 Nephi 29:8). While this statement is certainly true in broad terms—the Lord teaches the same truths to all men everywhere—at least in the

English-language versions of the scriptures, it is also literally true.[7] In the Bible, the Book of Mormon, and the Doctrine and Covenants, the Lord literally and extensively speaks the same words to different generations. His purpose in doing so, as he explains it, is to serve as a witness that "I am God, that I remember one nation like unto another" and to prove "that I am the same yesterday, today, and forever" (2 Nephi 29:8–9).

In this passage, the Lord also declares that in the last days his word "shall be gathered in one" (2 Nephi 29:14). While the immediate context for this statement is Nephi's prophecy of the coming forth of the Book of Mormon, we should note that it is realized perhaps even more fully in the Doctrine and Covenants, as that book extensively weaves the Lord's words together. Elsewhere, in speaking of the joint role of the Bible and the Book of Mormon, the prophet Lehi lists several other reasons that the scriptures will "grow together" into one: to confound false doctrines, lay down contention, establish peace, and bring the remnants of the house of Israel to a knowledge of their fathers and of the covenants of the Lord (see 2 Nephi 3:12). Certainly the Doctrine and Covenants, in its extensive use of language from the Bible, works with the Book of Mormon to fulfill these purposes. It literally melds the dispensations into "one."

Another possible reason for the use of biblical language in modern revelations may grow out of the inherent difficulties of expressing revelation adequately in human language. The few eyewitness accounts we have of Joseph Smith receiving revelations suggest that it was essentially a process of dictation: Joseph felt or heard the words in his mind and then spoke them aloud to be written down. Parley P. Pratt, for example, described the process this way: "Each sentence was uttered slowly and very distinctly, and with a pause between each, sufficiently long for it to be recorded by an ordinary writer, in long hand. This was the manner in which all his written revelations were dictated and written."[8]

There is good reason to believe, however, that for Joseph Smith, the process was not quite so easy. Joseph had to struggle with both the process of receiving revelation and with the difficulties of then "translating" that revelation into written language. We know that receiving revelation was, first and foremost, work. This was the lesson Oliver Cowdery had to learn when he desired to translate and found that he could not do it because, as the Lord explained, he "took no thought save it was to ask." Instead, he had to "study it out in [his] mind" and then ask for confirmation from the Spirit (D&C 9:7–9). While receiving and understanding the whisperings of the Spirit undoubtedly accounted for a large proportion of the work involved, it was also a struggle to find the right words to express that inspiration, and both Joseph and the Lord recognized that there would be a complex and sometimes difficult relationship between revelation—the language of God—and the language of men.

The Lord himself acknowledged this issue, declaring that the revelations in the Doctrine and Covenants "were given unto my servants in their weakness, after the manner of their language, that they might come to understanding" (D&C 1:24), implying that the Lord considers our language a necessary but "weak" vehicle for his communications to us. Undoubtedly, as Joseph Smith translated the Book of Mormon—perhaps the formative experience through which he learned how to receive and record revelation—he had sympathized with Moroni, who spoke poignantly of the difficulties he and his fellow Nephite prophets had encountered in putting their inspired words into writing. "When we write we behold our weakness, and stumble because of the placing of our words," Moroni lamented (Ether 12:25). While Moroni's difficulties may have been compounded by the physical realities of engraving on metal plates, certainly the primary problem was the disparity between inspiration and human language: "Thou hast also made our words powerful and great, even that we cannot write them" (Ether 12:25). Joseph Smith himself poignantly expressed his frustration with this disparity, pleading for deliverance from "the little, narrow prison, almost as it were, total darkness of paper, pen and ink;—and a crooked, broken, scattered and imperfect language."[9]

Getting from revelation to text, then, was a complex process that involved rendering the still, small voice of the Spirit into English words that would be coherent and meaningful to Joseph and his nineteenth-century American associates. While it is true that the language of the revelations in the Doctrine and Covenants is comprehensible to us as modern English, it is also clear that, in expressing the revelations in modern English, Joseph Smith held definite ideas about what sacred, scriptural language should sound like. In short, it should sound like the Bible—and in Joseph Smith's day, the Bible meant the King James Version, that magnificent accomplishment of English prose that had stood for two centuries as the apex of the English language. As one recent assessment puts it, "The translators of the King James Bible attuned the ears of English speakers everywhere as to how the Bible is supposed to sound."[10]

Indeed, it may be that the language of the Bible provided a vital escape from that "narrow prison" of "scattered and imperfect language."

As I have already discussed, we do not know the exact relationship between the ideas or words the Lord spoke or placed in Joseph's mind and heart and the words and phrases that were recorded as the textual form of those revelations. But whether we attribute the words of the revelations as we now have them more to the Lord or to Joseph Smith, it seems clear that the language of the Bible was equally useful to each "author" in expressing himself. For the Lord, it offered a means of communicating with his people in language that was already familiar and authoritative. It brought the dispensations together and served as a further witness of his word. For Joseph Smith, struggling to write his way out of that narrow prison of language, the Bible offered both a model and a storehouse of words and phrases that enabled him to express his revelations in meaningful terms.

The same was true for Joseph's listeners, and this brings us to the third reason for the extensive biblical intertextuality in the Doctrine and Covenants: the language of the Bible was thoroughly familiar and authoritative to Americans of the early nineteenth century and therefore provided an important point of reference for the new revelations. The early Saints recognized in the revelations a blend of familiar words and new doctrines that mutually illuminated and validated each other. It is probably impossible for us today to fully appreciate just how central and fundamental an element the Bible was in the culture of English-speaking people in the early nineteenth century. The historian Perry Miller famously remarked that "the Old Testament is truly so omnipresent in the American culture of 1800 or 1820 that historians have as much difficulty taking cognizance of it as of the air people breathed."[11] Through centuries of use and repetition, the language of the King James Version had become part of the cultural DNA. People owned and read Bibles, to be sure, but we should remember that the culture was much more organized around face-to-face interaction and that the spoken word (sermons, dramatic readings, storytelling) provided the most common and fundamental forms of entertainment and education. Joseph Smith and his contemporaries knew the language of the Bible not only because they read it but because they *heard* it all around them—directly from the book, but also as part of the deeply embedded idioms of everyday speech.

This fact should make us even more sensitive to the many uses of "hear" or similar terms in the Doctrine and Covenants. The first word of the book, indeed, is "hearken," and the word "hear" appears in the revelations over eighty times, usually in imperative form as the Lord instructs us to listen to his words (see D&C 18:36; 41:1; 133:16). For many of the early Saints, undoubtedly, *hearing* was a primary means by which they learned the word of the Lord, and it is likely that Joseph and his contemporaries retained an auditory orientation to the scriptures that we have largely lost. In other words, the revelations *sounded* familiar to them because they had *heard* such language repeatedly throughout their lives.

It is important to stress, I think, that we cannot know for certain which intertextual expressions in the revelations would have been previously familiar to Joseph Smith himself or to his listeners; certainly we cannot assume that any given person had essentially memorized the Bible. Therefore, it would be a highly variable matter to account for the biblical resonances in any given verse. Nevertheless, it seems safe to say that, on the whole, the biblical language used in the Doctrine and Covenants circulated widely in early-nineteenth-century America, and when Joseph Smith's listeners did recognize it as such, the use of that language in these texts communicated more than words alone. Joseph Smith and his contemporaries would have heard not only the words of the modern revelation but also those words in the context of the biblical passages to which they refer, often expanding or enriching their meaning in ways that we miss if we are not aware of the original.

Moreover, we should also acknowledge that the intertextuality of the Bible with both the Doctrine and Covenants and the Book of Mormon has been cited by some observers as evidence that Joseph Smith simply composed the revelations himself by patching together biblical phrases and pseudo-scriptural language. In my view, this explanation is much too easy. Looking at section 4, for example, we find in just seven short verses a complex and beautiful text that draws on over eight different biblical sources with little self-conscious marking of itself as quotation or allusion. It is a text that simultaneously stands on its own while resonating with the meanings and music of its sources. In order to have "composed" this passage, Joseph Smith would have had to be a literary mind of no small proportion. Yet Emma, his wife, describing him during the same period in which section 4 was received, adamantly asserted that Joseph "could neither write nor dictate a coherent and well-worded letter."[12] Critics have long tied themselves in knots trying to explain away Joseph Smith's revelations, but the texts themselves provide the best evidence for their own validity. For those of us who accept the veracity of those revelations, the biblical intertextuality in the Doctrine and Covenants provides yet another witness of their authenticity.

Functions of Biblical Intertextuality

Having considered the *why* of biblical intertextuality in the Doctrine and Covenants, we can now turn to the *how*: How does this intertextuality function in the texts of the revelations? We can discuss only a few examples here, but I would like to identify three general patterns. First, biblical intertextuality in the Doctrine and Covenants works to reaffirm and reframe prophecy. Second, it serves to amplify previous scripture, adding new insight or information. Third, it functions to motivate and help develop the identity of the recipients.

Sometimes we find all of these functions simultaneously. I have already mentioned the phrase "a marvelous work," which first appears in section 4. Throughout the scriptures, God's works are referred to as "marvelous," as in Psalm 9:1 ("I will shew forth all thy marvellous works") or Revelation 15:3 ("Great and marvellous are thy works, Lord God Almighty"). In section 4, however, this language echoes a specific prophecy in Isaiah 29 where the Lord declares that he will "proceed to do a marvellous work among this people, even a marvellous work and a wonder" (Isaiah 29:14), referring to the coming forth of the Book of Mormon and the Restoration of the gospel in the latter days. This revelation simultaneously places the work of Joseph Smith within that larger framework, affirming and reframing prophecy, and clarifies the older biblical passage, making clear that it would be fulfilled through the Book of Mormon and the work of Joseph Smith.

The intertextuality in this revelation also functioned to powerfully reorient the lives and identities of those who heard it. Joseph Smith Sr. was confirmed in his faith that his son had been called of God and was informed that he, too, had a role to play. Likewise, the reference to "a marvelous work" is repeated in early revelations given to several other individuals who had asked Joseph to inquire of the Lord regarding their standing and duties. Through this language Oliver Cowdery (see D&C 6:1), Hyrum Smith (see D&C 11:1), Joseph Knight (see D&C 12:1), and David Whitmer (see D&C 14:1) were each invited to recognize, accept, and become part of the "marvelous work," with the intertextual relationship of the modern revelation and the biblical passage mutually illuminating one another. In this simple phrase first found in section 4, we find all three functions of biblical intertextuality in the Doctrine and Covenants: it affirms prophecy, expands the meaning of a previous scripture, and invites actual people, then and now, to identify with and participate in the work of God.

Considering the functions of intertextuality separately, we first find that the revelations in the Doctrine and Covenants often invoke biblical language in reference to prophecy. One powerful example is the poignant declaration of the Lord that he will "gather his people even as a hen gathereth her chickens under her wings" (D&C 29:2; see also D&C 10:65 and 43:24). This promise echoes the lament of the Savior not long before his death: "O Jerusalem, Jerusalem, . . . how often would I have gathered thy children together, even as a hen gathereth her chickens under her wings, and ye would not" (Matthew 23:37; see also Luke 13:34). It takes an expression from the Bible that could refer to one particular historical moment and transforms it into a prophecy that applies to all. It tells us something about the Savior and his eagerness to watch over and bless his people, those who "will" as opposed to those who "would not." I find it significant that Christ himself speaks these words in the New Testament, the Book of Mormon, and the Doctrine and Covenants, spanning dispensations and cultures. He seems to feel that it is a particularly apt metaphor for helping us understand his love for and watchcare over us.

Prophecy of the last days occurs frequently in the Doctrine and Covenants. Sections 29, 45, 88, and 133 contain some of the better known millennial prophecies. In these sections, the biblical intertextuality is especially dense, and Isaiah figures heavily as a point of reference. Consider, for example, the first five verses of section 133 (see table 1). This passage introduces an extended revelation in which the Lord imparts much information about the "preaching of the Gospel to the inhabitants of the earth, and concerning the gathering" (section heading). Some of the phrases used seem to be direct references to the prophecies invoked ("shall suddenly come to his temple" and "make bare his holy arm"), while others simply speak in language familiar from the Bible ("all the nations that forget God" and "sanctify yourselves"). All come together to create a new, unified text.

This pattern continues throughout the revelation. In D&C 133:42–53, to take another example, the text quotes extensively from or alludes directly to Isaiah 64:2–5 and Isaiah 63:1–9, weaving together many phrases from the original but also omitting some and adding new language. Taken together, the intertextuality in section 133 serves to affirm that the day is near—"the great day of the Lord" (D&C 133:10, echoing Zephaniah 1:14 and many other Old Testament references)—when ancient prophecies will be fulfilled in modern times, bringing the dispensations together and fulfilling the covenants and promises made by the Lord from the beginning of this earth. On this subject, perhaps more than any other, the Doctrine and Covenants brings the Lord's words into one.

A second function of intertextuality in the Doctrine and Covenants is to expand upon the biblical source. Perhaps the most powerful example of this function is also one of the most indirect. It is found in D&C 19:18, where the Savior describes his own suffering in completing the Atonement: "Which suffering caused myself, even God, the greatest of all, to tremble because of pain, and to bleed at every pore, and to suffer both body and spirit—and would that I might not drink the bitter cup, and shrink." This description stands powerfully on its own, but it also refers unmistakably to the description in Luke 22:44 of Jesus' agony, in which "his sweat was as it were great drops of blood falling down to the ground." And the modern revelation's declaration that he shrank from drinking the "bitter cup" also echoes Matthew's account, in which Jesus prayed that the Father would "let this cup pass from me" (Matthew 26:39). Here we have a modern revelation that adds to the biblical accounts by providing profound detail that expands our understanding of the scope of the Atonement.

Section 29 includes another brief intertextual reference that provides expanded doctrinal understanding to a puzzling biblical term. Verse 7 of that revelation instructs the elders that they are "called to bring to pass the gathering of mine elect." "Elect" is a term that appears in several places in the New Testament. Jesus himself uses it (see Mark 13:20, 22, for example), and it appears in various epistles, such as Colossians 3:12, which refers to "the elect of God." These usages led the Christian world to much discussion and speculation about how we might know who "the elect" are. Calvinists believed that God would save only a few; Universalists believed that God would save everyone. Either way, "the elect" were chosen by God. Section 29 invokes the term and then offers a simple definition: "mine elect hear my voice and harden not their hearts" (v. 7). This definition radically reconfigures the biblical term. The "elect" are not such because God chooses them; they are "elect" because they choose God. We have agency.[13] This one brief intertextual reference clears up centuries of speculation.

Finally, as we saw in conjunction with section 4, some of the most powerful uses of intertextuality in the Doctrine and Covenants come in revelations addressed to specific individuals. In the March 1832 calling of Frederick G. Williams to become a counselor in the First Presidency, for example, he is instructed to "succor the weak, lift up the hands which hang down, and strengthen the feeble knees" (D&C 81:5). This counsel repeats the counsel given in Hebrews 12:12 ("lift up the hands which hang down, and the feeble knees"), a passage that in turn echoes one in Isaiah 35:3 ("Strengthen ye the weak hands, and confirm the feeble knees"; see also Job 4:4). This language encouraged Brother Williams to see himself as connected to the servants of previous dispensations and to develop characteristics of service and compassion that would likewise qualify him for his calling.

Perhaps the most significant uses of this kind of intertextuality occur in revelations concerning the apostleship. Section 18 was given in June 1829, in part to commission Oliver Cowdery and David Whitmer to "search out the Twelve" (v. 37). In this revelation the Lord employs language associated with his New Testament Apostles, often repeating verbatim instructions and counsel given to those ancient servants. The Twelve "are called to go into all the world to preach my gospel unto every creature" (v. 28, echoing Mark 16:15). They are told, "My grace is sufficient for you," repeating words that the Apostle Paul reported the Lord had spoken to him (D&C 18:31; 2 Corinthians 12:9). Six years later, the Lord once again addressed the recently called Twelve Apostles with counsel and instruction delivered through intertextual language. "Take up your cross," he commanded, and "feed my sheep" (D&C 112:14; see, for example, Matthew 16:24 and John 21:16). Here, the command to "go ye into all the world, and preach my gospel unto every creature" includes the rest of the original reference: "And he that believeth and is baptized shall be saved, and he that believeth not, and is not baptized, shall be damned" (D&C 112:28–29; see Mark 16:15–16).

The modern Twelve would certainly have known these verses well. The words would have served to confirm, even to create, a self-image and identity for these brethren as Apostles—an office that was at once familiar and brand-new to them. By speaking to these brethren in the same language he used to teach his original Apostles, the Lord tied together the dispensations and provided an unmistakable model, replete with biblical precedent, for the modern Church to follow.

Appreciating Intertextuality

In the revelations contained in the Doctrine and Covenants, we see clearly that the Lord "speak[s] the same words unto one nation like unto another" and gathers his word into one (2 Nephi 29:8, 14). The use of biblical language in modern revelations marks them with authority and familiarity, expands on ancient sources, and develops identity and motivation in both the original recipients and modern readers. These functions, we might note, parallel the reasons discussed above for the presence of intertextuality. The Lord declares his authority and imparts truth by reaffirming prophecy. Biblical language bridges the gap between the familiar and the new by adding additional information and insight. And the use of intertextuality capitalizes on biblical precedent to profoundly orient and develop the commitment of the new Saints being forged for the new dispensation.

Clearly, many other examples of biblical intertextuality in the Doctrine and Covenants could be enumerated, and there is yet room to investigate this subject much more fully, identifying patterns and implications that cannot be explored here. I offer these observations not by way of a comprehensive or definitive treatment but in hopes of prompting us to be more sensitive readers of scripture. By attuning ourselves to the biblical intertextuality in the Doctrine and Covenants, we can increase our understanding of modern revelation, and we can also gain new appreciation for the Bible—especially, perhaps, the Old Testament. As we look for the interrelationships in these magnificent texts, we will come to search the scriptures with new eyes, looking for connections and resonances we might otherwise miss—connections and resonances that continue to reverberate powerfully for us, just as they did for Joseph Smith and the early Saints.

Table 1:
Biblical Intertextuality in D&C 133:1–5

Verse	D&C Phrase	Biblical Reference	Biblical Phrase
2	"The Lord who shall suddenly come to his temple"	Malachi 3:1	"The Lord, whom ye seek, shall suddenly come to his temple"
	"[The Lord] shall come down upon the world with a curse to judgment"	Isaiah 34:5	"[My sword] shall come down upon Idumea, and upon the people of my curse, to judgment"
	"Upon all the nations that forget God"	Psalm 9:17	"The wicked shall be turned into hell, and all the nations that forget God"
3	"For he shall make bare his holy arm in the eyes of all the nations, and all the ends of the earth shall see the salvation of their God"	Isaiah 52:10	"The Lord hath made bare his holy arm in the eyes of all the nations; and all the ends of the earth shall see the salvation of our God"
4	"Prepare ye, prepare ye"	Isaiah 40:3; Mark 1:3; Luke 3:4	"Prepare ye the way of the Lord"
	"Sanctify yourselves"	Leviticus 11:44, seven other references in OT	"Sanctify yourselves"
	"Gather ye together"	Matthew 13:30	"Gather ye together first the tares . . ."
5	"Be ye clean that bear the vessels of the Lord"	Isaiah 52:11	"Be ye clean, that bear the vessels of the Lord"

Notes

1. For historical background on section 4, see Steven C. Harper, *Making Sense of the Doctrine and Covenants* (Salt Lake City: Deseret Book, 2008), 29.

2. Joseph Fielding Smith, *Church History and Modern Revelation* (Salt Lake City: Deseret Book, 1946), 1:35.

3. There is also a great deal of interdependence between the Doctrine and Covenants and the Book of Mormon. For example, though Joseph Smith Sr. and his son would not have fully recognized it yet, many of the biblical expressions in section 4 are also found in the Book of Mormon. The prophecy of a "marvelous work" is quoted directly from Isaiah in 2 Nephi 27:26 and again by Mormon in 3 Nephi 28:32, and it appears elsewhere in 1 and 2 Nephi. Ammon speaks of thrusting in the sickle in Alma 26:5, and the sacred triumvirate of "faith, hope, and charity" appears in several places (Alma 7:24; Ether 12:28; Moroni 7:1, 42–48; 10:20–22). The Savior teaches the Nephites about the importance of having an "eye single" (3 Nephi 13:22) and exhorts them to "ask" and to "knock" (3 Nephi 27:29). This subject is worthy of further exploration. However, most of the expressions that appear in the Doctrine and Covenants from the Book of Mormon are also found in the Bible, and it was the Bible that held a place of cultural familiarity and authority, especially for those who did not know the Book of Mormon; therefore, I am focusing this discussion on the Bible and the Doctrine and Covenants.

4. A complete discussion of the concept of intertextuality is found in Graham Allen, *Intertextuality* (London and New York: Routledge, 2000). Allen stresses that postmodern theorists, who coined the term, use it to challenge the idea of authority in language and texts (209). In this view, all language is interrelated and all human thought and interaction take place through language; therefore, they argue, there is no ultimate authority outside of language. I would argue that God and his communication with us (i.e., revelation) do exist outside of human language, radiating from a realm of ultimate truth and reality and therefore making the only legitimate claim to authority we can know—despite the difficulties, as I discuss below, of translating that revelation into human language. In any case, we do not have to accept all of the uses or possible implications of the term to find it helpful in discussing the interrelationship of texts.

5. Professor D. Kelly Ogden has written an impressive study of biblical expressions, analogies, and imagery used in the Doctrine and Covenants. While his essay provides an exhaustive cataloging of those items, I want to explore more fully the question of *why* this intertextuality exists and how it functions. See D. Kelly Ogden, "Biblical Language and Imagery in the Doctrine and Covenants," in *Doctrine and Covenants, A Book of Answers*, ed. Leon R. Hartshorn, Dennis A. Wright, and Craig J. Ostler (Salt Lake City: Deseret Book, 1996), 169–87.

6. We should note that technology has made it much easier to identify scriptural intertextuality by allowing us to search for specific words and phrases. The "search the scriptures" function on lds.org, for example, works well to identify shared language across the standard works. Because the footnotes in our scriptures are geared toward topics and principles, rather than language, they tend to identify only the most obvious instances of intertextuality.

7. As discussed below, the relationship of revelation and language is complex, and we cannot completely recover or pinpoint that relationship. In the case of the Bible, we have added layers of complexity because of the process of transmission and translation from the original languages in which the scriptural texts were originally written. Acknowledging all of these factors, it still seems safe to assume that the translators of the King James Version were divinely guided in their choice of language, which became the basis for the language used in subsequent revelation, including the Joseph Smith Translation.

8. *Autobiography of Parley P. Pratt*, ed. Scot Facer Proctor and Maurine Jensen Proctor, revised and enhanced ed. (Salt Lake City: Deseret Book, 2000), 72; paragraphing altered. Pratt reported that he had witnessed the reception of "several communications" (i.e., revelations to Joseph Smith) but did not specify which ones.

9. Joseph Smith to William W. Phelps, November 27, 1832. See *The Personal Writings of Joseph Smith*, ed. Dean C. Jessee. rev. ed. (Salt Lake City: Deseret Book, 2002), 287. Joseph's statement about language appears at the end of the letter; the central section of the letter contains the instructions now canonized as section 85 of the Doctrine and Covenants.

10. John S. Tanner, "The King James Bible in America: Pilgrim, Prophet, President, Preacher," *BYU Studies* 50, no. 3 (2011): 6.

11. Perry Miller, "The Garden of Eden and the Deacon's Meadow," *American Heritage* 7 (December 1955): 54, quoted in Tanner, "The King James Bible in America," 5.

12. Quoted in Mark L. McConkie, *Remembering Joseph: Personal Recollections of Those Who Knew the Prophet Joseph Smith* (Salt Lake City: Deseret Book, 2003), 303.

13. I am indebted to Steven Harper's discussion of section 76 for this insight. See Harper, *Making Sense of the Doctrine and Covenants*, 262.

8

Isaiah in the Doctrine and Covenants

Terry B. Ball and Spencer S. Snyder

Isaiah is the most quoted Old Testament prophet in the Book of Mormon and arguably the most quoted Old Testament prophet in the Doctrine and Covenants as well. Our survey of the Doctrine and Covenants found that nearly two-thirds of the sections, 86 out of 138, share some characteristic language, phrases, or terms with the words of Isaiah. In this study, we evaluate how and why Isaianic language is used in the revelations and other writings that compose the D&C.

How Isaianic Language Is Used in the D&C

Through computer-assisted analysis, we identified 312 occurrences of Isaianic language in the D&C (see tables 1, 2).[1] Our list includes wording that clearly originates in Isaiah (72 percent of our total count),[2] as well as wording that in our opinion likely originates with Isaiah but may be found in other scriptures as well (28 percent of our total count).[3] When we refer to Isaianic language in this study, we draw upon all 312 occurrences. We calculated that the D&C averages nearly three usages of Isaianic language for every thousand words of text.

Terry B. Ball is dean of Religious Education at Brigham Young University. Spencer S. Snyder is an exercise science major at Brigham Young University.

While some of the shared language in the D&C occurs in the form of extended passages taken from Isaiah's writings, the preponderance of the common language found in the two texts is in the form of short phrases such as "blossom as the rose" (Isaiah 35:1; D&C 49:24), "see eye to eye" (Isaiah 52:8; D&C 84:98) and "prepare ye the way" (Isaiah 62:10; D&C 33:10; 65:1, 3; 133:17). Only D&C 113:1–10, which comments on the identities of individuals and the meaning of phrases found in Isaiah 11 and 53, and D&C 138:42, which speaks of the Redeemer's work as described in Isaiah 61:1, openly identify Isaiah as the source of the language. In every other instance, the D&C incorporates the Isaianic language without referring to the book of Isaiah itself.[4]

In our analysis, we found that the D&C draws not only regularly but also broadly from the words of Isaiah. We found 171 different Isaianic terms or phrases used in the D&C. While some of the terms and phrases such as "stakes," "an ensign," and "everlasting covenant" occur in the D&C text fifteen or more times each, surprisingly, 86 percent of the shared Isaianic language or phrases (147 out of 171) are used three times or less. This suggests that the frequent appearance of Isaiah's words in the D&C is not merely a function of a few favorite phrases being used repetitively but is rather the wording of one who is widely familiar and deeply acquainted with the entire text of the King James Version of Isaiah.

We observed that the revelations recorded in the D&C draw language and phrases from 82 percent of the chapters of Isaiah (fifty-four of sixty-six). We calculated an index of usage for each chapter of Isaiah to determine if there were particular chapters that more frequently share language with the D&C. This was done by dividing the total number of times language from a given chapter occurs in the entire D&C by the total number of words in that chapter. The twenty Isaiah chapters with the highest indices of usage are reported in table 3. We found that thirteen of the twenty chapters with the highest indices of usage (Isaiah 40, 42, 45, 47, 51–55, 58, 61–63), including the top three (Isaiah 61, 54, 55), come from the closing portion of Isaiah. Students of Isaiah typically recognize that the first thirty-five chapters of the book (Isaiah 1–35) focus primarily on themes of warning, chastisement, and judgment, followed by four historical chapters that chronicle events that transpired during King Hezekiah's reign (Isaiah 36–39). The last twenty-seven chapters (Isaiah 40–66), which share more language with the D&C,

tend to focus on God's ability and plans to restore and redeem his people. In fact, overall we found that 55 percent of the occurrences of Isaianic language found in the D&C come from the last twenty-seven chapters of Isaiah rather than the first thirty-nine.

To further consider if Isaiah's restoration and redemption language is more common in the D&C than his judgment and rebuke language, we categorized each of the 171 different Isaianic phrases found in the D&C into one of three types: (1) rebukes or warnings for apostasy and sin, (2) counsel or advice, and (3) prophecies of future events such as the gathering, restoration, and redemption of Israel and the coming of the Messiah. We then calculated the percentage of the total each type represented (see table 4). We found that, although warning and rebuke language is abundant in the book, the D&C does not draw significantly upon Isaiah for the wording, with only 10 percent of the total shared Isaianic phrases being of this type. When it occurs, Isaianic rebuke language is typically used to describe the apostate world into which the gospel was and will be restored (for example, compare D&C 1:15–16; 112:23 with Isaiah 24:5; 60:2).

The second type, Isaiah's language of counsel and advice, appears slightly more frequently in the D&C, with 21 percent of the total Isaianic phrases in the text being in this category. For example, individuals and groups are variously counseled and admonished to "be . . . clean, that bear the vessels of the Lord" (compare D&C 38:42; 133:5 with Isaiah 52:11), to seek the Lord "early" and "call upon" him while he is "near" (compare D&C 88:62, 83 with Isaiah 26:9; 55:6), and to "bind up" and "seal" the law and their testimonies as they proclaim the word of God (compare D&C 88:84; 109:38 with Isaiah 8:16).

Representing 69 percent of the total, Isaiah's language prophesying of the Messiah and the future gathering, restoration, and redemption of his people is by far the most abundant. Often prophetic phrases from Isaiah are used in the D&C to describe the latter-day Restoration that has occurred and is still occurring. For example, the "marvelous work" of the Restoration has begun causing the "wisdom of the wise" to "perish" (compare D&C 4:1; 6:1; 11:1; 12:1; 14:1; 18:44; 76:9 with Isaiah 29:14). The latter-day "voice in the wilderness" has cried out, "Prepare ye the way of the Lord" (compare D&C 65:1; 133:17 with Isaiah 40:3), as the "light" of the gospel is sought out by the "Gentiles" (compare D&C 45:9, 28; 86:11 with Isaiah 42:6; 60:3).

Truth is being revealed "line upon line, precept upon precept" (compare D&C 98:12; 128:21 with Isaiah 28:10, 13) as God performs his "strange act" (compare D&C 101:95 with Isaiah 28:21). The desert has begun to "blossom as the rose" (compare D&C 49:24 with Isaiah 35:1) as Zion prepares to "arise and put on her beautiful garments" (compare D&C 82:14 with Isaiah 52:1). Isaiah's prophetic language foretelling the coming of Christ is also common in the Doctrine and Covenants. For example, at the advent of the Millennial Messiah, the "nations" will "tremble" at his presence (compare D&C 34:8 with Isaiah 64:2), "the scorner shall be consumed," and those who "watched for iniquity" will be destroyed (compare D&C 45:50 with Isaiah 29:20). When he appears, the "valleys" will "be exalted," "the mountains" will "be made low" (compare D&C 49:23; 109:74 with Isaiah 40:4), and an "overflowing scourge" shall cover the land (compare D&C 45:31 with Isaiah 28:15). Jesus will appear, proclaiming that he has "trodden the winepress alone" (compare D&C 76:107; 88:106 with Isaiah 63:3). "All flesh shall see" him "together" (compare D&C 101:23 with Isaiah 40:5), and "every knee shall bow, and every tongue shall confess" that he is the Christ (compare D&C 88:10 with Isaiah 45:23) as he becomes their "lawgiver" (compare D&C 38:22 with Isaiah 33:22). Eventually, the righteous shall dwell in Zion, having "songs of everlasting joy upon their heads" (compare D&C 66:11; 101:18; 133:33 with Isaiah 35:10).

To further analyze how Isaianic language is incorporated into the D&C, we calculated the rate of occurrences of Isaianic wording per thousand words of text for each of the D&C sections. We found a wide distribution for the rate of occurrences of Isaianic language among the 138 sections. The twenty sections with the most occurrences of Isaianic language per thousand words are reported in table 5. We observed that of these twenty sections, sixteen included significant prophecy concerning the Restoration of the gospel, the last days, and the Second Coming of Christ.[5] The other four sections (D&C 30, 71, 115, and 125) are primarily counsel on contemporary Church administration.

This observation led us to categorize each of the 138 sections as either contemporary or prophetic and then calculate the number of occurrences of Isaianic language per thousand words of text for each category (see table 6). We classified as contemporary those sections that primarily contain doctrine and instructions for Church organization and administration, as well as personal instruction for individuals or groups contemporary with the Prophet Joseph Smith. We classified as prophetic any sections that significantly touch upon events that are to occur in the future for the Church or the world, such as the Second Coming and the Millennium. We found that contemporary sections contain about two Isaianic phrases per thousand words of text, while prophetic sections contain nearly four and a half occurrences per thousand words.

In our study, we observed that in 109 sections of the D&C, the voice of the Lord is recorded in the first person. In the remaining 29 sections, others are the voice and refer to the Lord in the third person. Curious to know if the "voice" of the prophecy influences the amount of Isaianic language usage in the D&C, we calculated the rate of occurrences of Isaianic language per thousand words of text for both voices (see table 7). We found that in sections where the Lord speaks in the first person, there are about 2.9 occurrences of Isaianic language per thousand words, and when others are the voice, there are 2.36 occurrences, a difference we are not confident is significant.

In summary, our study of how Isaianic language is used in the D&C indicates that the shared language is drawn broadly and abundantly from throughout the 66 chapters of Isaiah's writings and is incorporated broadly and abundantly throughout the 138 sections of the D&C. While the voice of the prophecy does not seem to influence the rate of Isaianic wording in the D&C, the type of prophecy does. It appears that, typically, when a D&C revelation begins to speak of the future, the words of Isaiah echo from the past.

Why Is Isaianic Language Often Used in the D&C?

The broad and prevalent occurrence of Isaianic language in the D&C suggests either that the Prophet Joseph Smith was extraordinarily familiar with Isaiah's writings and accordingly borrowed terminology from them extensively as he communicated the revelations he received from God, or that the shared language finds its way into the D&C because the Lord chose to use King James Translation Isaianic language to communicate, inspire, and reveal truths to the Prophet. The question that arises is intriguing. Does the choice of words in the revelations recorded in the D&C belong to Joseph Smith or to God—or to both? The answer to that question has the potential to tell us much about how Joseph Smith received and communicated revelation.[6] We felt that some insights to addressing the question could be gained by looking for explanations regarding why Isaianic language is so prevalent in the D&C.

We began by looking for any particular time in Joseph Smith's life wherein the revelations he received contained more Isaianic language than others. We reasoned that if there were, then perhaps we could make inferences about events or experiences he had at those particular times of his life that may have influenced the amount of Isaianic language in the D&C. We first calculated the number of occurrences of Isaianic language per thousand words of text for the D&C sections received during each year. We found that from 1828 to 1835 the amount of revelation the Prophet received, as well as the rate of Isaianic language usage in the text, rose and then fell, peaking in 1831, but after 1836 the values show no predictable pattern (see table 8).[7] These results suggest that for the first portion of Joseph's prophetic career, the amount of Isaianic language used in the D&C is in part a function of the amount of revelation the Prophet was receiving. Generally, the greater the volume of revelation received during a year, the greater the use of Isaianic language per thousand words of text. We could not, however, identify any other significant pattern that pointed to an experience or event to explain the rate of usage of Isaianic wording in the D&C.

We next looked for evidence that Joseph Smith had ever intensely studied the writings of Isaiah during his life, reasoning that if so then perhaps such study may have been a contributing factor to the ubiquitous occurrence of Isaianic language in the D&C. As we considered the life of Joseph Smith, we identified translating the Book of Mormon and working on the Inspired Version (JST) as two experiences in his life that could have given him an exceptional expertise in and affinity for the writings of Isaiah.

If translating the Book of Mormon, with its frequent and long quotations from Isaiah, gave the Prophet a special familiarity with Isaiah's wording and moved him to incorporate Isaianic language in the D&C revelations, then, we reasoned, the passages of Isaiah quoted in the Book of Mormon should be the source of more of the shared language in the D&C than those chapters of Isaiah not represented in the Book of Mormon. Accordingly, we calculated an index of usage for the Isaiah passages quoted in the Book of Mormon[8] and compared it to the same index of usage for passages not quoted there. The indices of usage were once again derived by dividing the number of times wording from the Isaiah passages occur in the D&C text by the total number of words in the passages. We found that with values of 0.86 compared to 0.83 respectively, the Isaiah passages quoted in the Book of Mormon did not have a significantly higher index of usage in the D&C than the nonquoted passages (see table 9).[9] The data appear to argue against any expertise Joseph Smith obtained from translating the Book of Mormon being a prime reason for the abundant Isaianic wording in the D&C.

We observed further that Isaianic language does not appear to be used in the Book of Mormon in the same way it is used in the D&C. As noted above, the D&C does not contain much in the way of long quotations from Isaiah, but rather regularly incorporates short phrases and terms from the King James Version of the Old Testament prophet's writings without identifying their source. In contrast, the Book of Mormon contains many lengthy quotations from Isaiah and usually identifies them as such. We found that if we remove the lengthy Isaiah quotations from the Book of Mormon and then evaluate the remaining text for Isaianic language, not much is found. While the D&C uses nearly three Isaianic phrases for every thousand words, the Book of Mormon text that is not directly quoting Isaiah averages only two for every ten thousand words of text.[10] Obviously, in terms of the use of Isaianic language, Joseph Smith's prophetic experience in translating the Book of Mormon was very different from that of receiving the D&C revelations.

If Joseph Smith's work on the JST, particularly the JST of Isaiah, influenced the amount of Isaianic language in the D&C text, then we would expect a significant increase in the occurrence of Isaiah's words in the revelations received during and, for a reasonable period, following the time he worked on the Isaiah portion of the JST. To consider whether the expertise the Prophet may have gained while working on the JST of Isaiah influenced how much Isaianic terminology appears in the D&C, we considered the timing of the work. We believe that the Prophet likely worked on the JST of Isaiah during the summer of 1833 and most certainly between July 1832 and July 1833.[11] Accordingly, we compared the number of occurrences of Isaianic language per thousand words for D&C revelations received during 1832 and 1833 to those received during other years. We found that revelations received during the years the Prophet would have been working on the JST of Isaiah do not show a significant increase in the occurrences of Isaianic language. In fact, the 1832 and 1833 revelations, with 2.7 occurrences of Isaianic language per thousand words, are actually significantly less rich in Isaianic language than the 1831 revelations, with 3.4 occurrences, and not significantly different than the 1830 revelations, with a value of 2.5 (see table 8). Thus, while Joseph Smith likely learned much while working on the JST of Isaiah, that learning did not appear to influence how much Isaianic language made its way into the D&C.

We considered the possibility that Joseph Smith habitually incorporated Isaianic language into his writings and sermons, reasoning that if so, then the abundant Isaianic language in the D&C is no special phenomenon but rather simply a product of his regular way of communicating. Accordingly, we calculated the rate of occurrences of Isaianic language per thousand words for approximately 15,000 words of Joseph Smith's personal letters and correspondence and for approximately 160,000 words of his sermons and teachings. We then compared our results with the rate of occurrences in the D&C.

For the text of the personal letters, we consulted Dean C. Jessee's *The Personal Letters of Joseph Smith*. We purposely selected letters and correspondence from the corpus in which Joseph Smith appears to be speaking as a prophet.[12] Finding texts of Joseph Smith's sermons and other teachings that we were confident he personally recorded, dictated, or edited proved problematic. We finally determined to consult Ehat and Cook's *The Words of Joseph Smith* and the corpus of teachings gathered by Joseph Fielding Smith in *Teachings of the Prophet Joseph Smith*. These were better than most options, but far from ideal. For the most part, *The Words of Joseph Smith* contains the journal and diary entries of Joseph Smith's contemporaries wherein they recorded what they heard the Prophet say in sermons he delivered from 1839 to 1844. We chose those texts from this collection wherein the entries report the Prophet speaking in the first person, in hopes that they closely reflected his actual words.[13] Likewise, *Teachings of the Prophet Joseph Smith* contains much that was recorded by others as they recalled what the Prophet taught or as it was dictated to them, but we hoped the collection generally represented Joseph's own words. We analyzed this entire collection for Isaianic language.[14]

We found that while the D&C contains 2.9 occurrences of Isaianic language per thousand words, the personal letters and correspondence that we considered in this study contained only 1.4 occurrences, and the other teachings of the Prophet we analyzed contained only 0.4 occurrences per thousand words (see table 10). We suspect that had we considered all of Joseph Smith's letters rather than selecting only those in which he assumed a prophetic voice, the rate of Isaianic language usage would likely have dropped considerably from the 1.4 per thousand words that we calculated. Moreover, if we had the full and accurate text of all of Joseph Smith's public sermons rather than secondhand reports, the rate of Isaianic language usage would perhaps increase from 0.4. In spite of these limitations, the data suggest that the Prophet did not habitually use Isaiah's wording in his personal correspondence or regular teachings at a rate comparable to the D&C usage. It appears that prophetic wording of his D&C revelations is something beyond his typical pattern of communication.

We wondered if other early Church leaders with whom Joseph Smith associated or contemporary preachers and prophets of other faiths regularly used Isaiah's language in their communications, sermons, and prophetic teachings. If so, we reasoned, perhaps the abundant usage of Isaianic language in the D&C simply reflects the influence of Joseph's colleagues in his prophetic wording or a common style of religious leaders of his day.

To consider the question, we calculated the number of occurrences of Isaianic language per thousand words in recorded sermons and writings of three groups of individuals. First, we analyzed the writings and sermons of some of Joseph Smith's contemporary Church leaders with whom he associated. In this group we included Sidney Rigdon,[15] Parley P. Pratt,[16] Brigham Young,[17] Orson Hyde,[18] and Orson Pratt.[19] Next, we analyzed sermons and writings from preachers contemporary with Joseph Smith as well as some that came before him whose works he may have known. In this group we included Alexander Campbell,[20] Benjamin T. Onderdonk,[21] Jonathan Edwards,[22] Charles Finney,[23] Charles Hodge,[24] John Wesley,[25] Asahel Nettleton,[26] and William Miller.[27] Finally, we analyzed the prophecies of individuals of other faiths who were roughly contemporary with Joseph Smith and who reported visions or spoke in the name of God. In this group we included Ellen White,[28] Philemon Stewart,[29] and Paulina Bates.[30]

We found that none of the early Church leaders who were contemporary with Joseph Smith incorporated Isaianic wording in the sermons and writings we analyzed at a rate comparable to the D&C revelations (see table 11). Even though Sidney Rigdon was specifically commissioned to "call upon the holy prophets to prove [Joseph Smith's] words" (D&C 35:23), like the other early leaders of the Restoration we evaluated, he used Isaianic language at about only one-third the rate of the D&C revelations (0.9 compared to 2.9). Moreover, in most cases where Isaianic language is used in these early Church leader's teachings and writings, it typically occurs in the form of long passages quoted from the text of Isaiah in distinct blocks, in contrast to the abundant short Isaianic phrases and terms scattered throughout the D&C.

We likewise found that none of the writings and sermons of religious leaders and teachers of other faiths we analyzed, whether preacher or prophet, incorporated Isaiah's words in their works at a rate comparable to the D&C revelations, the highest being Bates, at a rate of 1.6, and the lowest Hodge, at 0.1 (see tables 12, 13). Interestingly, we observed that in the writings of those we classified as "preachers" (see table 12), Isaianic language once again typically occurs in the form of long passages quoted from the text of Isaiah in distinct blocks, while in the writings of those we classified as "prophets" (see table 13) the Isaianic language more commonly occurs in short phrases and terms, similar to the D&C pattern, but at only one-third to one-half the rate.

Thus our analysis indicates that it would be difficult to make the case that the abundant shared language between Isaiah and the D&C is simply a product of Joseph Smith copying the practice and language of his associates or contemporaries. The phenomenon appears to be more profound in the D&C than in any comparable text.

Summary

This study has produced some insight into how the revelations of the D&C use Isaianic language. We observed that the D&C incorporates the words of the ancient prophet frequently and broadly. We noted that the majority of the D&C sections contain Isaianic language and that the language is drawn from the majority of the chapters of Isaiah. We identified 171 different Isaianic terms and phrases in a total of 312 instances in the D&C. Most of those 171 different phrases occur three times or less in the D&C text. We observed that the rate of Isaianic language usage increases significantly when the D&C speaks of latter-day events such as the Restoration of the gospel, the building of Zion, and the Second Coming of Christ. Clearly, the language of the revelations recorded in the D&C was influenced by someone who was extraordinarily familiar with Isaiah's writings.

We feel our findings in this study provide no definitive answers to the question of why Isaianic wording is so common in the D&C, but perhaps they help us eliminate some possible explanations. While the revelations Joseph Smith received in some years used more of Isaiah's words than those he received in other years, we could not identify any particular time, experience, or event that could account for the phenomenon. Overall, the rate of Isaianic language usage seems to flow and ebb throughout his prophetic life with no clear patterns. Our findings suggest that any special familiarity or expertise with the writings of Isaiah that the Prophet may have gained while translating the Book of Mormon or working on the JST did not significantly impact the content or rate of Isaianic language usage. Furthermore, we could not comfortably conclude that the use of Isaianic language in the D&C simply reflects Joseph Smith's typical patterns of communication, for he apparently did not use Isaianic language nearly as often in his regular teachings and sermons or in his personal correspondence. Likewise, we could not find evidence that the use of Isaianic wording in the D&C was simply a reflection of the style of preaching and prophesying of his day or that it was fostered by his association with other Church leaders in the Restoration with whom he worked. The abundance of Isaianic language in the D&C is truly remarkable and unique.

Accordingly, the question remains, does the choice of words in the revelations recorded in the D&C belong to Joseph Smith or to God—or to both? Is the language of the revelations internal or external to the Prophet? We conclude that if the language is internal to Joseph Smith, then he must have had an extraordinary mastery of Isaiah—one that far exceeds our expectations. If the language is external, then Joseph Smith must have received the revelations with remarkable clarity and detail. We are comfortable with either being the case.

Table 1:
Verses with Shared Wording between Isaiah and the D&C

Book	Verses with Shared Wording
D&C	1:1, 13–16, 22, 36; 4:1; 6:1–3; 11:1, 3; 12:1–3; 14:1, 3, 9; 18:44; 19:15, 36; 21:1; 22:1; 24:2, 15; 25:12, 14; 27:18; 29:12, 21, 23–24, 29, 42, 64; 30:4, 11; 33:1, 9, 10; 34:1–2, 8; 35:6, 8, 25; 36:1; 38:17, 22, 33, 42; 39:8; 41:1; 42:2, 6, 39, 45, 53; 43:11, 25; 45:1, 9, 10, 25, 28, 31, 36, 45–48, 50, 71; 49:9, 23–24, 27; 50:10; 52:43; 56:1, 16; 57:10; 58:5, 7–8, 64; 59:8–9; 60:7, 15; 61:20; 63:6; 64:9, 34–35, 42; 65:1, 3; 66:2, 11; 67:6; 68:25–26; 70:2; 71:8–9; 76:1, 9–10, 26–27, 44, 101, 107–8, 110; 78:3, 11; 81:5; 82:13–14; 84:24, 69–70, 98–100, 108; 85:3, 7; 86:11; 87:6; 88:7–8, 45, 66, 73–74, 84, 87, 94, 104, 106, 119, 131, 133; 89:20; 90:10; 93:51; 94:1; 95:4; 96:1; 97:23–24, 26; 98:12; 100:13; 101:12, 18, 21, 23, 30–31, 39, 53–54, 58, 75, 89, 95, 101; 103:11, 25; 104:4, 7, 14, 40, 48; 105:15, 30, 39; 106:3; 107:4, 36–37, 74; 109:8, 13, 16, 25, 38–39, 45–46, 50–51, 59, 74, 80; 111:14; 112:5, 23; 113:1–10; 115:5–6, 18; 117:7, 9; 119:7; 121:1, 4, 7, 12; 122:4, 6; 123:6; 124:2, 7–8, 10–11, 18, 21, 23, 26, 36, 60–61, 128, 131, 134, 142; 125:4; 128:19, 21–22; 131:2; 132:4, 6, 19, 26–27, 41–42, 49; 133:3, 5, 7–9, 16–17, 20–21, 24, 27, 29, 33, 40–44, 46–53, 57–58, 68–70, 72; 135:4; 136:10, 18; 137:2, 6; 138:18, 31, 42, 48
Isaiah	1:8, 16, 18–19, 24, 26, 27; 3:4, 16–17; 4:6; 5:5, 17, 24–26; 7:14; 8:8, 16; 9:2; 10:2–3, 22, 32; 11:4, 10–12, 16; 12:1; 13:5, 10; 14:6–7, 12; 15:4; 16:1; 18:2–3; 21:6, 9; 23:7, 9; 24:5, 14, 16, 20; 25:4, 6; 26:2; 28:2, 5, 10, 13–17, 19, 21, 23; 29:6, 14, 20; 30:2, 17, 19, 26–27, 29–30; 31:9; 32:2, 13; 33:1, 8, 14, 20, 22; 34:2, 5, 8, 16; 35:1, 3, 5–7, 10; 37:22, 26; 40:1, 3–8, 24, 31; 41:19, 21; 42:1, 5–6, 11, 23; 43:9, 11, 25; 44:3, 22–23; 45:8, 17–18, 22–23; 47:2, 7, 11, 14; 48:13, 20; 49:6, 13, 19, 13, 26; 50:2–3, 11; 51:2–3, 7, 9; 52:1–2, 7–12; 53:1, 7–8; 54:1–2, 7, 17; 55:2–3; 56:7; 58:1, 5, 8, 12; 59:1, 8, 17, 21; 60:1–2, 12–13, 19, 22; 61:1–2, 8, 10; 62:2–4, 6, 10–12; 63:1–9, 15, 18; 64:1–5; 65:5, 17, 20–22; 66:1–3, 15, 22, 24

Table 2:
Sample of Distinctive Quotes, Phrases, and Language from the King James Version of Isaiah Found in the Doctrine and Covenants

Quotes, Phrases, and Language	D&C	Isaiah
Islands of the sea	1:1	11:11
Broken mine everlasting covenant	1:15	24:5
Babylon the great, which shall fall	1:16	21:9
Marvelous work is about to come forth	4:1; 6:1; 11:1; 12:1; 14:1; 18:44	29:14
Rod of mouth	19:15	11:4
Helmet of salvation	27:18	59:17
New heaven, new earth	29:23, 24	65:17
Prepare ye the way of the Lord	33:10	40:3
All nations shall tremble	34:8	64:2
Mine arm is not shortened	35:8	50:2; 59:1
For I am your lawgiver	38:22	33:22
Go ye out. . . . Be ye clean that bear the vessels of the Lord.	38:42; 133:5	52:11
Laid the foundation of the earth	45:1	48:13
To be a light to the world . . . Gentiles	45:9; 86:11	42:6
Overflowing scourge	45:31	28:15
Earth shall reel to and fro	45:48; 49:23; 88:87	24:20
Scorner shall be consumed	45:50	29:20
Behold, I will go before you and be your rearward	49:27	52:12
And now come, saith the Lord, by the Spirit, unto the elders of his church, and let us reason	50:10	1:18
Day of visitation	56:1, 16; 124:8	10:3
Uttermost part of the earth	58:64	24:16
All flesh shall know	63:6	49:26
Prepare ye the way of the Lord, make his paths straight	65:1; 133:17	40:3
And push many people to Zion with songs of everlasting joy upon their heads	66:11; 101:18; 109:39; 133:33	35:10

Quotes, Phrases, and Language	D&C	Isaiah
No weapon that is formed against you shall prosper	71:9; 109:25	54:17
For the Lord is God, and beside him there is no Savior	76:1	43:11
Wisdom of the wise shall perish, and the understanding of the prudent shall come to naught	76:9	29:14
Put on her beautiful garments	82:14	52:1
The voice of one crying in the wilderness	88:66	40:3
Bind up the law and seal up the testimony	88:84; 109:46; 133:72	8:16
Every knee shall bow, and every tongue shall confess/swear	88:104	45:23
House of prayer	88:119; 109:8, 16	56:7
And shall run and not be weary, and shall walk and not faint	89:20	40:31
Line upon line, precept upon precept	98:12; 128:21	28:10
All flesh shall see me together	101:23	40:5
In that day an infant shall not die until he is old; and his life shall be as the age of a tree	101:30	65:22
Watchmen upon walls	101:53; 124:61	62:6
Avenge me of mine enemies	103:25	1:24
Clothed with salvation	109:80	61:10
Solitary places to bud	117:7	35:1
Bear him up as on eagles' wings	124:18, 99	40:31
O that thou wouldst rend the heavens, that thou wouldst come down, that the mountains might flow down at thy presence	133:40	64:1
I am going like a lamb to the slaughter	135:4	53:7
Zion shall be redeemed	136:18	1:27
Liberty to the captives	138:18, 42	61:1

Table 3:
Twenty Highest Indices of Usage in the D&C
for the Chapters of Isaiah[31]

Isaiah Chapter	Number of Words in the Chapter	Number of Times Words from the Chapter Occur in the D&C	Index of Usage (Number of Occurrences/ Number of Words)
61	380	26	6.84
54	493	31	6.29
55	399	22	5.51
33	585	29	4.96
24	592	25	4.22
52	405	17	4.20
35	277	11	4.00
11	519	20	3.85
62	362	13	3.59
28	814	22	2.70
58	521	13	2.50
40	796	16	2.01
45	774	15	1.94
63	538	9	1.68
42	676	11	1.63
1	758	12	1.60
18	255	4	1.57
51	771	12	1.56
53	387	6	1.55
47	471	7	1.49

Table 4:
Percent of Isaianic Language Categories in the D&C

Type	Number of Isaianic Phrases in D&C	Percent of Total
Rebuke	31	10%
Counsel	65	21%
Prophecy	216	69%

Table 5:
D&C Sections with the Highest Rate of Isaianic Language per 1,000 Words (Only Sections with 100 Words or More are Included)

Section	Number of Words	Occurrences of Isaianic Language	Rate
113	334	11	32.9
34	269	4	14.9
133	2,012	28	13.9
14	302	3	9.9
122	432	4	9.3
12	232	2	8.6
22	117	1	8.5
65	240	2	8.3
71	259	2	7.7
115	519	4	7.7
45	2,177	16	7.3
4	145	1	6.9
1	1,070	7	6.5
131	154	1	6.5
101	2,717	17	6.3
109	2,574	16	6.2
49	827	5	6.0
33	505	3	5.9
125	176	1	5.7
30	370	2	5.4

Table 6: Rate of Occurrences of Isaianic Language per 1,000 Words of Text for Two Types of D&C Sections

D&C Section Type	Sections	Total Number of Words in the Sections	Occurrences of Isaianic Language	Rate
Contemporary	3–9, 11–28, 30–32, 36–37, 39–42, 44, 46–47, 50–57, 59–62, 66–75, 77–81, 83, 85–86, 89–96, 98–100, 102, 104, 106–12, 114–20, 123–32, 134–38	74,225	147	1.98
Prophetic	1–2, 10, 29, 33–35, 38, 43, 45, 48–49, 58, 63–65, 76, 82, 84, 87–88, 97, 101, 103, 105, 113, 121–22, 133	37,323	165	4.42

Table 7: Rate of Occurrences of Isaianic Language per 1,000 Words of Text for The Lord's Voice and Others'

Voice	Sections	Number of Words	Occurrences of Isaianic Language	Rate
Lord's	1, 5–6, 8–11, 13–18, 20–46, 48–72, 74–76, 78–84, 86–101, 103–5, 107–8, 111, 113–15, 117–19, 123–26, 132	90,781	263	2.90
Others'	2–4, 7, 12, 19, 47, 73, 77, 85, 102, 106, 109–10, 112, 116, 120–22, 127–31, 134–38	20,767	49	2.36

Table 8:
Rate of Occurrences of Isaianic Language per 1,000 Words of Text for the D&C Revelations Received during Each Year

Year	Number of Words	Occurrences of Isaianic Language	Rate
1823	69	0	0
1828	2,546	1	0.4
1829	6,532	12	1.8
1830	10,956	27	2.5
1831	29,483	100	3.4
1832	15,579	42	2.7
1833	10,024	27	2.7
1834	6,482	11	1.7
1835	4,012	4	1.0
1836	3,305	19	5.7
1837	1,073	2	1.9
1838	1,978	18	9.1
1839	2,421	9	3.7
1841	5,698	20	3.5
1842	3,205	4	1.2
1843	4,280	9	2.1
1844	899	1	1.1
1847	1,108	2	1.8
1918	1,861	4	2.1

Table 9:
Indices of Usage in the D&C for Passages of Isaiah Quoted and Not Quoted in the Book of Mormon

Passages	Number of Words in the Passages	Number of Times Words from the Passages Occur in the D&C	Index of Usage (Number of Occurrences/Number of Words)
Quoted in the Book of Mormon	12,183	105	0.86
Not Quoted in the Book of Mormon	24,095	200	0.83

Table 10:
Rate of Occurrences of Isaianic Language per 1,000 Words of Text for Joseph Smith's Personal Correspondence and Sermon Reports Compared to the D&C

Text	Number of Words	Occurrences of Isaianic Language	Rate
D&C	107,366	312	2.9
Personal Correspondence	15,059	21	1.4
Sermons and Teachings	160,000	69	0.4

Table 11:
Rate of Occurrences of Isaianic Language per 1,000 Words of Text for Sermons and Teachings of Selected Colleagues of Joseph Smith Compared to the D&C

Colleague	Number of Words	Occurrences of Isaianic Language	Rate
D&C	107,366	312	2.9
Sidney Rigdon	51,507	47	0.9
Parley P. Pratt	49,689	39	0.8
Brigham Young	50,537	47	0.9
Orson Hyde	52,734	38	0.7
Orson Pratt	51,447	52	1.0

Table 12:
Rate of Occurrences of Isaianic Language per 1,000 Words of Text for Sermons of Joseph Smith's Contemporary Preachers of Other Faiths Compared to the D&C

Preacher	Number of Words	Occurrences of Isaianic Language	Rate
D&C	107,366	312	2.9
Alexander Campbell	50,828	34	0.7
Benjamin T. Onderdonk	50,243	28	0.6
Jonathan Edwards	49,981	36	0.7
Charles Finney	48,928	13	0.3
Charles Hodge	53,122	6	0.1
John Wesley	55,150	52	0.9
Asahel Nettleton	20,385	21	1.0
William Miller	5,495	8	1.5

Table 13:
Rate of Occurrences of Isaianic Language per 1,000 Words of Text for Prophecies of Joseph Smith's Contemporary Prophets of Other Faiths Compared to the D&C

Prophet	Number of Words	Occurrences of Isaianic Language	Rate
D&C	107,366	312	2.9
Ellen White	50,194	34	0.7
Philemon Stewart	50,877	37	0.7
Paulina Bates	51,731	86	1.6

Notes

1. For our analyses we used QDA Miner v4 by Provalis Research (2997 Cedar Ave, Montreal, QC. H3Y 1Y8, Canada). This program includes a feature that enables researchers to search for shared language up to seven words in length between two texts. Two earlier studies, Ellis T. Rasmussen, "Textual Parallels to the Doctrine and Covenants and Book of Commandments as Found in the Bible" (master's thesis, Brigham Young University, 1951) and Lois Jean Smutz, "Textual Parallels to the Doctrine and Covenants (Sections 65 to 133) as Found in the Bible" (master's thesis, Brigham Young University, 1971) likewise identified much Isaianic language in the D&C, but without the use of computer-assisted analysis, their findings were not as extensive. Although our study employed the enhanced search features of computer technology, we feel our list of shared language should be considered illustrative rather than exhaustive.

2. Seventeen percent of these phrases are not found quoted in any other book of scripture, while 55 percent occur not only in the D&C but also in other standard works, where they are clearly quoted from Isaiah.

3. We categorize this 28 percent as Isaianic because it occurs first in the book of Isaiah or is used more frequently there than in other books.

4. Elder Bruce R. McConkie perhaps explained this phenomenon when he observed, "Our understanding of the prophetic word will be greatly expanded if we know how one prophet quotes another, usually without acknowledging his source." "The Doctrinal Restoration," in *The Joseph Smith Translation: The Restoration of Plain and Precious Truths*, ed. Monte S. Nyman and Robert L. Millet (Provo, UT: Religious Studies Center, Brigham Young University, 1985), 17.

5. In a 1973 address to priesthood holders, President Harold B. Lee admonished the brethren to avoid being swept up in popular speculation about "calamities which are about to overtake us." Instead, he counseled those wanting a sense of what the future held to look to the scriptures and then listed particular passages they should read. Interestingly, his list from the D&C consisted of sections 38, 45, 101, 133, all of which are on our list of those with the most Isaianic language usage per thousand words. See "Admonitions for the Priesthood of God," *Ensign*, January 1973.

6. In the Lord's preface to the Doctrine and Covenants, the Lord declares, "Behold, I am God and have spoken it; these commandments are of me, and were given unto my servants in their weakness, after the manner of their language, that they might come to an understanding" (D&C 1:24). While this passage helps us understand that the Lord spoke to Joseph in language he would understand, it does not, in our view, indicate whether the choice of words used to communicate the revelations in the D&C originates with God or the prophet. Hence the discussion that follows.

7. We observed that the value for 1838 is skewed by section 113, which is devoted entirely to a discussion of Isaiah 11 and Isaiah 53.

8. Isaiah passages quoted in the Book of Mormon are Isaiah 2–14 (2 Nephi 12–24), Isaiah 29 (2 Nephi 26; 27), Isaiah 48–49 (1 Nephi 20–21), Isaiah 50 (2 Nephi 7), Isaiah 51, 52:1–2; 55:1–2 (2 Nephi 8; 9:50–51), Isaiah 52 (3 Nephi 20), Isaiah 53 (Mosiah 14), Isaiah 54 (3 Nephi 22).

9. We note that for the first fourteen Isaiah chapters quoted in the Book of Mormon (Isaiah 2–14, 29), the index of usage is 0.63 (52/8268) but for the last eight chapters quoted in the Book of Mormon (Isaiah 48–52:2), the index jumps up to 1.33 (52/3915), more than twice as much. This again indicates that the D&C more heavily quotes from the restoration chapters of Isaiah (40–66) than the judgment chapters (1–35).

10. The Isaiah quotes in the Book of Mormon text removed from this analysis are found in 1 Nephi 20–21; 2 Nephi 6:6–7, 16–18; 7–8; 9:50; 12–24; 26:18; 27:2–5, 25–35; 30:9, 11–15; Mosiah 12:21–24; 14; 15:6, 29–31; 3 Nephi 16:18–20; 20:34–45; 21:8; 22 (as identified by John W. Welch in *Charting the Book of Mormon*, accessible at: http://byustudies.byu.edu/januarybomcharts/index.html). After removing these quotes, we found sixty occurrences of Isaianic language in the remaining 261,469 words for a rate of usage of 0.2 per 1,000 words compared to 2.8 per 1,000 words in the D&C. We also evaluated just the D&C revelations received while Joseph Smith was translating the Book of Mormon from April to June 1829 (D&C 6–9, 11–18) to see if the rate of usage in those revelations varied significantly from that of the Book of Mormon non-Isaiah-quoting text. We found that the D&C revelations received while Joseph Smith was translating the Book of Mormon had an Isaianic language use rate of 1.5 per 1,000 words (10 usages in 6,802 words), still much higher than the Book of Mormon's 0.2 rate. We are not confident this represents a significant difference, however, due to the small sample size and the fact that the D&C rate of usage is perhaps inflated by the redundancy of the "marvelous work" phrase in sections 6, 11, 12, and 14.

11. In the Old Testament Manuscript 2 of the JST, which contains the book of Isaiah, Isaiah starts on page 97 and ends on page 111. Malachi starts on page 119 with the finishing date of July 2, 1833, written after it on that page. Thus of the 446 pages that ended on July 2, 1833, Isaiah finishes eight pages from the end. Accordingly, it appears the Prophet likely worked on the Isaiah portion of the JST in the summer of 1833 (personal correspondence with Kent P. Jackson). For a review of the history of the JST work, see *Joseph Smith's New Translation of the Bible*, ed. Kent P. Jackson, Robert J. Matthews and Scott H. Faulring (Provo, UT: Religious Studies Center, Brigham Young University, 2004), 3–8.

12. Texts included in our study were entries from the Joseph Smith Diary for November 19 and December 18, 1833; November 2–3 and December 10, 1835; November 29, 1844; letters written to Harvey Whitlock, November 16, 1835; William W. Phelps, July 31, 1832; William W. Phelps, John Whitmer, Edward Partridge, Isaac Morley, John Corrill, and Sidney Rigdon, August 10, 1833; William W. Phelps, John Whitmer, Edward Partridge, Isaac Morley, John Corrill, and Sidney Rigdon, August 18, 1833; the Church, December 16, 1838; and the Twelve, December 15, 1840. For the full text, see *The Personal Writings of Joseph Smith*, ed. Dean C. Jessee (Salt Lake City: Deseret Book, 1984).

13. The following is a list of dates and the names of those reporting sermons or the places in which the report is found for the sermons given by Joseph Smith that we included in this study: March 21, 1841, reported in the Howard and Martha Coray Notebook; December 19, 1841, March 10, 1842, April 9, 1842, April 10, 1842, January 22,

1843, June 30, 1843, July 4, 1843, January 21, 1844, March 24, 1844, April 7, 1844, reported in the Wilford Woodruff Diary; August 29, 1842, reported in the *Manuscript History of the Church*; August 31, 1842, reported in the Nauvoo Relief Society Minutes; January 29, 1843, April 6, 1843, April 13, 1843, April 16, 1843, October 15, 1843, reported in the Joseph Smith Diary by Willard Richards; April 8, 1843, reported by William Clayton; May 12, 1844, June 16, 1844, reported by Thomas Bullock; May 26, 1844, reported in *History of the Church*, 6:408–12; October 5, 1840, reported in an original manuscript in the hand of Robert B. Thompson. Ehat and Cook note that this last sermon is apparently the only one for which the Prophet prepared a text. For the full text of all the sermon reports listed here, see *The Words of Joseph Smith*, ed. Andrew F. Ehat and Lyndon W. Cook (Provo, UT: Religious Studies Center, Brigham Young University, 1980).

14. Some of the text in *Teachings of the Prophet Joseph Smith* is also found in *The Words of Joseph Smith*, but whereas this is a rate of usage, we were not concerned about duplicates skewing the results. In our analysis we tried to avoid including text from Joseph Smith's personal writings, teachings, or sermons that are also found in the D&C.

15. We reviewed about fifty thousand words of Sidney Rigdon text, taken primarily from early Church newspapers. Sidney Rigdon (February 19, 1793–July 14, 1876) was a popular preacher in Alexander Campbell's Disciples of Christ movement. The text we analyzed in this study consisted of his July 4, 1838, oration printed in the Journal Office at Far West, Missouri, a treatise on the Millennium he published in serial form in *The Evening and the Morning Star* 2, no. 15–17, 19–23n and the *Latter Day Saints' Messenger and Advocate* 1, no. 2–6, 8, and those portions of a treatise on the gospel he published in serial form in *The Evening and the Morning Star* 1, no. 11; 2, no. 24; and the *Latter Day Saints' Messenger and Advocate* 1, nos. 2–4.

16. We analyzed about 50,000 words of text from Parley P. Pratt's *A Voice of Warning*. An early convert to the Church, also from Alexander Campbell's Disciples of Christ movement, Parley P. Pratt (April 12, 1807–May 13, 1857) became a prominent leader, missionary, and preacher, as well as becoming the editor of the *Latter-day Saints' Millennial Star*. He was a close associate of Joseph Smith, in a position to exercise significant influence on the thinking and language of the Prophet. In this study we analyzed the first five chapters of Pratt's book *A Voice of Warning and Instruction to All People; or an Introduction to the Faith and Doctrine of the Church of Jesus Christ of Latter-day Saints*. For a review of the significance of this work and the text thereof, see Kent P. Jackson's introduction in the Barnes & Noble Library of Essential Reading Edition: Parley P. Pratt, *A Voice of Warning* (New York: Barnes & Noble, 2008).

17. Brigham Young (June 1, 1801–August 29, 1877) was baptized into the Church in 1832 and was a faithful associate of Joseph Smith from then on. He served as the second President of The Church of Jesus Christ of Latter-day Saints from 1847 until his death in 1877. The approximately fifty thousand words of Brigham Young's writings we analyzed were taken from the *Journal of Discourses*, 1:1–6, 37–42, 195–203, 233–45, 277–79, 376; 2:1–10, 29–33, 90–96, 121–45. These were chosen for their prophetic or doctrinal themes.

18. Orson Hyde (January 8, 1805–November 28, 1878) was an original member of the Quorum of the Twelve Apostles in The Church of Jesus Christ of Latter-day

Saints. He was the President of the Quorum from 1847 to 1875. The approximately fifty thousand words of Orson Hyde's writings we analyzed were taken from the *Journal of Discourses*, 1:71–73, 121–30; 2:61–70, 75–87, 112–20, 202–21; 4:257–63; 5:14–23, 67–72, 279–84. These too were chosen for their prophetic or doctrinal themes.

19. Like Orson Hyde, Orson Pratt (September 19, 1811–October 3, 1881) was an original member of the Quorum of the Twelve Apostles. He was the younger brother of Parley P. Pratt, who introduced him to the Church and baptized him in 1830. The approximately fifty thousand words of Orson Pratt's writings we analyzed were taken from the *Journal of Discourses*, 1:53–66, 280–94; 2:54–61, 96–104, 235–48, 259–66, 284–98. These too were chosen for their prophetic or doctrinal themes.

20. Alexander Campbell (September 12, 1788–March 4, 1866) was an early leader in the Second Great Awakening and was the driving force behind the Disciples of Christ movement. He emphasized New Testament Christianity. Many of the early Saints were converts from his movement, and several American churches trace their history to his leadership. He authored the polemical work *Mormonism Exposed*. In this study we analyzed text from three works: (1) chapters 1, 4–5, 8, and 22 of *The Christian System in Reference to the Union of Christians, and a Restoration of Primitive Christianity, As Plead in the Current Reformation* (Pittsburg, PA: Forrester & Campbell, 1839), (2) *Sermon on the Law* (1846), *The Millennial Harbinger*, series 3, vol. 3, no. 9 (Bethany, VA, September 1846); and (3) *Life and Death* (Cincinnati, OH: H. S. Bosworth, 1861). All of these texts are available at http://www.mun.ca/rels/restmov/people/acampbell.html.

21. Benjamin T. Onderdonk (July 15, 1791–April 30, 1861) was the bishop of the Episcopal Diocese of New York from 1830–61 and is remembered as one of the most controversial figures in the history of the diocese. In this study we analyzed the following sermons and writings: "A Sermon on the Excellence, the Benefits, and the Obligations of the Divine Law," "The Change at the Resurrection," "The Seventeenth Article of Religion Considered," "A Funeral Sermon on Occasion of the Death of the Rev. Lewis P. Bayard, D. D.," "A Sermon Preached on Occasion of Administering the Holy Rite of Confirmation in St. George's Church, New-York," "Sermon on Isaiah 1:13," "Address Delivered to the Recipients of Confirmation, Immediately After Its Administration," "The Edifying of the Church," "The Christian Ministry," and "A Sermon Preached in Trinity Church, New-York, at the Funeral of the Right Reverend John Henry Hobart, D. D." The text of all of these sermons is available at http://anglicanhistory.org/usa/btonderdonk/.

22. Jonathan Edwards (October 5, 1703–March 22, 1758) was a preacher and a missionary to Native Americans. Though not a contemporary of Joseph Smith, he played a critical role in shaping the First Great Awakening, and the Prophet likely would have been exposed to his theology and writings. In this study we analyzed the following sermon and writings: "Sinners in the Hands of an Angry God," "The Manner in Which the Salvation of the Soul Is to Be Sought," "The Justice of God in the Damnation of Sinners," and "Pressing into the Kingdom of God." All of these texts are available at http://www.jonathan-edwards.org/.

23. Charles G. Finney (August 29, 1792–August 16, 1875) was a leader in the Second Great Awakening. He has been called the "Father of Modern Revivalism." He is

known as an innovative revivalist, an advocate of Christian perfectionism, and a pioneer in social reforms. He was a president at Oberlin College. In this study we analyzed the following sermon and writings: "Sinners Bound to Change Their Own Hearts," "How to Change Your Heart," "Traditions of the Elders," "Total Depravity," and "Doctrine of Election." All of these texts are available at http://www.charlesgfinney.com/1836SOIS/indexsois.htm.

24. Charles Hodge (December 27, 1797–June 19, 1878) was the principal of Princeton Theological Seminary from 1851 to 1878. He was a Presbyterian theologian and a leading exponent of historical Calvinism in America during the nineteenth century. He argued that the authority of the Bible as the word of God had to be understood literally. In this study we analyzed the following sermon and writings: "The Protestant Rule of Faith," "Office of the Church as a Teacher," "For Whom Did Christ Die?," and "The Plan of Salvation" in *Systematic Theology*, vols. 1 and 2 (New York, NY: Charles Scribner, 1873). All of these texts are available at http://www.ccel.org/ccel/hodge?show=worksBy.

25. John Wesley (June 28, 1703–March 2, 1791) served in the clergy for the Church of England and, along with his brother Charles Wesley, was largely credited with the founding of the Methodist movement. The Prophet Joseph Smith mentioned that he felt "somewhat partial to the Methodist sect" (Joseph Smith—History 1:8), suggesting he may have had some exposure to John Wesley's writings. In this study we chose to analyze Wesley texts and sermons that started with a quote from Isaiah or had biblical or last-days themes. The texts we chose included the following sermons and writings: Sermon 107, "On God's Vineyard"; Sermon 134, "True Christianity Defended"; Sermon 66, "The Signs of the Times"; Sermon 129, "The Cause and Cure of Earthquakes"; Sermon 116, "Causes of the Inefficacy of Christianity"; Sermon 63, "The General Spread of the Gospel"; Sermon 65, "The Duty of Reproving Our Neighbor"; Sermon 56, "God's Approbation of His Work"; Sermon 20, "The Lord Our Righteousness"; Sermon 130, "National Sins and Miseries"; Sermon 102, "Of Former Times"; Sermon 111, "On the Omnipresence of God"; and Sermon 131, "The Late Work of God in North America." All of these texts are available at http://gbgm-umc.org/umhistory/wesley/sermons/.

26. Asahel Nettleton (April 21, 1783–May 16, 1844) was a theologian and pastor from Connecticut who was highly influential during the Second Great Awakening. The number of people converted to Christianity as a result of his ministry is estimated at 30,000. In this study we analyzed about 20,000 Nettleton words from the following sermon and writings: "The Final Warning," "The Destruction of Hardened Sinners," "Rejoice Young Man," "Regeneration," and "Professing Christians, Awake!" All of these texts are available at http://www.reformedreader.org/rbb/nettleton/neindex.htm.

27. William Miller (February 15, 1782–December 20, 1849) was a Baptist preacher credited with founding North American Adventism. Today's Seventh-Day Adventists and Advent Christians are influenced by Miller's teachings. His own followers were called Millerites. Written sermons by Miller are rare. In this study we only analyzed a single 5,000-word sermon entitled "The Kingdom of God," which was delivered by Miller on November 14, 1842. It is available at http://www.adventistheritage.org/article.php?id=38.

28. Ellen G. White (November 26, 1827–July 16, 1915) along with others formed what is now known as the Seventh-Day Adventist Church. She reported her visionary experiences to her fellow believers and viewed these experiences as the biblical gift of prophecy. During her lifetime she wrote more than five thousand periodical articles and forty books. In this study we analyzed the visions and writings found in her volume *Early Writings*, 14–190, available at http://www.gilead.net/egw/books2/earlywritings/ewindex.html.

29. Philemon Stewart was a prominent member of the Shakers and was considered a visionary man in that movement. His revelation *A Holy, Sacred and Divine Roll and Book* was published in 1842. The revelation is reported to have been received over a fourteen-day period from February 2 to February 16, 1842. God speaks in the first person throughout this revelation. In this study we analyzed chapters 1–3, 9, 11, 14, 16, 21, 23–27, 29–31, and 33 of this revelation, as well as visions entitled "A Word of Warning and Invitation by the Patriarch Noah" with Elmira Allard as the "inspired writer," "The Solemn Warning of A Holy Angel of God" with Paulina Bates as the "inspired writer," and "Words of the Holy Prophet Isaiah" with Roselinda Allard as the "inspired writer," all contained in *A Holy, Sacred and Divine Roll and Book*. The text is available at http://www.iinet.com/~passtheword/Shaker-Manuscripts/Sacred-Roll/rollndex.htm.

30. Like Philemon Stewart, Paulina Bates was a prominent member of the Shakers. She claimed to receive visionary messages and was called "a prophetess unto the Most High." Her 1849 publication, *The Divine Book of Holy and Eternal Wisdom*, is her most famous visionary work. As in other Shaker revelation, God speaks in the first person throughout this text. In this study we analyzed the following chapters from the volume: part 1, chapters 1–3, 7, 9, 11, 14, 16, 21, 23–27, 29–31, 33; part 2, chapters 3, 6–9, 11–12, 14, 17, 19–21. The text is available at http://www.iinet.com/~passtheword/Shaker-Manuscripts/Holy-Wisdom/wsdmndex.htm.

31. The index of usage equals the number of times words from the chapter occur in the D&C divided by total words in the chapter.

9

"Let Zion in Her Beauty Rise": Building Zion by Becoming Zion

Scott C. Esplin

The building up of Zion is a cause that has interested the people of God in every age," Joseph Smith editorialized in Nauvoo's *Times and Seasons* in May 1842. "It is a theme upon which prophets, priests, and kings have dwelt with peculiar delight."[1] Indeed, the Prophet himself seems to have pondered much about this topic. Numerous revelations in the Doctrine and Covenants trace what its Explanatory Introduction calls "the mighty struggles of the saints in attempting to build Zion on the earth in modern times." Moreover, Joseph Smith repeatedly returned to the subject in sermons throughout his life.[2] However, like many who dreamed of establishing the city of Zion before him, Joseph Smith "died without the sight."[3] Of this apparent failure, Elder Robert D. Hales summarized, "This promised Zion always seems to be a little beyond our reach. We need to understand that as much virtue can be gained in progressing toward Zion as in dwelling there. *It is a process as well as a destination.* . . . Many are perfected upon the road to Zion who will never see the city in mortality."[4]

Scott C. Esplin is an assistant professor of Church history and doctrine at Brigham Young University.

Though Zion certainly will be a place, throughout the Doctrine and Covenants, the Lord seems to have expanded the Prophet's vision beyond the destination to include Zion as a process. In particular, the revelations associated with Joseph Smith's first trip to Zion (see D&C 57–64) outline much about how Zion can be established. When we study the principles contained in these sections in their historical context and in conjunction with other scriptural passages, a pattern emerges for becoming Zion-like while laboring for the city's establishment.

Locating the City of Zion (D&C 57)

While the concept of Zion is frequently repeated biblically, the first Doctrine and Covenants reference to Zion is in an April 1829 revelation to Oliver Cowdery, wherein the Lord directed him to "seek to bring forth and establish the cause of Zion" (D&C 6:6). In subsequent sections, the Lord commanded Hyrum Smith and Joseph Knight Sr. to likewise "establish the cause of Zion" (D&C 11:6; 12:6). A year later, he introduced Zion as more than a cause, promising Emma Smith that if she was faithful, she would "receive an inheritance in Zion" (D&C 25:2). Shortly thereafter, the Lord called Zion a city for the first time, directing Oliver Cowdery to head a mission to the Lamanites in September 1830, when he declared, "It is not revealed, and no man knoweth where the city Zion shall be built, but it shall be given hereafter. Behold, I say unto you that it shall be on the borders by the Lamanites" (D&C 28:9). Joseph Smith's work on the translation of the Bible in December 1830 further highlighted the physicality of Zion, as this translation described the establishment of Enoch's city by the same name with the promise that in the last days there would be "an Holy City . . . called Zion, a New Jerusalem" (Moses 7:62). Finally, motivating the Saints to build this city, the Lord revealed that Zion would be "a land of peace, a city of refuge, a place of safety for the saints of the Most High God" (D&C 45:66).

Understandably, the Prophet and his associates quickly became interested in locating the promised city Zion. Commanded by the Lord in June 1831 to "journey to the land of Missouri" (D&C 52:3), the Saints were promised that "it shall also, inasmuch as they are faithful, be made known unto them the land of your inheritance" (D&C 52:5). In company with Sidney Rigdon, Martin Harris, Edward Partridge, William W. Phelps, Joseph Coe, and Algernon and Elizabeth Gilbert, Joseph Smith left Kirtland for Missouri on June 19, 1831. Traveling by wagon, canal boat, stagecoach, and steamer and on foot, the party arrived in Independence, Missouri, in the middle of July, where their thoughts naturally turned to questions about the location of Zion. On July 20, 1831, the Prophet Joseph inquired of the Lord further, "*When* will the wilderness blossom as the rose? *When* will Zion be built up in her glory, and *where* will Thy temple stand, unto which all nations shall come in the last days?" According to the Prophet's reminiscence, his "anxiety was soon relieved" by the receipt of Doctrine and Covenants 57.[5]

The incomplete nature of the response may have surprised some. In section 57, the Lord answered the question of where Zion would be located, designating Missouri as "the land which [he had] appointed and consecrated for the gathering of the saints" and as "the land of promise, and the place for the city of Zion" (vv. 1–2). Further answering where, he designated Independence as "the center place" with "a spot for the temple . . . lying westward, upon a lot which [was] not far from the courthouse" (v. 3). However, the twin questions of "when . . . the wilderness [would] blossom as the rose" and "when . . . Zion [would] be built up in her glory" went unanswered. Instead, the Lord directed how the city would be built and who would build it, instructing leaders that they were to purchase "every tract [of land] lying westward" (v. 4) while informing them which members were to "plant" themselves in this place (see vv. 6–15). For everything else regarding the establishment of Zion, the Lord promised, "Further directions shall be given hereafter" (v. 16).

A Pattern for Establishing Zion (D&C 58)

Understandably, the Prophet and his associates were anxious for additional instruction about Zion. Twelve days later, on August 1, 1831, section 58 was received, what John Whitmer later called "a Revelation given to the Elders who were assembled on the land of Zion" containing "Directions what to do &c &c &c."[6] The revelation began addressing both Zion as a people and Zion as a place. "Hearken, O ye Elders of my church, and give ear to my word," the Lord invited. "Learn of me what I will concerning you [Zion the people], and also concerning this land [Zion the place]" (D&C 58:1). However, in the section as well as in the revelations that follow, focus shifted from Zion as a place to Zion as a process as the Lord outlined how the Saints could become his promised people.

Section 58 parenthetically returned to the earlier question of when Zion would be established, indicating that "the hour is not yet, but is nigh at hand" (v. 4) and that "the time has not yet come, for many years, for [the Saints] to receive their inheritance in this land" (v. 44). In contrast to this brief discussion of timing, the Lord heavily emphasized principles of becoming Zion-like. In more modern times, President Ezra Taft Benson highlighted the fact that Zion will be built by living revealed principles. "Only a Zion people can bring in a Zion society," Benson noted. "And as the Zion people increase, so we will be able to incorporate more of the principles of Zion until we have a people prepared to receive the Lord."[7]

Received during Joseph Smith's first trip to Zion, section 58 outlined for the Saints principles required in the process of becoming Zion. Foreshadowing the immediate history of Jackson County, the Lord promised a reward "greater in the kingdom of heaven" for those who are "faithful in tribulation." He further declared that they "cannot behold with [their] natural eyes, for the present time, the design of [their] God," but that "after much tribulation [would come] the blessings" (vv. 2–4). For Zion to be built, Saints must faithfully overcome trials—this is a first principle for becoming Zion.

Section 58 continues by outlining obedience to law as a second principle upon which Zion must be built. "My law shall be kept on this land," the Lord declared (v. 19). Using Martin Harris as "an example unto the church, in laying his moneys before the bishop of the church," the Lord linked consecration specifically to the establishment of Zion, declaring that consecration is "a law unto every man that cometh unto this land [Zion] to receive an inheritance." To be a part of Zion, each man must do "with his moneys according as the law directs" (vv. 35–36).

Obedience to God is connected to the proactive use of agency, a third principle outlined in the section. While Saints committed to building Zion are to obey God's laws, they should also not wait "[to be commanded] in all things; for he that is compelled in all things, the same is a slothful and not a wise servant" (v. 26). Rather, the Saints "should be anxiously engaged in a good cause, and do many things of their own free will, and bring to pass much righteousness" because "the power is in them, wherein they are agents unto themselves" (vv. 27–28). We do not merely wait for Zion to be built; it is a goal we actively seek to achieve.

The section continued with a fourth principle upon which Zion and Zion-like lives are built—sharing the gospel. Because Zion was to be a place "unto which all nations shall be invited," the Lord's representatives had to "push the people together from the ends of the earth" (vv. 9, 45). Those who were "not appointed to stay in this land" were to "preach the gospel in the regions round about," the Lord commanded, "for, verily, the sound must go forth from this place into all the world, and unto the uttermost parts of the earth—the gospel must be preached unto every creature" (vv. 46, 64).

Finally, consistent with how Zion was later equated with "the pure in heart" (D&C 97:21), the Lord called both Martin Harris and William W. Phelps to repent in section 58. If Enoch's Zion was a group of people who were "of one heart" and who "dwelt in righteousness" (Moses 7:18), modern Zion was to become the same. Rebuking Harris and Phelps for seeking "the praise of the world" and "to excel" (D&C 58:39, 41), the Lord counseled them that they could purify their hearts by confessing and forsaking their sins (see v. 43).[8] Indeed, if they did so, the Lord promised he would "remember [their sins] no more" (v. 42). These principles of faithfully enduring trials, obeying God's laws, exercising agency, preaching the gospel, and purifying hearts—delivered as the Prophet sought instruction regarding Zion's establishment—provide a pattern for how the Lord's people would become a modern Zion.

Armed with the knowledge of where to establish Zion and the principles upon which it must be built, Joseph Smith moved forward with focus on its physical location while emphasizing the standards required for its establishment. The day after the receipt of section 58, he assisted recently arrived members of the Colesville Branch in laying the first log for a house "as a foundation of Zion." On the same occasion, "through prayer, the land of Zion was consecrated and dedicated by Elder Sidney Rigdon for the gathering of the Saints."[9] Committing the inhabitants of Zion to become Zion, Rigdon challenged the audience, "Do you receive this land for the land of your inheritance with thankful hearts from the Lord?" "We do," was the enthusiastic answer from all. "Do you pledge yourselves to keep the laws of God on this land, which you have never have [sic] kept in your own land?" Rigdon continued. Again, "we do" was the response. Finally, Rigdon asked "Do you pledge yourselves to see that others of your brethren, who shall come hither do keep the laws of God?" Following a third "we do" and a benedictory prayer, Rigdon concluded, "I now pronounce this land consecrated and dedicated to the Lord for a possession and inheritance for the Saints, (in the name of Jesus Christ having authority from him.) And for all the faithful Servants of the Lord to the rimotest [sic] ages of time."[10] The next day, in what was described as a "scene . . . solemn and impressive," Joseph Smith continued to focus on the physical location of Zion, likewise dedicating the spot for the temple.[11]

Implementing the Principles to Establish Zion (D&C 59–64)

While Joseph and his companions labored for Zion's physical establishment, additional revelations focused the early Saints back on the principles of how to become Zion-like. Just as Elder D. Todd Christofferson emphasized that "Zion is both a place and a people," the Lord returned to stressing the principles outlined in D&C 58.[12] On August 7, 1831, Joseph Smith's next revelation, D&C 59, again addressed two earlier themes. The revelation was received following the funeral of Polly Knight, who had traveled with her husband, Joseph Knight Sr., and the rest of the Colesville Branch at the Lord's direction to settle in Zion (see D&C 54:8). So ill on her journey that her son Newel "bought lumber to make a coffin in case she should die before we arrived at our place of destination," Polly Knight had her "greatest desire" fulfilled to "set her feet upon the land of Zion, and to have her body interred in that land."[13] Praising these Saints for having faithfully come to Zion in spite of tribulation, the revelation opened, "Blessed . . . are they who have come up unto this land with an eye single to my glory, according to my commandments. For those that live shall inherit the earth, and those that die shall rest from all their labors, and their works shall follow them; and they shall receive a crown in the mansions of my Father, which I have prepared for them" (D&C 59:1–2). As promised in the previous section, people become Zion-like after much tribulation, though their ultimate blessings might be delayed until eternity. Of Polly Knight, Joseph Smith later wrote, "a worthy member sleeps in Jesus till the resurrection."[14]

In addition to expounding the role of tribulation in becoming like Zion, the Lord praised obedience in section 59. "Blessed are they whose feet stand upon the land of Zion, who have obeyed my gospel," the revelation continued, "for they shall receive for their reward the good things of the earth. . . . And they shall also be crowned with blessings from above" (vv. 3–4). This revelation, however, went further than its predecessor in explaining the role of obedience in shaping Zion. Prohibiting specific sins like stealing, adultery, and murder, the Lord added the caution "nor do anything like unto it" (v. 6). Saints serious about becoming Zion are to live a higher standard of obedience. Furthermore, not needing to be commanded in all things, they go beyond merely not committing sin to avoiding even its very appearance.

While this section seems to cover a host of possible sins with its umbrella-like phrase "nor do anything like unto it," the Lord did go into significant detail regarding obedience to the fourth commandment, honoring the Lord's Sabbath. Received on Sunday, August 7, 1831, the text may have some connection to the day and also to the audience who, as farmers arriving late in the planting season, may have been tempted to make up for lost time.[15] However, like the other principles for building Zion, the section may also foreshadow a modern challenge, as the lack of Sabbath observance seems to stifle Zion's establishment. In 1997, President Gordon B. Hinckley cautioned:

> The Sabbath of the Lord is becoming the play day of the people. It is a day of golf and football on television, of buying and selling in our stores and markets. Are we moving to mainstream America as some observers believe? In this I fear we are. What a telling thing it is to see the parking lots of the markets filled on Sunday in communities that are predominately LDS.
>
> Our strength for the future, our resolution to grow the Church across the world, will be weakened if we violate the will of the Lord in this important matter. He has so very clearly spoken anciently and again in modern revelation. We cannot disregard with impunity that which He has said.[16]

Focusing specific attention on keeping the Sabbath holy, section 59 also subtly models the principle of proactively applying agency introduced in the previous revelation. Commanding obedience to the law of the Sabbath, the section outlines principles of proper Sabbath observance rather than prescribing specific behavior (see vv. 9–14), allowing the Saints in Zion the latitude for personal application. This blending of obedience with proactivity is part of the process of becoming Zion. Noting that we should follow this pattern, Elder Dallin H. Oaks observed, "Teachers who are commanded to teach 'the principles of [the] gospel' and 'the doctrine of the kingdom' (D&C 88:77) should generally forgo teaching specific rules or applications. For example, they would not . . . provide a list of *dos* and *don'ts* for keeping the Sabbath day holy. Once a teacher has taught the doctrine and the associated principles from the scriptures and the living prophets, such specific applications or rules are generally the responsibility of individuals and families." Teaching principles but allowing for individual agency brings power, for, as Elder Oaks concluded, "well-taught doctrines and principles have a more powerful influence on behavior than rules."[17]

Having accomplished the trip's purpose of locating and dedicating Zion, Joseph and his associates turned their attention toward their homes in Kirtland. The day after the delivery of section 59, another revelation was given in response to "some inquiry among the Elders what they were to do."[18] The sections associated with the return trip to Kirtland continue to hearken back to section 58 and the principles outlined for how to become a Zion people. In particular, they stress the declaration that "the gospel must be preached unto every creature" (D&C 58:64). The Lord instructed the elders "to return speedily to the land from whence they came" (D&C 60:1), and he reemphasized that they were to "bear testimony of the truth in all places" (D&C 58:47). To do so, the elders were to return "two by two, and preach the word" (D&C 60:8). After chiding them for having hidden their talents because of fear, the Lord challenged them to travel home "proclaiming [his] word, . . . not in haste" (v. 14).

Four days later, on August 12, 1831, the elders were rebuked for having disobeyed the counsel. Commenting on their canoe journey down the Missouri River, the Lord declared, "It is not needful for this whole company of mine elders to be moving swiftly upon the waters, whilst the inhabitants on either side are perishing in unbelief" (D&C 61:3). Though Joseph Smith, Sidney Rigdon, and Oliver Cowdery were to make their way speedily home, the "residue" of the elders were to "journey and declare the word among the congregations of the wicked" (D&C 61:30–33). Obeying the counsel, the Prophet pressed for home when the next day he met his brother Hyrum, together with John Murdock, David Whitmer, and Harvey Whitlock. Following "joyful salutations" with this group, who were still journeying to Zion, Joseph again received a revelation from the Lord which is now known as section 62.[19] Having complied with the command to preach by "contending for the faith once delivered to the Saints,"[20] these elders were "blessed, for the testimony which [they had] borne [was] recorded in heaven . . . and [their] sins [were] forgiven [them]" (D&C 62:3). While journeying to Zion, they were becoming Zion, furthering its cause by preaching the gospel.

In the midst of these revelations associated with traveling home, the Lord also expanded upon the principle of proactively exercising agency. When these elders asked what they were to do now that their missions to Zion were complete, the Lord declared, "Concerning your journey unto the land from whence you came. Let there be a craft made, or bought, as seemeth you good, *it mattereth not unto me*" (D&C 60:5; emphasis added). In a little-used phrase in the Doctrine and Covenants, the Lord indicated that some decisions may not matter to him. Rather, as these elders were told in section 58, "the power is in them, wherein they are agents unto themselves" (D&C 58:28).

Though the phrase "it mattereth not unto me" appears rarely in the revelations of the Doctrine and Covenants, it is used repeatedly in sections 60 through 63. After revealing that there were "dangers upon the waters . . . and especially upon these waters" and instructing the leaders to "forewarn [their] brethren concerning these waters," the Lord nevertheless encouraged them to make their own choice (D&C 61:4–5, 18). "*It mattereth not unto me*, after a little," he concluded, "if it so be that they fill their mission, whether they go by water or by land" (D&C 61:22; emphasis added). Traveling by water was physically dangerous, but requiring that the Lord direct every detail of their trip was spiritually damaging.

When Joseph encountered his brother Hyrum and his companions the next day, the Lord again used the phrase "it mattereth not unto me." Instructing them regarding the remainder of their journey, he counseled, "You may return to bear record, yea, even altogether, or two by two, as seemeth you good, *it mattereth not unto me*" (D&C 62:5; emphasis added). The Lord did, however, counsel them to "only be faithful, and declare glad tidings unto the inhabitants of the earth" (D&C 62:5), linking again two of the principles in becoming Zion: the Saints were to use their agency and share the gospel.

Continuing on their journey, the party arrived in Kirtland on August 27, 1831, where the residents were anxious to learn the results of the Prophet's mission.[21] "In these infant days of the Church," Joseph Smith later recalled, "there was a great anxiety to obtain the word of the Lord upon every subject that in any way concerned our salvation; and as the land of Zion was now the most important temporal object in view, I enquired of the Lord for further information upon the gathering of the Saints, and the purchase of the land, and other matters."[22] The responding revelation continued the theme of agency, directing the Saints in their acquisition of the land but again cautioning, "Let all the moneys which can be spared, *it mattereth not unto me* whether it be little or much, be sent up unto the land of Zion" (D&C 63:40; emphasis added).

Like other elements of the process for establishing Zion, doing "many things of [our] own free will" without waiting for a "command in all things" is a gospel principle. However, in these revelations, this admonition for the proactive use of agency seems especially applicable to those striving for Zion. Saints committed to this ideal don't wait for Zion to come about; they actively seek to establish it (see D&C 6:6). This principle is consistent with modern counsel. Elder Ezra Taft Benson observed that proper use of agency facilitates divine progression. "Usually the Lord gives us the overall objectives to be accomplished and some guidelines to follow," Elder Benson observed, "but he expects us to work out most of the details and methods. The methods and procedures are usually developed through study and prayer and by living so that we can obtain and follow the promptings of the Spirit." This process seems true regarding the early Saints' efforts to build Zion. Benson continued,

> Less spiritually advanced people, such as those in the days of Moses, had to be commanded in many things. Today those spiritually alert look at the objectives, check the guidelines laid down by the Lord and his prophets, and then prayerfully act—without having to be commanded "in all things." This attitude prepares men for godhood. . . .
>
> Sometimes the Lord hopefully waits on his children to act on their own, and when they do not, they lose the greater prize, and the Lord will either drop the entire matter and let them suffer the consequences or else he will have to spell it out in greater detail. Usually, I fear, the more he has to spell it out, the smaller is our reward.[23]

The final principle for establishing Zion as outlined by the Lord in D&C 58, namely, that people must purify and sanctify their hearts, was expanded in the revelations Joseph Smith received upon returning to Kirtland. In answer to questions about which people could move to Zion and how they were to purchase the land, the Lord directed, "Wherefore, let my disciples in Kirtland arrange their temporal concerns, who dwell upon this farm. Let my servant Titus Billings, who has the care thereof, dispose of the land, that he may be prepared in the coming spring to take his journey up unto the land of Zion" (D&C 63:38–39). Ironically, however, the property discussed in the revelation did not belong exclusively to Billings. Rather, he had "the care thereof" on behalf of his brother-in-law Isaac Morley, who was still returning from the mission to Missouri. Understandably, upon his return Morley learned of the directive that his farm be sold and must have questioned why. Addressing the concern, Joseph Smith received D&C 64, informing him that God "gave commandment that [Morley's] farm should be sold," so that "my servant Isaac Morley may not be tempted above that which he is able to bear, and counsel wrongfully to your hurt" (v. 20).

The sale of the farm highlights what may be the crowning principle in establishing Zion. "If our hearts are set too much upon the things of this world," Elder Neal A. Maxwell counseled, "they may need to be wrenched, or broken, or undergo a mighty change."[24] Combining both Zion the place and Zion the process, the Lord stressed, "I, the Lord, will not hold any guilty that shall go with an open heart up to the land of Zion; for I, the Lord, require the hearts of the children of men" (D&C 64:22). To test his people, the Lord declared that in this "day of sacrifice" (D&C 64:23) he "requireth the heart and a willing mind" (D&C 64:34). Like Isaac Morley, those who give their all, be it a farm or their heart, will "eat the good of the land of Zion in these last days" (D&C 64:34). As the Savior declared in the New Testament, "Where your treasure is, there will your heart be also" (Luke 12:34).

Morley obediently complied with the directive regarding the sale of his farm, a transaction he completed on October 12, 1831, prior to his moving to Zion.[25] Though achieving Zion was difficult, Morley and others personally experienced both the place and process of Zion. Elder Orson F. Whitney later penned, "The redemption of Zion is more than the purchase or recovery of lands, the building of cities, or even the founding of nations. It is the conquest of the heart, the subjugation of the soul, the sanctifying of the flesh, the purifying and ennobling of the passions." If Saints are to build Zion, they must surrender their hearts. "In her children's hearts," Whitney concluded, "must Zion first be built up and redeemed."[26]

Conclusion

In the Doctrine and Covenants, the Lord progressively expanded the Saints' understanding regarding Zion. While the concept continues to be both a cause and a place, the Lord also emphasized Zion as a process because of what it would cause his people to become. "Zion is Zion because of the character, attributes, and faithfulness of her citizens," summarized Elder D. Todd Christofferson.[27] Focused on the place, Joseph Smith inquired diligently regarding where and when Zion would be created. While the Lord did indicate "the place for the city of Zion," when it would be established remained, and remains, a mystery. The Prophet was told how to be Zion-like. God's people are counseled to follow the pattern established in section 58 of the Doctrine and Covenants and highlighted in the subsequent sections associated with the mission to Zion. By faithfully enduring trials, obeying God's law, properly using agency, sharing the gospel, and purifying our hearts, we will become Zion. Indeed, "we cannot wait until Zion comes for these things to happen," Elder Christofferson stressed. "Zion will come only as they happen."[28]

While elusive, establishing Zion was possible in Joseph Smith's day. In 1834, following the attempt by Zion's Camp to restore the Saints in Missouri to their lands of promise, the Lord declared, "Were it not for the transgressions of my people, speaking concerning the church and not individuals, they might have been redeemed even now" (D&C 105:2). Explaining the failure, he returned to the principles outlined on the first trip to Zion: "They have not learned to be obedient to the things which I required at their hands, but are full of all manner of evil, and do not impart of their substance, as becometh saints, to the poor and afflicted among them; and are not united according to the union required by the law of the celestial kingdom" (vv. 3–4). Declaring how the city must ultimately be established, the Lord concluded, "Zion cannot be built up unless it is by *the principles* of the law of the celestial kingdom; otherwise I cannot receive her unto myself" (v. 5, emphasis added).

Furthermore, becoming Zion and establishing the city remains possible today. Brigham Young counseled, "When we conclude to make a Zion we will make it, and this work commences in the heart of each person. . . . There is not one thing wanting in all the works of God's hands to make a Zion upon the earth when the people conclude to make it. . . . A Zion of God can always be built on the earth."[29]

In becoming Zion to establish Zion, early settler in Zion Edward Partridge penned a prayer that summarizes the process for all:

> Let Zion in her beauty rise;
> Her light begins to shine.
> Ere long her King will rend the skies,
> Majestic and divine,
> The gospel spreading thru the land,
> A people to prepare
> To meet the Lord and Enoch's band
> Triumphant in the air.
>
> Ye heralds, sound the golden trump
> To earth's remotest bound.
> Go spread the news from pole to pole
> In all the nations round:
> That Jesus in the clouds above,
> With hosts of angels too,
> Will soon appear, his Saints to save,
> His enemies subdue.
>
> That glorious rest will then commence
> Which prophets did foretell,
> When Saints will reign with Christ on earth,
> And in his presence dwell
> A thousand years, oh, glorious day!
> Dear Lord, prepare my heart
> To stand with thee on Zion's mount
> And nevermore to part.[30]

Notes

1. Joseph Smith, "The Temple," *Times and Seasons*, May 2, 1842, 776.
2. With twenty-two separate entries, "Zion" is tied as the tenth most frequently recurring topic in *The Teachings of Joseph Smith*. See Larry E. Dahl and Donald Q. Cannon, eds., *The Teachings of Joseph Smith* (Salt Lake City: Bookcraft, 1997), ix, 720–30.
3. Joseph Smith, "The Temple," *Times and Seasons*, May 2, 1842, 776.

4. Robert D. Hales, in *Conference Report*, April 1986, 38; emphasis added.

5. *History of the Church of Jesus Christ of Latter-day Saints*, ed. B. H. Roberts, 2nd ed. rev. (Salt Lake City: Deseret Book, 1957), 1:189; emphasis added. The date for this revelation comes from the Book of Commandments and Revelations, also known as Revelation Book 1. Robin Scott Jensen, Robert J. Woodford, and Steven C. Harper, eds., *Revelations and Translations, Volume 1: Manuscript Revelation Books*, vol. 1 of the Revelations and Translations series of *The Joseph Smith Papers*, ed. Dean C. Jessee, Ronald K. Esplin, and Richard Lyman Bushman (Salt Lake City: Church Historian's Press, 2009), "Revelation Book 1," 159.

6. Jensen, Woodford, and Harper, *Revelations and Translations, Volume 1: Manuscript Revelation Books*, 161.

7. Ezra Taft Benson, "Jesus Christ—Gifts and Expectations," *New Era*, May 1975, 18.

8. In a phrase that was later struck through, the copy of this revelation contained in the Book of Commandments and Revelation preserves the connection to the heart, warning that Phelps was "not sufficiently humble meek in his heart." Jensen, Woodford, and Harper, *Revelations and Translations, Volume 1: Manuscript Revelation Books*, 165.

9. *History of the Church*, 1:196.

10. *From Historian to Dissident: The Book of John Whitmer*, ed. Bruce N. Westergren (Salt Lake City: Signature Books, 1995), 86.

11. *History of the Church*, 1:199.

12. D. Todd Christofferson, "Come to Zion," *Ensign*, November 2008, 37.

13. *History of the Church*, 1:199.

14. *History of the Church*, 1:199.

15. Keeping the Sabbath of the Lord holy was a theme of early sermons in the Salt Lake Valley as well, as pioneers likewise arrived late in the season but were counseled by Brigham Young to honor the Sabbath. Wilford Woodruff recalled Young's Sabbath sermon on July 25, 1847, one day after their arrival in the valley. "President Young . . . Informed the brethren they must not work on Sunday," Woodruff wrote, and if they did, "they would loose [sic] five times as much as they would gain by it. . . . And there should not any man dwell among us who would not observe these rules. They might go & dwell whare they pleased," Young concluded, "but should not dwell with us." *Wilford Woodruff's Journal: 1833–1898 Typescript*, ed. Scott G. Kenney (Midvale, UT: Signature Books, 1983), 3:235–36.

16. Gordon B. Hinckley, "Look to the Future," *Ensign*, November 1997, 69.

17. Dallin H. Oaks, "Gospel Teaching," *Ensign*, November 1999, 79.

18. *History of the Church*, 1:201.

19. *History of the Church*, 1:205.

20. *History of the Church*, 1:205.

21. The Book of Commandments and Revelations dates the actual revelation as August 30, 1831. Jensen, Woodford, and Harper, *Revelations and Translations, Volume 1: Manuscript Revelation Books*, 181.

22. *History of the Church*, 1:207.

23. Ezra Taft Benson, in *Conference Report*, April 1965, 121–22.

24. Neal A. Maxwell, "'Swallowed Up in the Will of the Father,'" *Ensign*, November 1995, 24.

25. Lyndon W. Cook, *The Revelations of the Prophet Joseph Smith* (Salt Lake City: Deseret Book, 1985), 104.

26. Orson F. Whitney, *Life of Heber C. Kimball* (Salt Lake City: Bookcraft, 1996), 65–66.

27. Christofferson, "Come to Zion," 38.

28. Christofferson, "Come to Zion," 38.

29. *Discourses of Brigham Young*, comp. John A. Widtsoe (Salt Lake City: Deseret Book, 1954), 118.

30. Edward Partridge, "Let Zion in Her Beauty Rise," *Hymns* (Salt Lake City: The Church of Jesus Christ of Latter-day Saints, 1985), no. 41.

10

Revealing Parables: A Call to Action within the Doctrine and Covenants

Amy Easton-Flake

Figurative language and images communicate in ways that rational arguments cannot. By teaching in parables, Christ ignited his listeners' imaginations and made many difficult ideas comprehensible. Yet at times, Christ also used parables to conceal his message. Expanding on the sentiments Christ expressed in chapter 4 of the Gospel of Mark, Elder Bruce R. McConkie wrote, "When opposition to his message became bitter and intense, the master Teacher chose to present many of the truths of salvation in parables in order to hide his doctrine from those not prepared to receive it. It was not his purpose to cast pearls before swine."[1] The function of parables differs widely within the New Testament. Some are straightforward and require little explanation, while others are indefinite and have been copiously analyzed and debated. Centuries later, Christ again employed parables in the Doctrine and Covenants; however, the camouflage aspect of these parables is absent. This change invokes questions about the audience and the function of parables in the Doctrine and Covenants. How did Christ's latter-day audience differ from that of his day, and how do parables help the Lord communicate with

---

Amy Easton-Flake received her PhD in English from Brandeis University and currently teaches literature and writing courses at Brandeis and Framingham State.

his people? While his presentation of parables in the Doctrine and Covenants differs markedly—at times he references them briefly, and at times he offers an extended explanation—each instance reveals the Lord using parables to expand the Saints' understanding and to call them to action. This article focuses on the seven parables in the Doctrine and Covenants, with a particular emphasis on the three original to the text. By examining the content and form of these parables, we may identify principles of how the Lord works with individuals in addition to the doctrine revealed and the actions required.

The Power of Parables

Parables are a powerful literary device and teaching tool. Greek in origin, the word *parable* derives from a word that means a "comparison or analogy."[2] Rather than an abstract discussion about a divine truth, a parable is a brief and often simple narrative designed to convey a moral or religious lesson through comparison to commonplace events.[3] The benefits of using parables are many. First, parables often make abstract principles more comprehensible and may convey much quickly. Second, parables are often more memorable than abstract discussions or direct exhortations. They are more likely, as Elder Boyd K. Packer instructed, to live "after the students are out of class" because the commonplace items referenced in the parable will bring the teaching to individuals' minds when they see the objects in their daily lives.[4] Third, parables encourage listeners to discover embedded messages. "Parables," as Elder Bruce R. McConkie taught, "are a call to investigate the truth; to learn more; to inquire into the spiritual realities, which, through them, are but dimly viewed."[5] In exerting mental effort to comprehend a parable's divine message, listeners become active rather than passive recipients and are more likely to remember and put into effect the knowledge received.[6]

Fourth, parables may allow us to see what our current construction of the world keeps us from seeing. Using Søren Kierkegaard's treatment of indirect communication, New Testament scholar Klyne R. Snodgrass explains how parables, as indirect communication, skirt around individuals' defenses to confront "what one thinks is reality" and "provide new sets of relations that enable us (or force us) to see in a fresh manner."[7] Fifth, the narrative form of parables creates, as Northrop Frye explains, both centripetal and centrifugal meanings, as the structure simultaneously encourages both a closed reading and enables numerous connotations and layers of interpretations.[8] To understand the power of parables is to recognize that they can teach, as Elder Dallin H. Oaks noted, "several different and valuable principles."[9] Sixth, as explained in the Bible Dictionary, "the parable conveys to the hearer religious truth exactly in proportion to his faith and intelligence; to the dull and uninspired it is a mere story, 'seeing they see not,' while to the instructed and spiritual it reveals the mysteries or secrets of the kingdom of heaven."[10] In teaching with parables, Christ shows great mercy toward his listeners in that he keeps them from obtaining more knowledge than they are ready to receive. For, as we learn in the Doctrine and Covenants, "he who sins against the greater light shall receive the greater condemnation" (D&C 82:3).

Although many parables in the New Testament reveal and conceal simultaneously, depending on an individual's spiritual sensitivity, in the Doctrine and Covenants, the Lord most often takes away this dual potential by explaining the meaning of the parable. The reason for this alteration most likely lies in the listeners. When Christ spoke in the New Testament, he addressed an audience of believers and unbelievers. While his Apostles and disciples were among the multitudes who gathered to hear him speak, there were also Pharisees, scribes, chief priests, elders, lawyers, tax collectors, and many others who scoffed at his words. The parables in the Doctrine and Covenants, however, are addressed exclusively to believers: Joseph Smith, Sidney Rigdon, the elders of Israel, and other members of his restored Church. Consequently, the Lord no longer veils his message to protect those who are not spiritually prepared, but employs parables to help his disciples understand difficult principles, remember them more readily, and excite them to action.

Parables from the New Testament

Parable of the fig tree. The first parable to appear in the Doctrine and Covenants is the parable of the fig tree. In December 1830, Sidney Rigdon, a former Campbellite preacher, traveled to New York to meet Joseph Smith and inquire of the Lord what role he was to play in building the kingdom. Section 35 is the Lord's response: here Rigdon learns he was "sent forth, even as John, to prepare the way before [the Lord]" (v. 4)[11] and is then called to baptize people into the Church and act as Joseph Smith's scribe (see vv. 5, 20). The Lord also speaks to Rigdon of the "miracles, signs, and wonders" that he will show "unto all those who believe on [the Lord's] name" (v. 8)—significant because the possibility of miracles in the latter days had been a point of contention between Rigdon and Alexander Campbell[12]—and reveals that the "poor and the meek . . . shall learn the parable of the fig-tree, for even now already summer is nigh" (vv. 15–16).

For many, the reference to the parable of the fig tree would have been esoteric, but for Rigdon, it was illuminating. "Often called a 'walking Bible' by his peers in the Reformed Baptist Movement," Rigdon had devoted his life to studying scriptures and the life of Christ;[13] consequently, Rigdon was undoubtedly well aware of the parable of the fig tree and its reference to the signs of the Second Coming. Thus in referencing a parable, the Lord quickly conveys much to Rigdon. First, the parable effectively sums up the much-anticipated Second Coming of the Lord and possibly strokes Rigdon's desire to be a part of the work, since he learns the signs are soon to become apparent. Second, the repetition of a parable from the New Testament reinforces that the Lord who speaks to Joseph Smith, and now Rigdon, is not a new Lord, but the same Lord who lived on the earth. Since Rigdon had spent his adult life searching for a restoration of Christ's Church and judged all truth according to the Bible, he is a particularly fitting recipient of the first parable in the Doctrine and Covenants.[14] Looking at what this parable tells us about how the Lord works with humanity, we see evidence that the Lord knows us as individuals and works with us accordingly. The parable may be seen as a tender mercy given to Rigdon to assure him that he had found Christ's restored Church.

Parables of the fig tree and ten virgins. Three months later, in March 1831, the parable of the fig tree, accompanied by the parable of the ten virgins, makes another appearance in the Doctrine and Covenants. In what is now section 45, "Jesus reiterates his own sermon from Matthew 24, comments on it, and applies it to Latter-day Saints striving to replicate Enoch's Zion."[15] Throughout the revelation, the Lord makes it clear that many truths originally contained within the New Testament are in need of restoration and that these truths will prepare them "for the things to come" (D&C 45:61). Such insights likely motivated and prepared Joseph Smith to fulfill the command he receives at the end of the revelation to commence translating the New Testament, and these insights are an instance of the Lord supplying the motivation before the commandment.

The Olivet Discourse and the parables it contains are prime examples of the Doctrine and Covenants being a space for explanation as the Lord builds upon his previous teachings and explains their application to Latter-day Saints. With the parable of the fig tree, the Lord shares many of the signs that will precede his coming and directs the Saints to watch for them (see D&C 45:24–46). With the parable of the ten virgins, the Lord provides specific instruction to the Saints on how to be wise rather than foolish as they prepare for his Second Coming:[16] the wise virgins are wise because they "have received the truth, and have taken the Holy Spirit for their guide" (v. 57). Through this explanation, the Lord directs the Saints to gain truth and follow the Spirit in order to obtain the wise virgins' reward, a reward now made explicit in the Doctrine and Covenants: "the earth shall be given unto them for an inheritance; and they shall multiply and wax strong, and their children shall grow up without sin unto salvation" (v. 58). Turning to the form of this parable, we see evidence that the Lord expects Latter-day Saints to be familiar with his teachings in the Bible, because he references rather than recounts the parable. He builds rather than repeats.

Parable of the wheat and tares. The other parable to appear twice in the Doctrine and Covenants is the parable of the wheat and tares (see sections 86 and 101). After Christ gave this parable to the multitude, he explained its meaning to his disciples: he has planted wheat ("children of the kingdom"), but Satan has sown tares ("children of the wicked one"). He allows the two to grow together until the time of harvest ("the end of this world"), "lest while ye gather up the tares, ye root up also the wheat with them" (Matthew 13:29, 38–40).[17] On December 6, 1832, while Joseph was translating the Bible, he received a revelation explaining the parable of the wheat and tares. This revelation, recorded as Doctrine and Covenants 86, provides further information on how the gospel originally spread ("the apostles were the sowers of the seed" [v. 2]) and how the great apostasy occurred (after the apostles' deaths, Satan sowed the tares that "choke[d] the wheat and [drove] the church into the wilderness" [v. 3]). The parable also includes additional lines that bring the parable into the latter days—"But behold, in the last days, even now while the Lord is beginning to bring forth the word" (v. 4)—and indicate the Saints are a part of its fulfillment. The parable, as the Prophet Joseph Smith explained, had an "allusion to the setting up of the kingdom" in the Apostles' time and in the latter days.[18] Consequently, the Lord gave his disciples the information that would help them fulfill their role, and later, as President Joseph Fielding Smith explained, he provided the Latter-day Saints with "a more complete interpretation" because "it is to be in these last days that the harvest is gathered and the tares are to be burned."[19] The extended interpretation and expansion of this parable is an example of how the Lord often provides individuals with only the information pertinent to their role or progression.

The Lord's explanation of the parable culminates in the revelation of the priesthood's role in the harvesting of souls: "then ye shall first gather out the wheat from among the tares" (D&C 86:7). Significantly, the Lord has reversed the order of the gathering. First the wheat is gathered and then "the tares are bound in bundles" (v. 7). This reversal shifts the focus from the destruction of the wicked to the gathering of the righteous before the Second Coming, which in turn emphasizes the role Latter-day Saints are to play in gathering the righteous. "The servants of God," as Joseph Smith explained in regard to this parable, are "to go forth warning the nations."[20] As signaled by the conjunction *therefore*,[21] the parable is the jumping-off point for an explanation of the role of the priesthood and the Lord's purpose in preserving the lineage of those who carry it. Because the Lord needs gatherers in the latter days, "the priesthood hath continued through the lineage of your fathers" (v. 8), and by gathering the wheat and being "a light unto the Gentiles," they may be "a savior unto my people Israel" (v. 11). The parable becomes a clarion call, exciting the elders of Israel to fulfill their priesthood responsibility to gather the elect before the Lord's Second Coming. The Latter-day Saints are now a part of this profound biblical parable.

In a subsequent discourse from Joseph Smith, we see evidence that this revelation on the wheat and tares may have provided the Prophet with understanding on a more personal matter. Joseph received this revelation a mere three days after the excommunication of Jesse Gause, his counselor in the Presidency of the High Priesthood.[22] Apostasy by those close to him in leadership positions must have been difficult to understand, and surely Joseph wondered why this occurred. This revelation provides a partial answer, as the Lord assures the Prophet of the wisdom of letting the wheat and tares grow together because the faith of the wheat is currently too "weak" (v. 6). When Joseph later expounded on the parable to the Saints, he explained how Christ's "disciples would fain have plucked up, or cleansed the Church of [corruptions], if their views had been favored by the Savior."[23] Joseph, too, likely wished to cleanse the Church of apostates and iniquity, but his expansion on the Lord's response to his disciples indicates that this parable had taught him the importance of patience and restraint: "But he, knowing all things, says, Not so. As much as to say, your views are not correct, the Church is in its infancy, and if you take this rash step, you will destroy the wheat, or the Church, with the tares."[24] In studying past revelations, Joseph received direction for the Church and understanding for himself. Joseph's experience is another example of the inspiration the Lord promises to provide individuals who study his word (see 2 Nephi 32:3).

The Lord's second reference to the parable of the wheat and tares, in section 101, is much briefer and serves as a quick reminder to the Saints that the time of the parable's fulfillment is now. By reiterating that the "time of harvest is come" and that the reward of the gathered wheat is "to possess eternal life, and be crowned with celestial glory" (vv. 64–65), the Lord motivates them to follow his counsel. This visual image of harvesting would also reinforce the Saints' understanding of the Lord's command to literally "gather together" (v. 67).

Parable of the woman and the unjust judge. Section 101 also contains a new application of the parable of the woman and the unjust judge. In contrast to the Lord's use of other parables from the New Testament, he recounts this parable in its entirety: "There was in a city a judge which feared not God, neither regarded man. And there was a widow in that city, and she came unto him, saying: Avenge me of mine adversary. And he would not for a while, but afterward he said within himself: Though I fear not God, nor regard man, yet because this widow troubleth me I will avenge her, lest by her continual coming she weary me" (vv. 82–84). The identical preface to the parable—"for men ought always to pray and not to faint"—in both the New Testament (Luke 18:1) and Doctrine and Covenants (D&C 101:81) signals to the addressees that they are to listen to the parable for what it may teach them about prayer.[25] However, the different explanatory comments that follow reveal that the Lord's purpose in sharing the parable has changed. The emphasis in Luke is on the nature of God: God is merciful and will answer our prayers. If even an unjust judge will answer a repeated entreaty, surely a just and loving God will; consequently, men may pray in faith. In the Doctrine and Covenants, the emphasis shifts from the unjust judge to the widow. The Lord commands the Latter-day Saints to be like the widow. They are to "importune at the feet of the judge . . . the governor . . . [and] the president" for redress (D&C 101:86–89). Unwariness in seeking justice becomes the parable's dominant message.[26]

In bringing a different element to the forefront, Christ teaches an important lesson for understanding parables in general: parables can and should take on different meanings at various times for various people. The narrative aspect of parables gives them a flexibility that allows each individual to discover many principles and applications within them; consequently, studying with the Spirit allows us to discover how we may beneficially apply a parable to ourselves. Expanding on this idea, Elder Oaks explained that "scripture is not limited to what it meant when it was written but may also include what that scripture means to a reader today. Even more, scripture reading may also lead to current revelation on whatever else the Lord wishes to communicate to the reader at that time."[27]

Outside of the Doctrine and Covenants, Joseph Smith further demonstrated parables' multiple meanings when under inspiration he interpreted the parables in Matthew 13 to apply to the restored Church and its members. Joseph taught that the Book of Mormon and the restored Church of Jesus Christ are more specific fulfillments of the grain of mustard seed that becomes a great tree, that the Three Witnesses may be seen as the leaven in the parable of the kingdom of heaven and leaven, and that individual Saints are fulfilling the parables of the treasure in a field and of the merchant and the pearl as they sell all that they have in order to gather to Zion and be a part of God's kingdom.[28] Joseph's inspired interpretations of these parables demonstrate the advisability of placing ourselves within the parable. Are we a part of the fulfillment of the merchant and the pearl? Are we devoting all that we have and are to obtaining the kingdom of God? In applying the parables to ourselves, we may gain knowledge and strength.

Parables Original to the Doctrine and Covenants

Parable of the twelve sons. The Lord gave the first parable original to the Doctrine and Covenants to Joseph Smith at Fayette, New York, during the third general conference of the Church on January 2, 1831. The Church was almost nine months old, and Joseph Smith had recently received a revelation that the Saints were to gather to Ohio (see D&C 37). According to John Whitmer's account of the conference, at the congregation's request, "the Seer [Joseph Smith] enquired of the Lord in the presence of the whole congregation" for further information concerning the matter and received the revelation recorded as Doctrine and Covenants 38.[29] The Lord tells the Saints that the "commandment" to move to Ohio is for their "salvation" (v. 16). Like he did with the children of Israel, the Lord covenants to give to them "a land flowing with milk and honey" (v. 18); however, to qualify for this inheritance, they must seek it with all their hearts, follow his voice, teach one another, esteem their brother as themselves, and practice virtue and holiness before the Lord (see vv. 19–24). The instruction that "every man esteem his brother as himself" (v. 24) becomes the dominant requirement as the Lord repeats the phrase, offers a parable to illustrate his point, and then concludes the parable by telling them to "be one; and if ye are not one ye are not mine" (v. 27).

To help the Saints understand what it means to "esteem his brother as himself" and why the Lord requires this of his Saints, the Lord shares the following parable: "For what man among you having twelve sons, and is no respecter of them, and they serve him obediently, and he saith unto the one: Be thou clothed in robes and sit thou here; and to the other: Be thou clothed in rags and sit thou there—and looketh upon his sons and saith I am just?" (v. 26). The parable's family imagery is powerful because at the same time that it is accessible and clear-cut, it also holds multiple messages for the Saints. First, the image of a father and his sons encapsulates God's relationship to the Saints: he is a loving father who cares for all his children and is just in his rewards. Second, the parable emphasizes the familial relationship members of the Church enter into when they are baptized. Third, placed between a preface that announces the message of the story, "let every man esteem his brother as himself" (v. 24), and the conclusion that explains the consequence of not heeding this counsel, "if ye are not one ye are not mine" (v. 27), the parable makes a clear call to the Saints: they are to be unified and help the Lord fulfill his promise to be irrespective of persons. Fourth, the Saints learn from the imagery that they cannot be one and esteem their brethren as themselves as long as there are rich and poor among them.

For the Saints at the time, the parable was preparatory: it gave them specific instruction on how they should regard and treat one another so it would be easier for them to accept and live the law (see D&C 42), part of which was the law of consecration, which the Lord promised to give them once they gathered in Ohio. Here is further evidence of the Lord leading and teaching his people "line upon line, precept upon precept" (2 Nephi 28:30). Studying the history of the Saints, however, reveals the difficult time they had following the parable's counsel. In a later revelation to Joseph Smith, the Lord repeats the parable and states that the Apostles have failed to follow its counsel: "In consequence of their covetous desires, in that they have not dealt equally with each other in the division of the moneys which came into their hands."[30] The repetition and direct application of this parable to the Twelve reminds us that the parables have specific as well as universal applications. The Saints' failure to live the teachings of this parable also resulted in their failure to build Zion. As the Lord told the Saints after they were driven from Jackson County, they were "not united according to the union required by the law of the celestial kingdom; and Zion cannot be built up unless it is by the principles of the law of the celestial kingdom" (D&C 105:4–5); consequently, the redemption of Zion must wait.

Parable of the laborers in the field. Two years later, in December 1832, Joseph and a group of nine high priests received the next parable original to the Doctrine and Covenants, as part of what has come to be known as the Olive Leaf Discourse (D&C 88). In the middle of this glorious expansive revelation about light, glory, and sanctifying oneself to enter God's presence is the parable of the lord who sends his servants into the field and visits them in turn. At the lord's visit, each servant is "made glad with the light of the countenance of his lord" (v. 56). The Lord provides the key to understanding this parable when he concludes by likening it to his many "kingdoms, and the inhabitants thereof" (v. 61). Joseph Smith, and by extension the Saints, had learned of God's numerous worlds inhabited with his children in June 1830 while translating the Bible (see Moses 1:27–29). Two and a half years later, the Lord used this parable to reveal that he visits each of these worlds "in their several times and seasons."[31]

This new and profound truth may have been difficult for some to understand; as Elder Orson Pratt noted, the Lord "gave it as a parable, in order to assist our weak comprehensions."[32] Elder Pratt's statement recognizes that parables are often a tool for making difficult ideas comprehensible. The Lord teaches to the understanding of his listeners when he takes an allusive concept about God's many creations and renders it as a simple story about a lord and his many servants working in the field. Consequently, the parable is an example of the principle Nephi taught that the Lord "speaketh unto men according to their language, unto their understanding" (2 Nephi 31:3). Notwithstanding the ease with which the early Saints would likely have comprehended the parable, a significant dissonance does exist between the lived experience of the early Saints and the servants within the story. In particular, the democratic spirit of the United States is at odds with the gladness that each servant experiences as his lord visits him.

Scholars of Christ's parables in the New Testament have repeatedly noted how the details of his parables "are closely related to the listener's home, family, occupation, folkways, and customs";[33] however, the same cannot be as readily said of the parables original to the Doctrine and Covenants, because the Lord continues to use biblical and Middle Eastern rather than American imagery. References to robes, olive trees, lords, and servants distance the parables from the daily lives of the Lord's American audience. Since parables are powerful to a large degree because they draw on the familiar, one must consider the effect of using biblical language. What does the Lord accomplish with this approach, and what would be lost if he used imagery more in line with the Saints' everyday experience?

In keeping biblical imagery, the Lord promotes a serious study of the parables, displays a unity of message with his past and present teachings, and encourages the Saints to hold countercultural values. Since many of the Saints had been raised reading the Bible and learning the teachings of Christ, they were familiar with many biblical symbols and the importance of searching for spiritual truths within this imagery; consequently, biblical imagery within the Doctrine and Covenants signaled to the Saints to approach these teachings in a like manner. Using biblical and Middle Eastern imagery also connects the parables to those Christ uttered during his mortal ministry and, as D. Kelly Ogden has argued, shows the world that the Lord is "the same yesterday, today, and forever" (2 Nephi 29:9).[34] Returning to the parable of the laborer in the fields, the symbolically laden relationship of a nobleman and his servants, though not one most Saints could relate to, was particularly important to maintain because it highlights Christ's royal status as King of Kings and Lord of Lords. Through this parable, and this relationship in particular, the Lord encourages the Saints to place the Christian idea of submission to God above the American idea of freedom and democracy. By emphasizing the joy they will feel in his presence, the Lord motivates the Saints to submit willingly to heavenly authority and to look forward to the day when the Lord will be their king. Thus the parable becomes directive as well as informative.

Parable of the nobleman and the tower. The Lord gave the last parable original to the Doctrine and Covenants after the mobs forced the Saints to flee

Jackson County. From Joseph's letter to the Saints on December 10, 1833, we see a clear picture of his grief and confusion. He bemoans the suffering of the Saints and admits he does not know "why God hath suffered so great a calamity to come upon Zion; or what the great moving cause of this great affliction is[,] and again, by what means he will return her back to her inheritance with songs of everlasting Joy upon her head."[35] Disheartened and confused, Joseph sought inspiration from God. A week later he received a revelation that explained why Zion fell and how it will be redeemed (see D&C 101).

At the heart of the revelation is the parable of the nobleman and the olive trees, which signifies the "troubles and eventual redemption of Zion."[36] Sidney B. Sperry summed up well the common interpretation of the parable:

> The nobleman is the Lord, whose choice land in His vineyard is Zion in Missouri. The places where the Saints live in Zion are the olive trees. The servants are the Latter-day Saint settlers, and the watchmen are their officers in the Church. While yet building in Zion, they become at variance with each other and do not build the tower or Temple whose site had been dedicated as early as August 3, 1831. Had they built it as directed, it would have been a spiritual refuge for them, for from it the Lord's watchmen could have seen by revelation the movements of the enemy from afar. This foreknowledge would have saved them and their hard work when the enemy made his assault. But the Saints in Missouri were slothful, lax, and asleep. The enemy came, and the Missouri persecutions were the result.[37]

This most extensive parable in the Doctrine and Covenants is the culminating example of how the Lord uses parables to reveal knowledge and provide direction to his Saints, because in it he reveals the Saints to themselves. At this time, many of the Saints in Zion were not obeying the law of consecration. Elder Orson Pratt explained how the Saints "had imbibed the notions which had prevailed among the people of the whole earth.... The notions... were that every man must be for himself, every family for themselves, and they must labor with their might, mind and strength to gain all they possibly could gain.... These traditions had been instilled into our minds, and we were too full of covetousness and of false notions about property to carry out the law of God."[38] Pratt's explanation for the Saints' failure indicates the dueling ideas that many of the Saints were attempting to harmonize. Because these ideas of property and work were an integral part of their culture and mentality, many Saints may not have recognized how far they were from obeying the Lord's commandment to be one (see D&C 38:27). The Lord's method of using a parable would then be particularly effective because it would help them see their own weaknesses by viewing them in someone else.[39] The servants in the story did not build the tower and keep "the commandments of their lord," because "they were at variance with one another" (D&C 101:50), and the Saints in Zion "polluted their inheritances" and did not build the temple because there were "jarrings, and contentions, and envyings, and strifes, and lustful and covetous desires among them" (v. 6). Notably, the Saints lived out this third parable because they did not follow the counsel within the first parable original to the Doctrine and Covenants that "every man esteem his brother as himself" (D&C 38:24).

The parable's preface, however, indicates that the focus of the parable is not on past mistakes but on future action: "I will show unto you a parable, that you may know my will concerning the redemption of Zion" (D&C 101:43). Behind this preface is one of the great truths of how the Lord works with individuals: he helps us see our faults, but he also shows us a way to overcome them and return to the path of discipleship. This principle can be seen throughout the scriptures, perhaps most strikingly in the linking of the Fall and the Atonement throughout the Book of Mormon. As Robert L. Millet has observed, the Atonement and the Fall are a "package deal," and one does not appear without the other in the Book of Mormon.[40] In this revelation, the Lord illustrates this principle in both the parable and his opening statement to the Saints. For even as he begins the revelation by informing them they have been "cast out from the land of their inheritance . . . in consequence of their transgressions" (vv. 1–2), he immediately tempers this chastening by assuring, "Yet I will own them, and they shall be mine in that day when I shall come to make up my jewels" (v. 3). All is not lost, the Saints who endure this chastening will be better for it, and Zion will be redeemed. We can all take great comfort in the knowledge that the Lord is more interested in helping us change and overcome our weaknesses than in dwelling on our past sins and mistakes.

The second part of the parable encourages the Saints to move forward and take an active role in securing Zion. Just as the lord of the vineyard commands one of his servants to "take all the strength of mine house . . . and redeem my vineyard" (vv. 55–56), the Lord is preparing the Saints for the revelation that will soon come, the revelation to organize Zion's Camp. Two months later, the anticipated revelation came when the Lord revealed "that my servant Joseph Smith, Jun., is the man to whom I likened the servant" (D&C 103:21) and then commanded him to gather the brethren "together unto the land of Zion" (v. 22). In a highly accessible way, the parable illustrates how the Saints have misused their agency in the past and more importantly how they may now use their agency to regain Zion. Again, a parable in the Doctrine and Covenants reveals the Lord's recommended path and then motivates and calls the Saints to walk it.[41]

Conclusion

Through parables, the Saints of Joseph Smith's day heard the Lord calling them to action. The Lord directs them from the fig tree to look for the signs of the Second Coming; from the ten virgins to receive truth and take the Holy Spirit for their guide; from the wheat and tares to gather the righteous to the Church; from the woman and unjust judge to seek redress for their confiscated property; from the man with twelve sons to be one; from the laborers in the field to look forward to Christ's reign; and from the nobleman and the tower to focus on redeeming rather than losing Zion. This, however, is not all the guidance contained within these parables, nor are these Saints the only individuals to receive counsel from them. The focus of this paper has been on the Lord's directions to these early Latter-day Saints and what the forms of the parables teach us about his workings with mankind, but this exploration covers only a part of what these parables contain.[42] The majesty of these parables lies in the narrative form that allows them to contain multiple meanings and applications. From them we may learn principles of obedience, preparedness, patience, forgiveness, reliance, unity, justice, mercy, and sanctification, which enable us to walk the path of discipleship and become more like our Savior. In their universality, parables contain an invitation to study and receive direction for our lives and are an integral part of what Elder Neal A. Maxwell has referred to as "the inexhaustible gospel."[43]

Notes

1. Bruce R. McConkie, *Doctrinal New Testament Commentary*, vol. 1, *The Gospels* (Salt Lake City: Bookcraft, 1974), 283.

2. Warren S. Kissinger, *The Parables of Jesus: A History of Interpretation and Bibliography* (Metuchen, NJ: Scarecrow, 1979), xi.

3. How parables should be defined, classified, and interpreted has been rigorously debated. The definition I offer works well for the parables discussed in this paper, but as Klyne R. Snodgrass reminds us, "Every parable must be approached in its own right and not assumed to look like or function like other parables." Klyne R. Snodgrass, *Stories with Intent: A Comprehensive Guide to the Parables of Jesus* (Grand Rapids, MI: William B. Eerdmans, 2008), 7. Scholars often classify parables into three types: "figurative sayings, similitudes, and parables proper," but much melting and overlap occurs. C. H. Dodd, *The Parables of the Kingdom* (London: Nisbet, 1935), 18. For more information on these debates and an overview of the trends in interpreting parables, see Snodgrass, *Stories with Intent*, 4–15; Dodd, *Parables of the Kingdom*, 11–28; and Kissinger, *Parables of Jesus*, xi–xvi.

4. Boyd K. Packer, "Principles of Teaching and Learning," *Ensign*, June 2007, 86.

5. Bruce R. McConkie, *The Mortal Messiah*, vol. 2, *From Bethlehem to Calvary* (Salt Lake City: Deseret Book, 1980), 245.

6. C. H. Dodd, a well-respected New Testament scholar, explains how parables leave "the mind in sufficient doubt about its precise application to tease it into active thought." *Parables of the Kingdom*, 16.

7. Snodgrass, *Stories with Intent*, 8.

8. Northrop Frye, *The Great Code: The Bible and Literature* (San Diego: Harcourt, 1982), 61.

9. Dallin H. Oaks, "The Challenge to Become," *Ensign*, November 2000, 34.

10. Bible Dictionary, "Parables," 740–41.

11. Rigdon had fulfilled this role unaware during his nearly dozen years as a successful Reformed Baptist preacher and particularly with his Mentor congregation in the Kirtland area, who largely followed his leadership and joined the Church. F. Mark McKiernan writes, "Rigdon's conversion and the missionary aftermath which followed transformed Mormonism from a sect of about a hundred members to one which was a major threat to Protestantism in the Western Reserve." *The Voice of One Crying in the Wilderness: Sidney Rigdon* (Lawrence, KS: Coronado, 1971), 36. For an explanation of how the Reformed Baptist Movement prepared people to join the Church, see Richard S. Van Wagoner, *Sidney Rigdon: A Portrait of Religious Excess* (Salt Lake City: Signature Books, 1994), 61.

12. See McKiernan, *Voice of One Crying in the Wilderness*, 35; and Van Wagoner, *Sidney Rigdon*, 52–53.

13. Van Wagoner, *Sidney Rigdon*, 73.

14. Unfortunately, we do not have Rigdon's thoughts about this first revelation directed to him—quite possibly because his relative burned a 1,500-page manuscript upon his death (see McKiernan, *Voice of One Crying in the Wilderness*, 171). However, we can

safely conjecture a limited response based on what we do know about Rigdon. As Van Wagoner writes, "A biblical scholar with a reputation for erudition, he was more learned, better read, and more steeped in biblical interpretation than any other early Mormon." *Sidney Rigdon*, 73.

15. Steven C. Harper, *Making Sense of the Doctrine and Covenants: A Guided Tour Through Modern Revelation* (Salt Lake City: Deseret Book, 2008), 154.

16. In biblical scholarship, this parable has generally been understood to encourage people to be ready and prepared for either Christ's Second Coming or the coming of God to judge Israel (for more information, see Dodd, *Parables of the Kingdom*, 174; and Snodgrass, *Stories with Intent*, 511, 513–14, 518), but what the Doctrine and Covenants adds is specific understanding of how this is to be accomplished.

17. Many interpretations and questions abound about this parable in biblical scholarship. Snodgrass writes, "Both the traditional and modern critical approaches see the parable as a call to patience or as a warning about judgment for the church." *Stories with Intent*, 199. He then proceeds to explain how he and others have discounted this interpretation in favor of the following interpretation: "Its primary teaching is that the kingdom is present despite the presence of evil *and* that evil will be dealt with at the judgment." *Stories with Intent*, 212; emphasis in original. The explanation of this parable in the Doctrine and Covenants supports both of these readings but then shifts the focus to the end of the world and the priesthood's role in the gathering process. For more information on interpretations and questions about this parable, see Snodgrass, *Stories with Intent*, 198–214.

18. *Discourses of the Prophet Joseph Smith*, ed. Alma P. Burton (Salt Lake City: Deseret Book, 1977), 257.

19. Joseph Fielding Smith, *Church History and Modern Revelation* (Salt Lake City: Council of the Twelve Apostles of The Church of Jesus Christ of Latter-day Saints, 1953), 1:353.

20. *Discourses of the Prophet Joseph Smith*, 261.

21. Steven Harper has also pointed out that the Lord develops his point through four consecutive *therefores*. Harper, *Making Sense*, 308.

22. "While the ms history does not note it, Jesse Gause, Joseph Smith's (1st?) Counselor in the Presidency of the High Priesthood, was excommunicated on December 3rd." Note 31 from Annotated History of the Church, vol. 1, chap. 21 [September 1832–December 1832], Book of Abraham Project, http://www.boap.org/LDS/History/HTMLHistory/v1c21history.html.

23. *Discourses of the Prophet Joseph Smith*, 258.

24. *Discourses of the Prophet Joseph Smith*, 258.

25. The inclusion of this preface is significant within the context of biblical scholarship because scholars have generally concurred that it is a Lukan introduction. See Snodgrass, *Stories with Intent*, 455. That Christ repeats this preface when he shares the parable with Joseph Smith suggests otherwise, or at the very least, it affirms that Christ sanctioned this introduction to his parable. Similarly, a large debate surrounds the explanations attributed to Christ in the New Testament for the parable of the woman and the unjust judge and the parable of the wheat and tares. Many prominent scholars of

Jesus' parables, such as C. H. Dodd, believe that these explanations were not original to Christ but were added by the authors of the Gospels or their sources. See Dodd, *Parables of the Kingdom*, 184; and Snodgrass, *Stories with Intent*, 455–57. The Doctrine and Covenants may offer insight into these debates. The explanation of the parable of the wheat and the tares as recorded in Doctrine and Covenants 86 would affirm that Christ did offer the explanation recorded in Matthew 13 to his disciples. The explanation of the parable of the woman and unjust judge from Luke 18, however, is missing in Doctrine and Covenants 101, and a different one is in its place. I would argue that the inclusion of a different explanation of the parable does not indicate that Jesus did not offer the explanation recorded in Luke but rather that his reason for sharing the parable has changed.

26. Interestingly, many scholars who exclude the explanation and limit their interpretation of the parable to the parable itself conclude that the parable is about seeking justice. See Snodgrass, *Stories with Intent*, 454, for an overview of a few of these interpretations.

27. Dallin H Oaks, "Scripture Reading and Revelation," *Ensign*, January 1995, 8.

28. *Discourses of the Prophet Joseph Smith*, 258–60.

29. John Whitmer, "Book of John Whitmer," 3. Note 1 from Annotated History of the Church, vol. 1, chapter 13 [January 1831–February 1831], Book of Abraham Project, http://www.boap.org/LDS/History/HTMLHistory/v1c13history.html.

30. Revelation, Kirtland, Ohio, November 3, 1835; handwriting of Warren Parrish; in Joseph Smith, Journal, September 1835–April 1836, 17–19, Joseph Smith Collection, Church History Library, http://josephsmithpapers.org/paperDetails/revelation-3-november-1835.

31. Hyrum L. Andrus, *God, Man, and the Universe*, vol. 1, *Foundations of the Millenial Kingdom of Christ* (Salt Lake City: Bookcraft, 1968), 415, further explains "John Taylor quoted, and thereby sanctioned, a statement from the *Times and Seasons* that the twelve kingdoms in the above parable 'are governed by the same rules, and [are] destined to the same honor." In referring to this parable, Elder Taylor said, "It is further stated in this section [of the Doctrine and Covenants]: 'Therefore, unto this parable will I liken all these kingdoms, and the inhabitants thereof; every kingdom in its hour, and in its time, and in its season; even according to the decree which God hath made.'"

32. Orson Pratt, in *Journal of Discourses* (London: Latter-day Saints' Book Depot, 1854–86), 17:331.

33. Melvin R. Brooks, *Parables of the Kingdom* (Salt Lake City: Deseret Book, 1965), 4.

34. D. Kelly Ogden, "Biblical Language and Imagery in the Doctrine and Covenants," *Doctrine and Covenants, A Book of Answers*, ed. Leon R. Hartshorn, Dennis A. Wright, and Craig J. Ostler (Salt Lake City: Deseret Book, 1996), 189.

35. Joseph Smith, Kirtland, Ohio, to all Saints in Independence, Missouri, 10 December 1833, Joseph Smith Letterbook 1, in handwriting of Frederick G. Williams, 70–75, Church History Library, http://josephsmithpapers.org/paperDetails/letter-to-edward-partridge-and-others-10-december-1833?tm=expanded&dm=image-and-text&zm=zoom-right&p=2&s=&sm=none.

36. Chapter heading to D&C 101.

37. Sidney B. Sperry, *Doctrine and Covenants Compendium* (Salt Lake City: Bookcraft, 1979), 521–22.

38. Orson Pratt, in *Journal of Discourses*, 16:5.

39. Richard Lloyd Anderson, "How to Read a Parable," *Ensign*, September 1974, 58. "The parable is a teaching method recognizing the fact that one sees his own weaknesses better by viewing others who display the same weaknesses." Perhaps the best example of this is found in the Old Testament when Nathan tells David the parable of the ewe lamb to help him recognize the horrible sin he has committed by taking Bathsheba, the wife of Uriah, and deliberately arranging to have Uriah sent to his death (see 2 Samuel 12:1–6).

40. Robert L. Millet, *Grace Works* (Salt Lake City: Deseret Book, 2003), 27.

41. The parable also helped the Saints understand the importance of temples. In the parable, the servants begin to lay the foundation of the tower but then question "what need hath my lord of this tower" (D&C 101:47). They believe that the money might be better used if "given to the exchangers" because they see "no need" for a tower at this time (v. 49). The same was true of Saints in Jackson County who made no effort to build the temple beyond marking the foundation site and instead put their resources into other projects because they did not comprehend the importance of temples and temple covenants in 1833. A temple would not be dedicated in this dispensation until 1836; consequently, in 1833, the Saints had little understanding of how temples and temple covenants would bless their lives. Through the parable, the Lord teaches the Saints that the temple is key to their safety.

42. Charles Swift, for instance, has written about the major themes that become apparent in D&C 101 when the section is studied with a literary approach. "The Literary Power of the Doctrine and Covenants," *Religious Educator* 10, no. 1 (2009): 28–30.

43. Neal A. Maxwell, "The Inexhaustible Gospel," *Ensign*, April 1993, 71.

11

A Culmination of Learning: D&C 84 and the Doctrine of the Priesthood

Matthew C. Godfrey

One of the most significant doctrinal revelations that Joseph Smith received was Doctrine and Covenants section 84. Focused on an explication of the priesthood, the revelation delineated the existence of a greater and lesser priesthood while also explaining the duties and responsibilities assumed by those who obtained it. One recent commentator noted that section 84 "is a landmark revelation with a breathtaking scope," as it "explained the priesthood's past and projected its future use in temples."[1] Because of its significance, one might expect that Joseph and other Church leaders had kept a careful record of the circumstances surrounding its reception. Although they may have done so, no such explanation is extant today. A manuscript history of Joseph begun in 1838 devotes only one small paragraph to the context behind the revelation. However, a careful examination of early documents provides clues into the revelation's background. Using conference minutes, other revelations, journal entries, Joseph's work on his inspired translation of the Bible, and personal histories, this paper will show that section 84 did not just spring into being in September 1832 but rather that many of the concepts

---

Matthew C. Godfrey is a volume editor of The Joseph Smith Papers *and a coeditor of the* Document *series in which this document appears.*

revealed therein were taught to Joseph prior to that time. This paper is not meant to discuss in great detail the meaning of these concepts; it is only to show that Joseph was aware of many of them before they were consolidated in section 84.

Context and Background to Section 84

Section 84 was revealed over the course of two days: September 22 and 23, 1832. The six months leading up to this revelation were eventful for Joseph. In February 1832, he and Sidney Rigdon had experienced their vision of "the economy of God and his vast creation throug[h]out all eternity," which provided knowledge about premortal life; the celestial, terrestrial, and telestial kingdoms; and the fate of Satan and his followers.[2] In April, Joseph, in company with Rigdon, Newel K. Whitney, Jesse Gause, and Peter Whitmer Jr., had traveled to Missouri, where they organized the United Firm, an organization that joined together those responsible for the Church's mercantile and publishing concerns, and held one of the first meetings of the Literary Firm, a group included in the United Firm with the specific charge to manage the Church's publications. On the trip back to Ohio in May, the stage in which Rigdon, Whitney, and Joseph were riding crashed, breaking Whitney's ankle. Joseph stayed with Whitney in Greenville, Indiana, for several weeks until Whitney could travel. With Whitney spending most of his time in bed, Joseph had ample opportunity for solitary meditation and told his wife, Emma, that he had "visited a grove which is Just back of the town almost every day where I can be secluded from the eyes of any mortal and there give vent to all the feelings of my heart in meaditation and prayr."[3] Such solitude may have allowed Joseph to gain spiritual insights about many Church doctrines, including the priesthood.

After Whitney had recuperated to the point that he could travel, the pair returned to Ohio, arriving in June. Joseph then took his family back to John Johnson's home in Hiram, Ohio (where he and his family had been staying since September 1831), so that he could continue his translation of the Bible. On September 12, 1832, Joseph relocated his family to Kirtland, where they began residing in Newel K. Whitney's white store.[4]

After moving his family to Kirtland, Joseph began hearing accounts of elders returning to the town from missions to the eastern United States. As Joseph recounted in a later history, "The elders began to return from their missions to the eastern states, and present the histories of their several stewar[d]ships in the Lord's vineyard; and while together in these seasons of Joy, I enquired of the Lord and received [section 84]."[5] Joseph likely heard these elders' reports in either the "translating room" or the "council room" in the upstairs portion of Whitney's white store.[6] It may have been in one of these meetings that section 84 was given. The revelation itself states that the initial group in attendance was Joseph "and six elders" and that they had "united their hearts and lifted their voices on high" (D&C 84:1).

At least one account indicates that the revelation was given beginning in the evening of September 22 and continuing into the early morning hours of September 23.[7] Early manuscript copies support this view, suggesting that a pause in the dictation came at some point on September 23. The three existing manuscript copies of the revelation (one of which was made by Frederick G. Williams, one by Williams and Joseph, and one by John Whitmer) all contain a clear break between verses 102 and 103, suggesting an interruption in the dictation.[8] Whitmer's copy even inserts "Received on the 23 day of September 1832" between those two lines. However, the three manuscripts also include "viz 23d day of September A[D] 1832" as a notation several pages before this break, indicating that material presented before the interruption was also given on September 23. It may be, then, that the dictation began the evening of September 22, continued into the early morning hours of September 23, halted for a period of time, and then recommenced later that day.

At some point, the audience of the revelation shifted from the six elders to "Eleven high Priests save one," a notation in the copy inscribed by Williams that was not included in the 1981 edition of the Doctrine and Covenants.[9] At this point, the revelation provided direction as to what missionaries should proclaim, how they should receive sustenance while serving, and what would happen to those who did not accept their message. These instructions paralleled New Testament accounts of the resurrected Jesus Christ's directions to the eleven Apostles before his ascension into heaven. Calling the ten high priests "Eleven high Priests save one" was a clear reference to the eleven Apostles to whom Christ spoke, a point that was emphasized when the revelation called the high priests "mine apostles" (D&C 84:63).[10] These ten high priests were likely Joseph, Sidney Rigdon, Joseph Smith Sr., Hyrum Smith, Ezra Thayer, Zebedee Coltrin, Newel K. Whitney, John Murdock, Frederick G. Williams, and Joseph Coe.[11]

Pre–June 1831 Understanding of the Priesthood

According to the index to the Kirtland Revelation Book—one of the volumes where this revelation was recorded—the revelation "explain[ed] the two priest hoods and commission[ed] the Apostles to preach the gospel."[12] Apparently in 1832, the concept of priesthood, especially what the high priesthood was, was still nebulous among Church members, even though both the Bible and the Book of Mormon contained teachings about it. In the book of Alma, for example, Alma delivered a lengthy exposition on high priests and the priesthood. Calling the high priesthood God's "holy order, which was after the order of his Son" (Alma 13:1), Alma explained that high priests were "called [to] and prepared" for that office "from the foundation of the world according to the foreknowledge of God, on account of their exceeding faith and good works" (v. 3). The high priesthood, Alma continued, was "without beginning of days or end of years" and included the responsibility of proclaiming God's "commandments unto the children of men, that they also might enter into his rest" (vv. 7, 6). Alma taught that Melchizedek was a high priest in the high priesthood and that he was one of the greatest high priests; therefore the scriptures "particularly made mention" of him (v. 19). However, others who exercised "exceeding faith and repentance" and showed "righteousness before God" could also obtain the high priesthood (v. 10).

In addition to these Book of Mormon teachings, other churches at the time—including ones with which many early Church members were familiar—taught about the priesthood. The Disciples of Christ, from which many early members of the Church converted, for example, had developed its own priesthood doctrines, influenced by Alexander Crawford, a Scottish minister living in Canada. In 1827, Crawford had delineated the existence of three distinct priesthoods: a patriarchal priesthood (which he also called a priesthood after the "order of Melchisedec"), an Aaronical priesthood (originally held by Aaron), and a priesthood held by Jesus Christ. Crawford regarded Melchizedek as a greater priest than Abraham, citing the fact that Abraham paid tithes to him; indeed, according to Crawford, Melchizedek was one of the key players in the order of the patriarchal priesthood. Crawford also considered the patriarchal priesthood and the Aaronical priesthood as branches of the Levitical priesthood. Alexander Campbell and the Disciples of Christ were influenced by Crawford's ideas, although Campbell differed somewhat in his conception of the priesthood, arguing that God had given a "priesthood" to the tribe of Levi and a "high priesthood" to Aaron and his sons.[13] Regardless, as one historian has claimed, Campbell taught his understanding of priesthood "to many of his followers who [became] part of the Mormonite community and continued to believe the same doctrine."[14]

Despite the Book of Mormon's teachings and the presence of priesthood concepts in other religions, some early Church members still expressed confusion about what the priesthood really was. Levi Hancock, for example, recalled in his autobiography that in January 1832, he and Lyman Wight conversed with a woman in Jefferson City, Missouri, who "said She liked the Doctrine for we had the Priesthood and that looked like Sense." After this conversation, Hancock continued, he and Wight "had some conversation on the priesthood and neither of us understood what it was." Both Hancock and Wight were present at a June 1831 conference where elders were first ordained to the high priesthood (with Wight performing some of the ordinations), yet, as Hancock put it, "I did not understand it and [Wight] could give me no light."[15] Likewise, William McLellin remembered that when he was presented to an October 1831 conference for ordination to the high priesthood, he "was willing to do anything that was the will of God, but [he] did not understand the duties of the office."[16]

Also unclear was the way that the priesthood connected to different offices in the Church. The Articles and Covenants of the Church (as well as the Book of Mormon) had explained the different duties of Apostles, elders, priests, teachers, and deacons, but it did not associate these offices with any particular branch of the priesthood.[17] Indeed, the term *priesthood*—while appearing in both the Book of Mormon and Joseph Smith's biblical revisions—did not appear in any other contemporary documents (meaning documents that were actually written before September 1832) until the minutes of the June 1831 conference, which noted that several individuals "were ordained to the high Priesthood."[18]

Throughout 1831, however, Joseph increasingly revealed more information about the priesthood to Church members. As explained below, he obtained some of this information through his translation of the Bible; other concepts came through additional revelations from God. Some of the information that Joseph received was present in Alma's discussion of the high priesthood in the

Book of Mormon, but the principles revealed in 1831 and 1832 clarified these teachings and applied them directly to the Saints.

Developments in Priesthood Understanding, June 1831 to September 1832

As mentioned above, the first recorded ordinations of elders to the high priesthood occurred in a June 1831 conference in Kirtland, Ohio. Exactly what the term "high priesthood" meant to Joseph or other Church members at this time is difficult to determine. It apparently referred to both the authority of the greater priesthood (which would later be called the Melchizedek Priesthood) and the specific office of high priest. Jared Carter, for example, recorded in his journal that his brother Simeon, who had been ordained to the high priesthood at the June 1831 conference, was "an elder in the high prie[s]thood." In this instance, Carter appears to be using "high priesthood" to refer to a specific authority, not to an office.[19] At a conference held October 25–26, 1831, in Orange, Ohio, however, Joseph Smith and Sidney Rigdon used the term "High priesthood" to refer to a specific office with specific duties.[20] By the end of 1831, "high priest" was generally used to refer to the office, reducing some of the confusion surrounding the term.[21]

Because some of those present at the October 1831 conference exhibited "indifference" to obtaining the office of high priest, Joseph, assisted by Sidney Rigdon, taught the elders at that meeting of the dignity and responsibilities of that office. Joseph explained that "the order of the High priesthood is that they have power given them to seal up the Saints unto eternal life." Such sealing, Rigdon declared, would occur after God's people had "give[n] all for Christ's sake." Several conference participants then reiterated their covenant to "give all to the Lord." Since, as the minutes say, the high priesthood had the duty of sealing up the Saints to eternal life, and since such sealing could not come until one had consecrated all to the Lord, apparently those performing the sealing, first and foremost, had to have consecrated all as well. Nearly all the participants who expressed their willingness to consecrate all at the conference were those who had been ordained to the high priesthood or those who would be ordained at that meeting, suggesting, at the very least, a connection between the high priesthood and consecration.[22]

The October 1831 conference also indicated that one progressed through different offices in the Church in an orderly fashion, rather than haphazardly, until one attained the office of high priest. Joseph told the gathered members that "it was the privilege of every Elder present to be ordained to the High priesthood" and that "those who had been previously ordained Priests would be ordained Elders, & the others would be ordained Priests." As these ordinations occurred, the orderly nature of priesthood progression was emphasized.[23] This order was reiterated in a November 11, 1831, revelation, presently incorporated in section 107 of the Doctrine and Covenants. That revelation stated that one progressed from deacon to teacher, from teacher to priest, and from priest to elder before reaching the office of high priest, which was "the greatest of all."[24]

The November 11 revelation also stated the need for presiding officers to be called over each office in the Church, including the high priests. It explained that the president of the high priesthood had different duties from those of a bishop. A revelation received just a few days previously specified that a bishop's duties included being a worthy high priest (see D&C 68:15); though the president of the high priesthood had to meet that same qualification, his administrative duties were different from a bishop's. "The office of a Bishop is not equal unto" the president of the high priesthood, the revelation declared, "for the office of a bishop is in administering all temporal things." The president of the high priesthood, on the other hand, was responsible for "the administring of ordinances & blessings upon the Church, by the Laying on of the hands."[25] Describing the differences between the president of the high priesthood and the bishop in these ways indicated that the high priesthood dealt primarily with spiritual matters in the Church.

Indeed, the high priesthood was a sacred thing that had both great responsibilities and great power, a concept that was emphasized in another November 1831 revelation to Orson Hyde, Luke Johnson, Lyman Johnson, and William McLellin (all of whom had just recently been ordained to the office of high priest). This revelation (section 68 in the Doctrine and Covenants) stated that the four, together with "all the faithful elders of my church" (D&C 68:7), were "to proclaim the everlasting gospel, by the Spirit of the living God, from people to people, and from land to land" (v. 1). As they did so, they would have "power to seal" Saints "up unto eternal life" (v. 12).[26] The revelation also declared that when "those who were ordained unto this priesthood," or the high priesthood, spoke by the power of the Holy Ghost, such utterances would "be scripture, ... the mind of the Lord, ... the word of the Lord, ... the voice of the Lord, and the power of God unto salvation" (vv. 2, 4).

Answers that Joseph received in March 1832 to questions he had about the book of Revelation emphasized the responsibilities of high priests to preach the gospel throughout the world. One of the Prophet's questions dealt with the 144,000 that Revelation 7 says were "sealed" out of "all the tribes of the children of Israel" (v. 4). According to Joseph's list of questions and answers (section 77 in the Doctrine and Covenants), these 144,000 were "high priests, ordained unto the holy order of God, to administer the everlasting gospel." Taken "out of every nation, kindred, tongue, and people," their primary responsibility was "to bring as many as will come to the church of the Firstborn" (D&C 77:11). This explanation clearly emphasized the duty of high priests to preach the gospel, thereby gathering Israel from all corners of the earth. With the great responsibilities of preaching the gospel, however, came great rewards—even the ability to see the Lord. Late in 1831, the Lord promised a conference attended by several high priests, "Inasmuch as you strip yourselves from jealousies and fears, and humble yourselves, ... the veil shall be rent and you shall see me and know that I am" (D&C 67:10).[27]

As 1832 progressed, Joseph also came to understand more about the different forms of the priesthood. That summer, he composed a history of "his marvilous experience" and "an account of the rise of the church of Christ in the eve of time" that delineated his reception of two forms of priesthood authority. Joseph noted that he had received two types of authority: one, given to him through "the ministring of Aangels," allowed him "to administer the letter of the Gospel." The other, which gave him "power and ordinance from on high to preach the Gospel in the administration and demonstration of the spirit," was "the high Priesthood after the holy order of the son of the living God."[28] According to Webster's 1828 *Dictionary of American Language*, one meaning of "ordinance" at this time was "appointment,"[29] which clarifies that Joseph believed that his reception of the high priesthood appointed him to preach the gospel—a concept in line with what had been revealed to him before this time about the responsibilities of the high priesthood. In addition, this account shows that Joseph understood that there were two different authorities that he had, although he did not go so far as to call them greater and lesser forms of the priesthood. That would not come until the revealing of section 84.[30]

Joseph's work on his new translation of the Bible in 1831 and 1832 also revealed more about the priesthood, especially its eternal nature and its lineal passage through ancient patriarchs and prophets. As Robert J. Matthews has argued, "In the . . . translation of the Old and New Testaments many revelations were received which contained much information and gave expanded views on the gospel."[31] Joseph's revisions to Genesis 14 and Hebrews 7 (completed around February or March 1831 and February or March 1832, respectively), for example, revealed that because the priesthood was embedded in God, it was an eternal thing, something, as mentioned above, that Alma also explained in the Book of Mormon (see Alma 13:6–7). "The order of the Son of God . . . came not by man nor the will of men neither by father nor Mother neither by begining of days nor end of years but of God," Joseph's revision of Genesis 14 declared.[32] Likewise, his revision of Hebrews 7:3 clarified that the description "without father, without mother, without descent, having neither begining of days, nor end of life" pertained to "the order of the son of God."[33] In making these changes, Joseph showed that since the priesthood was something instituted by God, it was eternal and did not have a beginning or an end.

In a similar way, the new translation provided more details about some of the patriarchs who held the priesthood—namely Melchizedek (a concept, as discussed above, also present in the Book of Mormon). Joseph Smith revised Genesis 14 to explain that Melchizedek was a "high Preist after the order of the covenent which God made with Enock it being after the order of the Son of God." Called "a man of faith who wrought righteousness," Melchizedek blessed the sacrament, received tithes from Abraham, and blessed Abraham as well. The translation of Genesis 14 further explained that Melchizedek led his people in seeking the "City of Enock" and "was called the King of heaven by his people or in other words the King of peace."[34] In addition, Joseph's revision to Hebrews 7:3 stated that "Melchisedec was ordained a priest after the order of the son of God."[35]

Building on this discussion, the vision of the celestial, terrestrial, and telestial kingdoms that Joseph and Sidney Rigdon experienced in February 1832 emphasized that the high priesthood carried the name of Melchizedek. Those who inherited the celestial kingdom, the vision declared, were "priests of the Most High, after the order of Melchizedek, which was after the order of Enoch, which was after the order of the Only Begotten Son" (D&C 76:57). Joseph may have taught even earlier than this revelation that the high priesthood bore the name of Melchizedek. Ezra Booth, a former Church member writing in the fall of 1831, for example, asserted that many members of the Church had "been ordained to the High Priesthood, or the order of Milchesidec."[36]

Section 84's Contributions to Priesthood Understanding

With this background, section 84 can be seen as a culmination of revealed concepts and teachings that Joseph had been given prior to September 1832. Much of its doctrine did not just suddenly appear in September 1832 but had been revealed to Joseph "line upon line, precept upon precept" (2 Nephi 28:30; see also Isaiah 28:10). In accordance with the concepts discussed above, the September 22–23 revelation outlined the existence of two priesthoods: a greater priesthood that "holdeth the key of the mysteries of the kingdom, even the key of the knowledge of God," and a lesser priesthood—also termed the preparatory priesthood—holding "the key of the ministering of angels and the preparatory gospel," defined as "the gospel of repentance and of baptism" (D&C 84:19, 26–27). The authority of the greater priesthood, according to the revelation, allowed man to "see the face of God, even the Father, and live" (v. 22)—much like the Lord had promised high priests late in 1831 (see D&C 67:14). The revelation traced the lineages of the two priesthoods, noting that the greater priesthood was held by Moses, who received it from a line of individuals (including Melchizedek) who ultimately had received it from God. Aaron, meanwhile, held the lesser priesthood, which passed to his descendants until it reached John the Baptist. As Joseph's translation of the Bible emphasized, both priesthoods were of an eternal nature (see D&C 84:6–27).

Yet in other ways, section 84 went further than these earlier teachings. For example, although earlier revelations had noted the different offices of the Church, section 84 provided a concrete explanation of how these offices were connected to the greater and the lesser priesthoods. The offices of elder and bishop, it stated, were "necessary appendages belonging unto the high priesthood," while the offices of teacher and deacon were "necessary appendages belonging to the lesser priesthood."[37] High priests, elders, and priests, the revelation continued, had an obligation to travel to proclaim the gospel (just as section 68 had told Orson Hyde and other high priests in November 1831), while teachers and deacons were responsible for watching over the Church where it already existed (see D&C 84:29–30, 111).

Moreover, section 84 expanded on the duties of high priests to preach the gospel by providing a general discussion of who should serve missions, how they should serve, and what they should proclaim. Revelations from 1830, 1831, and 1832 had called specific individuals on missions,[38] but only a few revelations gave procedural instructions about missionary work.[39] Section 84, however, gave lengthy instructions to those who were to "go . . . into all the world"; the Lord called those who answered the call "mine apostles, even God's high priests," as well as "my friends" (D&C 84:62–63). Much like the direction Jesus provided to his Apostles after his Resurrection, these "friends" were to preach the gospel to all inhabitants of the world, reproving them of their wickedness. They were to use members who held the lesser priesthood "to make appointments, and to prepare the way, and to fill appointments that [they themselves were] not able to fill," thus allowing those holding the lesser priesthood to be strengthened and trained for their own missionary service (v. 107). Those who would not receive the message to repent and be baptized would be damned, and God would scourge the wicked nations and issue plagues upon them for their disobedience (see vv. 74, 96–97). Spiritual gifts would follow those who believed, which gifts included the casting out of devils; the healing of the sick, blind, deaf, and dumb; and protection from the effects of poison (see vv. 65–72). In practical terms, the revelation instructed missionaries to go without purse or scrip, relying on those to whom they preached for subsistence (vv. 77–78, 86, 89–90). The Lord would "go before [their] face," the revelation told the elders; furthermore, the Savior said, "I will be on your right hand and on your left, and my Spirit shall be in your hearts, and mine angels round about you, to bear you up" (v. 88).

In addition to these teachings—and perhaps most significantly—section 84 instructed Church members as to how the promises of the priesthood could become a tangible reality to them. Having provided the lineage of the greater priesthood from Adam to Moses and the lesser priesthood from Aaron to his sons, the Lord declared that "whoso is faithful unto the obtaining these two priesthoods . . . and the magnifying their calling" would "become the sons of Moses and of Aaron and the seed of Abraham" (D&C 84:33–34)—thus connecting those laboring in the latter days with ancient Israel. Those who received the priesthood, the revelation continued, would receive God's kingdom; the Savior said, "All that my Father hath shall be given unto him" (v. 38). Such a promise is likely what Sidney Rigdon and the Prophet Joseph referred to when they told a group of high priests and elders in October 1831 of the "power" of the high priesthood.[40] It also likely reflected the declaration in a December 1831 revelation that the Lord had given "the kingdom and power" unto "the high priests of [his] church" (D&C 72:1). In addition, it built on what Joseph and Sidney saw in their vision of the three degrees of glory—that those who inherited the celestial kingdom were "priests of the Most High, after the order of Melchizedek," who had "received of [the Father's] fulness, and of his glory" (D&C 76:57, 56).

Conclusion

Section 84 thus culminated Joseph's learning about the priesthood to that date, presenting much of the already-revealed doctrine in a consolidated section that also instructed the Saints as to how the priesthood could bless their lives. The Lord taught these truths to Joseph through a variety of means, including providing inspiration as Joseph worked on his translation of the Bible and giving Joseph additional revelations that clarified priesthood doctrine and responsibilities. Joseph, in turn, conveyed these teachings through his revelations and through conferences of elders and high priests. Such teachings helped members such as Levi Hancock, who did not understand what the priesthood was in 1831. Section 84 solidified priesthood doctrine—of the presence of a greater and lesser priesthood, of the eternal nature of the priesthood, of the power of the priesthood, of the offices of the priesthood, and of the duties of the priesthood to preach the gospel—by presenting them as one cohesive whole and by making them directly applicable to Church members. "All those who receive the priesthood, receive this oath and covenant of my Father, which he cannot break, neither can it be moved," the revelation declared. Because of this, Church members could receive "all that [the] Father hath" (D&C 84:40, 38). In the years that followed, the Lord would reveal more to the Prophet about priesthood; by 1835, for example, the greater priesthood, or the umbrella under which all offices of the priesthood exist, was known as the Melchizedek Priesthood, and the lesser priesthood was called the Aaronic Priesthood. But the doctrines revealed in the Church's initial years provided the foundation for this understanding, making what Joseph taught about the priesthood in the early years of the Church even more significant.

Notes

1. Steven C. Harper, *Making Sense of the Doctrine and Covenants: A Guided Tour through Modern Revelations* (Salt Lake City: Deseret Book, 2008), 295, 303.

2. Vision, February 16, 1832 (D&C 76), in Robin Scott Jensen, Robert J. Woodford, and Steven C. Harper, eds., *Revelations and Translations, Volume 1: Manuscript Revelation Books*, vol. 1 of the Revelations and Translations series of *The Joseph Smith Papers*, ed. Dean C. Jessee, Ronald K. Esplin, and Richard Lyman Bushman (Salt Lake City: Church Historian's Press, 2009), 414–15 (hereafter referred to as *JSP R1*); Doctrine and Covenants 76.

3. Joseph Smith to Emma Smith, June 6, 1832, holograph, ALS, Chicago Historical Society, Chicago.

4. [Emma Smith], List, ca. 1845, in Lucy Mack Smith, History, 1845, Church History Library, The Church of Jesus Christ of Latter-day Saints, Salt Lake City (hereafter referred to as CHL); Mark Lyman Staker, *Hearken, O Ye People: The Historical Setting of Joseph Smith's Ohio Revelations* (Salt Lake City: Greg Kofford Books, 2009), 251. Whitney had two stores in Kirtland: a red store and a white store.

5. Joseph Smith, 1838 Manuscript History, vol. A-1, 229, CHL.

6. Staker, *Hearken, O Ye People*, 251.

7. Lula Greene Richards, "A Sketch of the Life of Evan M. Greene," 2, copy provided to author by Steven Harper, gives the revelation's date as "the night of the 22 and 23 of September 1832." However, this may not be accurate, as other details in this account are incorrect. It states, for example, that Oliver Cowdery came into the room as the revelation was being dictated, but minutes from Missouri meetings place Cowdery in Missouri at both the end of August and the first of October, making it highly unlikely that he had the time to travel to Kirtland in September. See "Far West Stake (Mo.): The Conference Minutes and Record Book of Christ's Church of Latter Day Saints," 29, 31, CHL (hereafter referred to as Minute Book 2).

8. For copies of the Whitmer and Williams and Joseph Smith manuscripts, see *JSP R1*, 275–89, 453–75. Newel K. Whitney had a copy of the revelation in Williams's handwriting. Vision, February 16, 1832, in Newel K. Whitney Papers, L. Tom Perry Special Collections, Harold B. Lee Library, Brigham Young University, Provo, Utah.

9. If this notation remained, it would come in the middle of verse 42 after the phrase "you who are present this day."

10. I am indebted to Richard Jensen and Mark Ashurst-McGee of the Joseph Smith Papers Project for this insight.

11. According to a January 14, 1833, letter from Orson Hyde and Hyrum Smith that mentions this revelation, the high priests in attendance were the same twelve that met in a conference on January 13–14, 1833. Orson Hyde and Hyrum Smith to "the Bishop his councel and the inhabitants of Zion," January 14, 1833, Letterbook 1, Joseph Smith Collection, CHL. Those high priests were the ten mentioned above plus Samuel H. Smith and Orson Hyde. See Kirtland High Council, Minutes, Dec. 1832–Nov. 1837, 5, CHL (hereafter referred to as Minute Book 1). However, in September 1832, Samuel H. Smith and Orson Hyde were proclaiming the gospel in the eastern states and had not

yet returned to Kirtland. See Orson Hyde, diary, September 22, 1832, transcript, 31, CHL; Samuel H. Smith, diary, September 22, 1832, transcript, 19, CHL. Subtracting them from the number leaves "Eleven high Priests save one," if Joseph is included as one of the high priests.

12. *JSP R1*, 413.

13. Alexander Campbell, *Delusions: An Analysis of the Book of Mormon; with an Examination of Its Internal and External Evidences, and a Refutation of Its Pretences to Divine Authority* (Boston: Benjamin H. Greene, 1832), 11; see also Staker, *Hearken, O Ye People*, 148–50.

14. Staker, *Hearken, O Ye People*, 150. As a former associate of Campbell, Sidney Rigdon was probably familiar with these ideas.

15. Autobiography of Levi Ward Hancock, holograph, 43, CHL.

16. W. E. McLellan, M.D., to Davis H. Bays, May 24, 1870, in *The William E. McLellin Papers, 1854–1880*, ed. Stan Larson and Samuel J. Passey (Salt Lake City: Signature Books, 2007), 458. According to McLellin, after he expressed his concern, Joseph told him "to take upon [them] the office, and it would explain its duties."

17. Articles and Covenants, April 10, 1830 (D&C 20), in *JSP R1*, 75–87. The Articles and Covenants did not mention the priesthood office of Seventy, which apparently was not revealed to Joseph until 1835.

18. Minute Book 2, June 3, 1831, 4.

19. Journal of Jared Carter, typescript, 4, CHL.

20. Minute Book 2, October 25, 1831, 11.

21. See, for example, D&C 72:1, from a revelation given on December 4, 1831.

22. Minute Book 2, October 25, 1831, 10–15.

23. Minute Book 2, October 25, 1831, 11, 14.

24. Revelation, November 11, 1831-B (D&C 107:64), *JSP R1*, 216–17.

25. Revelation, November 11, 1831-B (D&C 107:65–68), *JSP R1*, 216–17.

26. This power to seal apparently worked in another way as well. Doctrine and Covenants 1, given in November 1831, stated that "they who go forth, bearing these tidings unto the inhabitants of the earth, to them is power given to seal both on earth and in heaven, the unbelieving and rebellious . . . up unto the day when the wrath of God shall be poured out upon the wicked without measure" (D&C 1:8–9).

27. The minutes of this conference declare that it was a conference of elders, and the revelation is addressed to those "elders of my church, who have assembled yourselves together" (D&C 67:1). However, all of the individuals except for Lyman Johnson listed as "Elders Present" in the minutes had previously been ordained high priests (Johnson would be ordained a high priest at the conference). See Minute Book 2, November 1–2, 1831, 15; Minute Book 2, October 25, 1831, 14; Minute Book 2, June 3, 1831, 4; Minute Book 2, August 28, 1831, 5. "Elders" in this sense appears to be used as a general title for Church leaders.

28. Joseph Smith, "A History of the life of Joseph Smith Jr. . . . ," ca. summer 1832, in Letterbook 1, Joseph Smith Collection, CHL.

29. *American Dictionary of the English Language*, 1828, s.v. "ordinance."

30. Joseph probably had an understanding of higher and lower authorities before the summer of 1832, as both biblical texts and the Book of Mormon referred to different authorities in the priesthood. In the case of the New Testament, for example, John the Baptist had the authority to baptize but, as the account in Matthew states, did not have the authority to "baptize . . . with the Holy Ghost, and with fire." That would come with Christ, who was "mightier" than John (Matthew 3:11).

31. Robert J. Matthews, "The 'New Translation' of the Bible, 1830–1833: Doctrinal Development During the Kirtland Era," *BYU Studies* 11, no. 4 (Summer 1971): 403.

32. JST Old Testament Manuscript 1, in Scott H. Faulring, Kent P. Jackson, and Robert J. Matthews, eds., *Joseph Smith's New Translation of the Bible: Original Manuscripts* (Provo, UT: Religious Studies Center, Brigham Young University, 2004), 127.

33. JST New Testament Manuscript 2, Folio 4, in Faulring, Jackson, and Matthews, *Joseph Smith's New Translation of the Bible*, 539.

34. JST Old Testament Manuscript 1, in Faulring, Jackson, and Matthews, *Joseph Smith's New Translation of the Bible*, 126–28.

35. JST New Testament Manuscript 2, Folio 4, in Faulring, Jackson, and Matthews, *Joseph Smith's New Translation of the Bible*, 539.

36. Ezra Booth to Ira Eddy, October 2, 1831, "Mormonism—No. II," *Ohio Star*, October 20, 1831. Hebrews 5:6, of course, stated that Christ was "a priest for ever after the order of Melchisedec."

37. While bishop is an office in the Aaronic priesthood, a November 1831 revelation indicated that bishops "shall be high priests" (D&C 68:15; see also v. 19).

38. See, for example, D&C 24 (given July 1830), D&C 31 (given September 1830), D&C 33 (given October 1830), D&C 52 (given on June 7, 1831), and D&C 80 (given March 1832).

39. Section 68, for example, was directed toward Orson Hyde, Lyman Johnson, Luke Johnson, and William E. McLellin, but it told "all the faithful elders of [the Lord's] church" to preach the gospel to the world, "acting in the authority which [the Lord] ha[d] given [them]." The elders were to baptize those that believed, who would then "be blest with signs following" (D&C 68:7–8, 10).

40. Minute Book 2, October 25, 1831, 11.

12

The Olive Leaf and the Family of Heaven

Samuel Morris Brown

In the days around New Year 1833, Joseph Smith received a revelation that he termed the "Olieve leaf which we have plucked from the tree of Paradise, the Lords message of peace to us."[1] Now Doctrine and Covenants 88, the Olive Leaf is a rich scripture with a complex history, both before and after its revelation. The Olive Leaf both directed the School of the Prophets toward the Kirtland Temple and its grand dedication in spring 1836 and provided important insight into the meaning of the Old Testament, the New Testament, and the plan of salvation. In its basic structure, the Olive Leaf contains two interrelated themes: an expansion of the Vision of February 1832, and the revelatory foundations for the School of the Prophets.

In this essay I want to draw attention to the relevance of the Olive Leaf to the restored doctrine of the family of heaven. Specifically, I suggest that the Olive Leaf contained the kernels of the doctrines that constitute what I have termed the divine anthropology, in which God, humans, and angels are all members of the same family, the family of heaven.[2] Understanding this restored doctrine requires that we understand the ways the Prophet Joseph

---

Samuel Morris Brown is a medical professor and cultural historian at the University of Utah.

corrected and supplemented an ancient philosophical concept, the Great Chain of Being, as well as other fragments of truth scattered throughout Western religious and intellectual history.

After discussing the immediate context of the Olive Leaf, I consider briefly the history of the Chain of Being and then analyze the text of the revelation with an eye toward the ways Joseph Smith and the early Latter-day Saints integrated and modified fragments of truth from ancient traditions.

Historical Setting for the Olive Leaf

When the Olive Leaf arrived, the Church had moved from New York and Pennsylvania to Ohio and Missouri. Zion was slowly growing, and the miseries of the Missouri Mormon War were yet in the future. Hopeful expectation of the Second Coming of Christ coexisted with the brutal realities of life on the American frontier. In late 1832, Joseph and his close associates were just beginning the work of organizing the Church and restoring the temple. In a quest for knowledge and the respectability associated with it, the Saints founded a frontier seminary they called the School of the Prophets. As the Olive Leaf would clarify, the School of the Prophets was much more than a Protestant seminary, though. The school began the restoration of the temple ordinances, revised ancient understandings of the structure of the universe, and directed the priesthood organization of the Church.[3]

The Olive Leaf arrived as 1832 transitioned into 1833. Though we associate late December with Christmas, in early America many of the holidays we take for granted were not celebrated in the same way, if at all.[4] For many early Americans, including the Saints, the beginning of a new year was a sober time to reflect on how quickly mortality passes. For the Prophet, such personal reflections often intersected with concerns over the fate of the entire earth. In the months leading up to the Olive Leaf, Joseph Smith received a revelation about the destruction of the earth and wrote a letter to a newspaper editor warning about the end of times.[5] We must keep this immediate historical context in mind—a developing church with two centers of power, New Year reflections, a growing priesthood hierarchy, and the imminent end of the world—to understand the meanings of the Olive Leaf. More context is required, though, especially an understanding of the reigning scientific paradigm from Ancient Greece to the European Enlightenment.

The Great Chain of Being, a dominant philosophical system that organized all of creation into a single hierarchy, derived from Aristotle's interpretation of Plato. Based on the principles of plenitude (all things that could exist do exist), gradation (all types of things are unique and hierarchically ordered), and continuity (there are no gaps between adjacent types of creatures), the chain extended from the highest demigods through humans and animals to the lowliest particles of dust. This was a taxonomy of life that saw God's hand in the patterns of biological diversity. The chain stood largely undisputed in religion and science for over two millennia. Christian thinkers employed a version of this chain, also called the Scale of Nature (*Scala Naturae*), to explain the harmony of the universe as well as the importance of social hierarchies. Throughout its history, thinkers saw the Chain of Being as describing the hierarchies of celestial bodies—planets, stars, comets, and meteors followed perfectly their decreed orbits or trajectories. These celestial bodies were seen as parallel to the organization of beings on earth. The original Chain of Being had been a static system in which different types of beings stayed forever in their original state. By the late eighteenth century, various thinkers had proposed what historians have called the "temporal" Chain of Being. In this eternally progressive version, the hierarchical relationships among different types of beings never changed, but every individual's level of glory increased endlessly as the entire chain progressed in glory.[6] While this new version had varied implications, many thinkers saw it as compatible with the eternal progression of humans. Reminding us of the dangerous corruptions that humans seem wont to impose on heavenly doctrines, the chain had been used to justify moral atrocities from the grinding of the face of the poor in Dickensian Britain to the genocide of native peoples in America to the brutal enslavement of Africans in the Atlantic world. Prior generations had seen in the Chain of Being support for social hierarchies that exploited and excluded vulnerable populations. As the British colonies became the American Republic, people tended to reject aristocracy and social hierarchy: the Chain of Being could not persist in the new nation in its original, static form.

The Prophet Joseph revealed a complex revision to the Chain of Being, one that drew on the temporal chain but made it genealogical. Joseph revealed that the Chain of Being, rather than representing social or ontological hierarchies, was in fact a family tree, a revision that I have called his Chain of Belonging.[7] This new chain was one of the most radical doctrines of the Restoration, and it had many repercussions. By transforming the Chain of Being into a heavenly family tree, the Prophet seems to have been clarifying the fact that human families parallel the structures of the universe, suggesting that what mattered most in the material and spiritual cosmos was the creation of family relationships.[8] Hierarchy and equality are present simultaneously in this solution to the problems of the chain. Just as the child grows into the adult and becomes a parent herself or himself, so will we all become parents within the family of heaven. The bonds that define our place in the chain are the tender sentiments of a parent for a child, not an existential scale of merit or power. Any height of authority or power achieved by one will ultimately be achieved by all as the entire chain progresses. This doctrine became central to the Restoration as the Church progressed through the Nauvoo and Utah periods. As the Saints attempted to understand this revelation, they saw in the family connections between God and humans the possibility that they were of one species with angels and other divine intelligences. This doctrine, difficult to separate from the basic structure of the Chain of Belonging, represents the core of the divine anthropology. Though there were occasional clues beforehand, the restoration of the divine anthropology is first clearly visible in the revelations of 1832–33.

The first of these revelations was the Vision of February 1832. Now Doctrine and Covenants 76, this revelation to Joseph Smith and Sidney Rigdon covered a staggering amount of ground, most famously the three degrees of heavenly glory. The Vision's discussion of degrees of glory was a revelatory clarification of Paul's sermon on the Resurrection in his first letter to the Church at Corinth, the scriptural passage used most consistently over the centuries to support the Chain of Being. In addition to many other sacred insights, the Vision highlighted the fact that human beings are the children of God in a literal way (specifically that saved Saints "are gods, even the sons of God"[9]) and that celestial bodies mirror the arcs of our lives and afterlives: heaven was divided into kingdoms based on the hierarchy of sun, moon, and stars. Almost a year later, the Olive Leaf returned to and clarified both of those themes from the Vision, employing a revelatory exegesis of Jesus' parable of the laborers in the vineyard to that end.

The Text of the Olive Leaf[10]

The Olive Leaf began by addressing and praising the Saints "who [had] assembled" themselves "together to receive [God's] will concerning" them (D&C 88:1). The Lord through Joseph then reassured those Saints that he was sending "another Comforter," the "Holy Spirit of promise," to guide and reassure faithful members (v. 3). The Olive Leaf continued to explain the close association between this second comforter and the "glory of the celestial kingdom" (v. 4), which encompassed a "light of Christ" (v. 7) that filled the "immensity of space" (v. 12), gave "life to all things" (v. 13), drove the planets in their orbits, and filled the minds of seekers with truth.[11] Christ is the "light of the sun, and the power thereof by which it was made" (v. 7). Explaining that each human soul would be "sanctified from all unrighteousness that it may be prepared for the celestial glory," Joseph Smith foresaw that the righteous would be "crowned with glory" (vv. 18–19). Though he was not explicit on this point, Joseph seems to have meant by this light something like a merger of power and spirit and knowledge, though the "light of Christ" was also probably a self-conscious reference to an actual force within the universe. The souls of believers would "receive of the same, even a fulness" (v. 29), as resurrected bodies "quickened by a portion of the celestial glory" (v. 29)—a reference to the replacement of mortal blood by eternal spirit in the vessels of resurrected bodies that merged human bodies with the energies of the cosmos.

As he explicated the Light of Christ, Joseph Smith returned to the celestial bodies and kingdoms of the vision. Christ's light animated the sun, the moon, and the stars. Joseph then extended the connection to celestial bodies by mentioning "the earth also, and the power thereof" (v. 10). The Lord in the Olive Leaf then reminded the Saints that it was "the earth upon which you stand" (v. 10), drawing attention to the close association between humans and the celestial body on which they lived. Joseph Smith then turned to the resurrection of the earth and the dead, by which the earth would acquire celestial glory. Joseph thereby tied the three kingdoms of the Vision of February 1832 to earth and the Light of Christ. After connecting laws of celestial order and human salvation, Joseph referred to the "many kingdoms" of heaven and then made an explicit reference to the chain, invoking plenitude and continuity: "there is no space in the which there is no kingdom; and there is no kingdom in which there is no space, either a greater or a lesser kingdom" (v. 37).

Joseph Smith then recalled images from the astronomical Chain of Being and juxtaposed them with Jesus' parable of the laborers in the vineyard. In the New Testament parable, poor agricultural workers start their labors at different times of day but ultimately receive the same wage, a denarius. Readers have interpreted the parable in many different ways over the centuries. Some have seen the reassurance that Gentiles could share in the same salvation as natural-born Israelites; others have seen the promise of heavenly reward to all who believe in Christ; still others have seen the absolute equality of the saved. In most interpretations, this parable recalls that of the prodigal son, emphasizing the power Christ had to save all, however lost or fallen. Even the worker who does not begin work until the very last hour, even the son who has squandered his inheritance, can find a place through Christ in the kingdom of God.

Joseph and the early Saints were open to all these interpretations, but the Olive Leaf opened a vista on a broader, if somewhat paradoxical, view of the parable. All would be saved in the family of heaven, but the "time" one began to labor in the vineyard represented one's place in that family. According to the parable, each different agricultural worker had a specific "time" or "season" (see v. 42), echoes of the planetary orbits that defined such seasons and times, to receive the Light of Christ. In this revelatory exegesis, the person who was called early in the morning was assigned that time as a reflection of his place in the process of sacred history. The times and seasons of the Olive Leaf's reading of the parable brought to mind the passage of generations; the relationships between ancestors, present individuals, and descendants far in the future; and the sense that each generation entered the world at a particular time for a particular purpose. When the Prophet Joseph brought the seven angels and seals of Revelation into conversation with the reinterpreted parable of the laborers, he drew attention to the role that angelic beings had in marking out sacred history. Those dispensational angels too were called at different points in the day, at different periods of human history. Those angelic beings, in their divine order, pointed toward a great final integration of humans into divine history, of human beings into divine beings. At the appearance of the seventh and final angel, Joseph Smith declared, "the saints shall be filled with his glory, and receive their inheritance and be made equal with him [God]" (v. 107).[12]

The early revelations to the Church often had a strong missionary focus. One central way that the family of heaven would be formed—the way that the Chain of Belonging would be created—was through preaching the gospel. One immediate meaning of the Olive Leaf's explanation of the parable of the laborers was that some missionaries, the "first laborers in this last kingdom," would be called to initiate the work in a new dispensation while others would follow in their footsteps. The dispensations of sacred time, marked by the seven seals and angels, mirrored the kingdoms of heaven, which themselves mirrored the order of celestial bodies.[13] We should not forget, however, that for the early Saints, the sealing of converts to salvation mirrored the connections among family members within the Church. Early Latter-day Saints understood that binding relationships could be created within the Chain of Belonging through sharing the gospel, through biological associations, or through both. The relationship between missionary and convert stood in for the relationship between parent and child.[14]

Joseph Smith took a parable that was generally understood as describing the complete lack of hierarchy, and he used it to highlight the revised chain. In doing so, Joseph emphasized the paradox at the center of the restored Chain of Belonging. Because the family of heaven was endless in extent, all would ultimately be equal; all would be the spiritual progenitors of a numberless kindred. The Chain of Belonging was a hierarchy of equality, a network of connection among equals, all sealed by the sacred tie of missionary and convert, parent and child. The head of that family was God. Understanding the temporal component of the Chain of Belonging is important. Because the chain was a family tree and members of it all advanced together, eventually everyone would pass through the phase of glory once associated with divine beings, such as God. The point of the parable of the laborers was that even though all had different times when they were called to act or arrive, they would all be a part of the kingdom and the chain. This meant that they would participate in the eternal progression that the Chain of Belonging promised. When the Olive Leaf revealed that humans would ultimately be "equal" with God, it did not mean that they would replace God or be the same as God. It meant that through the progress of the Chain of Belonging, they would one day be as mature as God had been at some time in the distant past. They would never catch up to or supplant God—they would always be his children. But they would have children of their own and would enjoy their own advanced forms of celestial glory.

The Olive Leaf's promise of equality was heady stuff. Critics promptly dismissed it as heresy,[15] while Parley P. Pratt enthusiastically embraced it in his *Voice of Warning*.[16] When Methodist polemicist La Roy Sunderland called the Olive Leaf "nonsense and blasphemy," Pratt responded strongly, identifying a variety of texts to suggest that scriptural promises to know "all truth" or to be able to do "all things" required eventual human "equality" with God.[17]

President Lorenzo Snow reported that the Olive Leaf's clarification of the parable of the laborers merged in his mind with a promise made by Joseph Smith Sr. "at a blessing meeting in the Kirtland Temple." From this flash of "inspiration," Snow recorded a couplet that now summarizes the divine anthropology for many observers: "As man now is, God once was; / As God now is, man may be."[18] According to President Snow, no matter where a believer joined the genealogical Chain of Belonging, he or she would eventually, through the progress of the entire chain, achieve a form of godhood. President Snow's language may sound somewhat odd to modern audiences, but he was pointing toward the fundamental unity of the family of heaven, which comprised God, angels, and humans, progressing within a family structure.

Conclusion

In the revelations of 1832, particularly the Olive Leaf, the Prophet Joseph sowed the seeds of the doctrines of the divine anthropology. He revealed that the Saints could join a Chain of Belonging and that their membership in that chain, which encompassed God himself, reflected a literal kinship with the Heavenly Father. As millenarian and evangelistic images merged with family images over the next few years, it became clear that the parental was the relationship of eternity, and the relationship of parent to child—the very relationship highlighted in Christ's status as Begotten Son—provided the key to a network of interconnection that was at once hierarchical and egalitarian.

Notes

1. Joseph Smith to William Phelps, January 11, 1833, Church History Library, The Church of Jesus Christ of Latter-day Saints, Salt Lake City. The "olive leaf" is an allusion to Genesis 8:11, in which a dove brings evidence to Noah that the floodwaters have begun to recede. The first manuscript copy of the revelation is available in Robin

Scott Jensen, Robert J. Woodford, and Steven C. Harper, eds., *Manuscript Revelation Books*, facsimile edition, vol. 1 of the Revelations and Translations series of *The Joseph Smith Papers*, ed. Dean C. Jessee, Ronald K. Esplin, and Richard Lyman Bushman (Salt Lake City: Church Historian's Press, 2009), (hereafter *JSP R1*), 292–311.

2. On "divine anthropology," see Samuel Morris Brown, *In Heaven as It Is on Earth: Joseph Smith and the Early Mormon Conquest of Death* (New York: Oxford University Press, 2012), chapter 9.

3. On the School of the Prophets and the restoration of the temple, see Brown, *In Heaven as It Is on Earth*, chapter 6.

4. On the history of American holidays, see especially Leigh Eric Schmidt, *Consumer Rites: The Buying and Selling of American Holidays* (Princeton, NJ: Princeton University Press, 1995).

5. Robert J. Woodford, "The Historical Development of the Doctrine and Covenants" (PhD diss., Brigham Young University, 1974), 1093–95.

6. The best treatment of the Chain of Being is Arthur O. Lovejoy, *The Great Chain of Being: A Study of the History of an Idea*, 1933 William James Lectures (Cambridge, MA: Harvard University Press, 1948). A detailed discussion of Joseph Smith's repair of the Chain of Being is presented in Brown, *In Heaven as It Is on Earth*, chapters 8–9.

7. Brown, *In Heaven as It Is on Earth*, 208.

8. This idea mirrored traditions about metaphysical correspondence. On correspondence, see Nicholas Goodrick-Clarke, *The Western Esoteric Traditions: A Historical Introduction* (New York: Oxford University Press, 2008), esp. 8–9, 23, 72, 155–72.

9. *JSP R1*, 249 [D&C 76:58].

10. Compare the text of Doctrine and Covenants 88, cited here, to that in *JSP R1*, 292–311.

11. Joseph expanded this theme several months later in the revelation that became D&C 93 (see *JSP R1*, 332–39).

12. Compare Matthew 20:1–16.

13. Joseph's brother Samuel, for example, understood the parable in precisely those terms: Woodford, "Doctrine and Covenants," 1128.

14. On the close connection between missionaries and parents within the priesthood, see Brown, *In Heaven as It Is on Earth*, chapter 8; and Samuel Morris Brown, "Early Mormon Adoption Theology and the Mechanics of Salvation," *Journal of Mormon History* 37 no. 3 (Summer 2011): 3–52.

15. A probably ghostwritten early attack on Campbellites decried Campbellite leaders for "exalting themselves to the stations of gods": Joseph Smith [possibly Sidney Rigdon], "Dear Brother," *Evening and Morning Star*, September 1834, 192.

16. Parley Pratt, *A Voice of Warning and Instruction to All People* (New York: W. Sandford, 1837), 145.

17. Parley P. Pratt, *Mormonism Unveiled: Zion's Watchman Unmasked, and Its Editor, Mr. L. R. Sunderland, Exposed: Truth Vindicated: The Devil Mad, and Priestcraft in Danger!* (New York: printed by author, 1838), 26–27; compare La Roy Sunderland, *Mormonism Exposed and Refuted* (New York: Piercy & Reed, 1838), 35.

18. Eliza R. Snow (Smith), *Biography and Family Record of Lorenzo Snow: One of the Twelve Apostles of the Church of Jesus Christ of Latter-day Saints* (Salt Lake City: Deseret News, 1884), 10, 46. Snow may have been following Orson Pratt, whose 1844 "Mormon Creed" asked "What is his [humanity's] final destiny? To be like God. What has God been? Like man." Orson Pratt, *Prophetic Almanac for 1845* (New York: printed by author, 1845), 5.

13

"Health in Their Navel and Marrow to Their Bones"

Kate Holbrook

In section 89 of the Doctrine and Covenants, the Word of Wisdom promises, "All saints who remember to keep and do these sayings, walking in obedience to the commandments, shall receive health in their navel and marrow to their bones; and shall find wisdom and great treasures of knowledge, even hidden treasures; and shall run and not be weary, and shall walk and not faint. And I, the Lord, give unto them a promise, that the destroying angel shall pass by them, as the children of Israel, and not slay them" (D&C 89:18–21). That leaders and members alike speak of section 89 in terms of health is no surprise; health, physical strength, and longevity are among its major rewards. Other than the law of chastity, the Word of Wisdom is one of the few guidelines relating directly to the physical body in a tradition where possession of a physical body is the essential component of both spiritual progression and salvation.

Following a brief history of the Word of Wisdom's reception, this paper explores how members have associated health with the Word of Wisdom and what this interpretation might reveal. Health is rarely the only consequence

---

Kate Holbrook is the specialist in women's history at the Church History Department.

mentioned when Church leaders advocate the Word of Wisdom; they also mention spiritual blessings or the blessing of wisdom or both. But this paper looks specifically at the discussion of health to decipher how a preoccupation with health has affected interpretations of the Word of Wisdom. I suggest that a fixation with health and the Word of Wisdom has resulted in two trends. First, some members have taken the health quotient of a substance as a way to expand Word of Wisdom boundaries either in the direction of allowances or prohibitions. Second, linking the Word of Wisdom with health has permitted some proponents (such as Leah and John Widtsoe) to expand notions of what this principle can accomplish. These trends represent the thinking of some members, but not the majority.

Lizzie Belle Gardner Fillmore drank black tea every morning of her life. And when she prayed to bless her food, she covered her tea cup with her hand.[1] "I have to do this so the Lord won't see what's in my cup," she would say. Lizzie Belle was a practicing Mormon and the granddaughter of early Church Apostle and martyr Parley P. Pratt. The God she prayed to was omniscient and omnipotent; she knew he could see the tea beneath her hand. But she covered that tea nonetheless as an acknowledgment that she knew her tea was against the rules. The God she worshipped was also all-loving, and that is why she continued to pray every day over the meals but not the tea.

Lizzie Belle's life (1876–1961) spanned an era of development in Word of Wisdom observance. The Word of Wisdom was born in 1833, three years after Joseph Smith organized The Church of Jesus Christ of Latter-day Saints. Reaching consensus about a minimum standard of how to obey the Word of Wisdom, and what the penalty for noncompliance would be, took a hundred years. Thus, following the Word of Wisdom looked different in the nineteenth century than it does now.

For example, where the text of Doctrine and Covenants 89 says "And, again, strong drinks are not for the belly, but for the washing of your bodies" in verse 7, present-day Saints think only of abstaining from alcohol. But early members of the Church observed this injunction by washing their bodies with cinnamon-infused whiskey as a ritual preparation for holy gatherings and ceremonies.[2] Similarly, verse 5 instructs, "Inasmuch as any man drinketh wine or strong drink among you, behold it is not good, neither meet in the sight of your Father, only in assembling yourselves together to offer up your sacraments before him." This verse alludes to how early Saints used wine to recall Christ's blood during the sacrament. Today, Saints use only water.

Early Church leaders encouraged members to follow the Word of Wisdom, but doing so was not strictly a commandment, and how to do so was not clearly defined. For many, living the Word of Wisdom was a process; President Brigham Young himself did not finally give up tobacco until 1860.[3] Paul Peterson has shown that it was not until 1883–84 that the Quorum of the Twelve renewed their commitment to following the Word of Wisdom, simultaneously admitting they had fallen short in that regard.[4] As President of the Twelve, Wilford Woodruff stated, "We have come to the conclusion that we will more fully observe the word of wisdom, as we have all more or less been negligent upon that point."[5] On November 24, 1886, John D. T. McAllister and David H. Cannon from the St. George Temple wrote to President John Taylor saying they understood from the teachings of the Apostles that those who do not "fully keep" the Word of Wisdom should not participate in temple ordinances. They wondered "how far we are expected by the Lord, and those who preside over us, to judge in this matter. We find that people come here, with their recommends duly signed, who bear the evidence with them that they do not observe the Word of Wisdom, so far as Tobacco is concerned; and we have good reason to state that others come here who habitually use tea or coffee, or both."[6] Several decades would pass before Word of Wisdom adherence was uniformly required for temple attendance.[7]

Although leaders encouraged members to obey the Word of Wisdom, when they saw that members would not and when they learned how much money was exported out of the community by members purchasing these commodities, they told them if they were going to partake of these things, then they should produce their own. "Over a five-year period beginning in 1861, many statements were made by Young, Wells, Kimball and especially Apostle George A. Smith, encouraging local production of tea, coffee, tobacco and alcoholic beverages for the Mormon market in order to save the money that was being sent out of the territory to purchase these items."[8]

Furthermore, Church leaders had differing interpretations of what it meant to follow this commandment. Lorenzo Snow, for example, felt that Church members should not eat meat. Defining and legislating compliance with the Word of Wisdom was a process—one heavily influenced by Joseph F. Smith, Heber J. Grant, and Leah and John A. Widtsoe. In 1902, President

Joseph F. Smith told stake presidents to refuse temple recommends to "flagrant" violators of the Word of Wisdom but to exercise leniency with older members who used tobacco or drank tea.[9] Under Heber J. Grant's presidency in 1921, obedience to the Word of Wisdom (now officially defined as abstinence from coffee, tea, tobacco, and all forms of alcohol) was again declared a requirement for admission to the temple.[10] But not until 1933, when the revelation was one hundred years old, did the *General Handbook of Instructions* explicitly state that those desiring temple recommends must keep the Word of Wisdom.[11] According to the text itself, adherents should also eat many fruits and vegetables in season, lots of grain, and little meat. But individual members do so according to their own discretion.

Lizzie Belle's grandchildren watched her cover her teacup when they were children, during the 1940s and '50s. Because Word of Wisdom adherence was linked by then with temple worthiness, her grandchildren's reminiscence about the tea is quickly followed by reassurance on how assiduously she kept her temple covenants. When Lizzie Belle was born on August 21, 1878, in Richfield, Utah (a year after Brigham Young's death), many members of the Church still considered aspects of the Word of Wisdom to be optional. But by the time of her death in April 1961, keeping the Word of Wisdom was understood to be an important component of Mormon living.

Nevertheless, even as late as the 1960s, cultural attitudes towards coffee and tea were more relaxed than they are now.[12] Fifty years after Lizzie Belle's death, her granddaughter, whom I will call Eloise, still drinks black tea every morning. She, too, is a practicing Mormon and a Church volunteer. Born around the time of Lizzie Belle's death, Eloise's daughter would never drink tea. Lizzie Belle drank tea sufficiently long ago that it makes for a good family story. Her granddaughter's tea habit, on the other hand, is worrisome.

This pattern of slow change over time, in addition to defining the Word of Wisdom as a health law, has provided some members with a sense of license in interpretation. For example, when Eloise considers her own tea habits, her first impulse is to talk about health and to use the concept of health to expound on the text's limitations. In this case, Eloise suggests that drinking tea is not an egregious transgression, because tea might not be bad for health. If the Word of Wisdom is only about health, and some forbidden substance is proven to promote health, then that substance becomes permissible. When medical science found benefit to resveratrol and flavonoids in red wine, for example, a few members interpreted these findings as permission to drink red wine.[13] This is the kind of interpretation that Eloise suggests regarding tea: "For every study that says what in tea is bad for you, there is another telling you why it is good," she asserts. "So I don't think you can say one way or another whether it's bad for you. . . . That depends on who is paying for the study. But I understand the part about obedience; I do get that." Eloise initially evaluates her tea drinking in light of nutrition, as though the main goal of the Word of Wisdom is to safeguard health. However, Eloise also refers to the fact that when General Authorities speak about the Word of Wisdom, they often include another scripture as well: "There is a law, irrevocably decreed in heaven before the foundations of this world, upon which all blessings are predicated—and when we obtain any blessing from God, it is by obedience to that law upon which it is predicated" (D&C 130:20–21). Church leaders teach that even when one does not see the purpose of following a rule, blessings come from following that rule, including an understanding of why the rule exists.[14]

Health can thus become the interpretive lens for discussions about what the Word of Wisdom will and will not allow. If someone learns that a substance is not harmful, she or he argues it should not be against the Word of Wisdom. On the other hand, upon learning that a substance is deleterious, some people will argue that it is against the Word of Wisdom. Coca-Cola is a primary example of the latter situation. When members have asked whether Coca-Cola is against the Word of Wisdom, the answer has generally been no. However, in 1917, Frederick J. Pack said Mormons should not drink it because it contains the same drugs as tea and coffee.[15] Similarly, Joseph Fielding Smith, then President of the Quorum of the Twelve, responded to a 1965 question about cola drinks by focusing on health instead of the language of the original revelation: "I was definitely informed by a chemist that the cola drinks are just as harmful as tea or coffee, and his advice was to leave all such substances alone."[16] In her devotional monograph, Doris T. Charriere argues that a person seeking to truly live the spirit of Word of Wisdom law will start by rejecting coffee, tea, alcohol, and tobacco but may eventually give up hot chocolate and pork and cease to eat significant amounts of starch and protein during the same meal.[17]

Leah and Elder John A. Widtsoe also spoke against cola drinks, and even chocolate, on the grounds of health. In addition, they expanded members' understanding of what the Word of Wisdom might accomplish. These two were the Church's most ardent and prolific advocates of Word of Wisdom observance. As a Harvard-trained chemist, John founded the Department of Agriculture at Brigham Young University and served as president of both Utah State University and the University of Utah. After earning degrees from the University of Utah and Brigham Young University (BYU), Leah trained at one of the country's leading schools for domestic science, the Pratt Institute in Brooklyn, New York.[18] By 1938, John and Leah completed their Church work for the European Mission and coauthored a book on the Word of Wisdom.[19] The First Presidency (President Heber J. Grant, first counselor J. Reuben Clark Jr., and second counselor David O. McKay)[20] embraced and designated this text as the official priesthood manual of study for 1938. A few years later, Leah Widtsoe wrote *How to Be Well*,[21] a work that aimed to review cutting-edge scientific information on nutrition that also served as a cookbook.

Elder Widtsoe's foreword to *How to Be Well* reads like a manifesto and shows the moral gravity with which both of the Widtsoes regarded alimentary habits. "Th[e] dark pall of ignorance has been swept away, during the last few decades, by the light of discoveries, unparalleled in volume and importance. We now know, as never before, what foods, and food combinations, will best promote the health of the body. Those who do not respect and use these findings by seekers after truth, are willful offenders of their bodily needs; and of course, sooner or later, must pay the penalty of their error."[22] In his view, scientific progress was a great blessing that at last provided knowledge about how best to care for the body. That anyone would have that knowledge and act against it was dreadful to him.

In Utah, both Leah and John Widtsoe became household names, and the Word of Wisdom was often called the "Word of Widtsoe." Many found it difficult to follow the Widtsoes' culinary standards, which prohibited refined sugar, white flour, too much meat, and even canned goods, as they represented an adulteration of fresh food and the possibility of eating items out of season. Leah insisted that even she had been unable to live the Word of Wisdom at times, because she did not grow her own food and modern agricultural methods polluted food. Leah believed that what we have come to call organic farming was central to the Word of Wisdom. She said, "I haven't lived the Word of Wisdom because I couldn't, can't get the food. Our food is nasty now-a-days, chemical fertilizer, doped with all kinds of dope conditioners and heaven knows what chemicals." She argued that Word of Wisdom "dos" were at least as important as the "don'ts." Though Winston Churchill smoked and drank, she said he lived to an old age because he lived the "dos": he grew his own food on his country estate.[23]

Widtsoe believed bodies fortified by the Word of Wisdom were better able to resist temptation: "If the body is fully nourished, it will help give the will power to say 'no' to the tempter even though dressed in the false front of the 'weed that soothes' or the social glass that is supposed to give cheer and exhilaration, but which leads to degradation, disgrace, and death."[24] In her view, good health makes it possible to resist the tobacco and wine that lead to the slow, insidious destruction of society. Widtsoe's work bears echoes of the trend Marie Griffith noted in American Protestantism, wherein the inner self can be judged by the outer appearance.[25] But Griffith's subjects focus on physical shape and slimness, while Leah looked inside the body to a physical interface between body and soul that could be controlled by good nutrition as stipulated by the Word of Wisdom.

In addition to believing that the Word of Wisdom would fortify individuals against temptation, Leah Widtsoe thought health was to some extent requisite for Saints to fulfill their earthly destiny. Here she diverges somewhat from Latter-day Saint theology, as well as from the domestic scientists.[26] Latter-day Saint teaching dictates that the purpose of life is the opportunity to gain a body and make choices while under the influence of that body. By learning to manage physical impulses and make appropriate choices, one can become godlike. But Widtsoe's distaste for sickness (a recurrent refrain both in her written work and in her oral history) extended to a sense that illness kept people from the active participation in life, the experience gathering that allowed them to realize life's purpose. Sickness interfered with the process of making choices while under the body's influence.

An interview Leah Widtsoe gave four months before her death illuminates her beliefs well. The year was 1965, Widtsoe was ninety-one, and her husband had been dead for thirteen years. As she described her career path, she expressed the same sentiments that were in *How to Be Well*. Initially, she wanted to be a nurse, but then, she says,

> I decided I didn't like to be around sick people. I'd much rather be around well people and I want to keep people well.... What's the use of being sick!... And, we shouldn't be sick, the Lord didn't intend it, I still feel that way.... The Lord gave us the Word of Wisdom to keep us well and if we're sick it's our own fault....
>
> *Interviewer (a BYU archivist)*: Some people feel that we are here to gain experience and have to go through considerable sickness and pain.
>
> *Widtsoe*: Fiddle! We gain experience in health rather than sickness.[27]

In Widtsoe's view, health was a condition necessary to fulfilling life's purpose. God revealed the Word of Wisdom when the Church was new because it would make a healthy people capable of completing his work. There was no redemption in physical suffering, just redemption from it, following the divine law of nutrition God had revealed.

Leah Widtsoe's enthusiasm for the Word of Wisdom turned both inward to the perfecting of her own religious community and outward with missionary zeal to the outside world. She was convinced that adherence to the Word of Wisdom would gather more of God's children to Zion. The good health of Mormons who followed the Word of Wisdom would attract others to the faith. Widtsoe saw the Word of Wisdom as a proselyting tool in two major respects. First, she saw the science of nutrition as a scientific, rational proof of the validity of the Word of Wisdom.[28] She believed that science had vindicated the calling of the Prophet Joseph Smith. God gave Joseph this law many decades before science had proved that the habits it outlined were optimal for human physical flourishing. As Leah and her husband argue in their own *Word of Wisdom* text:

> Throughout these pages fact has crowded upon fact in support of the declaration of Joseph Smith, the Prophet, that the Word of Wisdom was revealed to him from heavenly sources. He would have stood helpless before the problem of human health had he relied on current knowledge or upon his own shrewd guesses. There are statements in the revelation that, in the light of modern knowledge, cannot be explained by any other means than that of inspiration.

> Indeed, today, after more than 100 years the Word of Wisdom stands as one of the most convincing evidences of the divine inspiration of Joseph Smith, the "Mormon" Prophet.[29]

In addition to providing supporting evidence that God spoke to Joseph Smith, Widtsoe felt that the Word of Wisdom could bring others into the Church because they would see the remarkable health its members enjoyed. How could outsiders resist joining Zion and participating in its blessings once they witnessed its fruits? While her husband served as president of the European Mission, Widtsoe preached and wrote to Church members in Europe about the Word of Wisdom. She even compiled a small collection of recipes from local members and from her own experiments with local ingredients for dishes that exemplified Word of Wisdom standards as she saw them. She saw these writings as central to their proselytizing mission. Her introduction to the pamphlet shows her hope that people who follow God's teachings would so radiate good health that others would want to join them:

> This supplement is presented to you in the hope that an active participation in the teachings of the Word of Wisdom may be incorporated into the life of the members of the Church, who should be the healthiest, the happiest, as well as the best-living people on earth. To know a thing, or to know how it should be done is only half—to live the truth is as important as to know the truth....
>
> That diet is the greatest factor for health, few thinking people will deny. The Latter-day Saints are warned against the many "fads" which exist regarding food. An infallible guide is our inspired Word of Wisdom, which is a standard by which all advice is to be measured.
>
> The following recipes and menus are in strict accord with the latest rules of accepted food science, which, almost miraculously, harmonize with the advice given nearly a century ago by an inspired modern prophet.[30]

Near the end of her life, Leah Widtsoe expressed her disappointment that Church members had failed to flourish through observing her broadened vision of the Word of Wisdom and had thereby failed to attract the membership they otherwise could. Much of her disappointment focused on BYU, where she had founded the Home Economics Department, lectured, and served on the Board of Education and as dean of women. This was the university founded by and named for her grandfather, the second President of the Church, whom she adored and about whom she had coauthored a biography with her mother.

In her 1965 interview, she poignantly lamented the lack of health education at BYU. She was also disappointed in the Health Center, where ill students went to get well.

> *Interviewer*: You don't think we're setting a high standard for the world to follow?
>
> *Widtsoe*: This isn't a health center; this is a sickness center. . . . One of their leading men told me that that year they had over 33,000 applicants from sick students at the "Y," 33,000! Then the attendance was only 11,000. . . . Our people don't have any better health than the rest of the world.[31]

Leah understood Church membership and its leading educational institution to have failed, despite her life's work, in the task that could have brought millions into God's fold.

Health matters to the Latter-day Saints because only through having a body can people continue to develop. For example, Elder Robert L. Simpson taught, "[Our] Loving Father has not left us without specific instruction concerning the care of our physical bodies, for he created us, and he knows that true happiness and total growth, moral, spiritual, and intellectual, are largely dependent upon our physical well-being."[32] How one manages one's body affects one's spiritual development, and the two major guidelines regarding the physical body are the law of chastity (which, in addition to prohibiting sex outside of marriage, insists that members avoid impure thoughts and images) and the Word of Wisdom. Thus the Word of Wisdom becomes a key means by which one works out one's salvation. This somatism, or combining of body and spirit, means that those who obey laws governing the body are entitled to blessings that are less physically immediate as well, such as knowledge and wisdom. Elder Marion D. Hanks explained how he thought the Lord envisioned this process. After quoting D&C 88:15 ("the spirit and the body are the soul of man"), he said:

Later [the Lord] revealed again the truth that the elements—that is, the elements that make up our body—and the spirit in us, when they are combined, permit us to have a fullness of joy. These are eternally important principles. . . . One of the great purposes of mortal life is to take upon ourselves a mortal body (the elements), because in our eternal experience there will come a time of reunion of body and spirit. . . . It is vital that we do everything we can to preserve in honor and cleanliness and integrity this mortal body. It is part of our eternal soul.[33]

Despite such reminders of the Word of Wisdom's spiritual aspects, some Church members and leaders emphasized its health benefits to an extent that they used contemporary findings of nutrition science to either diminish or augment prohibitions. Some claimed that the relative harmlessness of a substance meant it did not violate the Word of Wisdom. Others believed that all deleterious items were against the Word of Wisdom. In addition, leaders like John and Leah Widtsoe expanded visions of what health resulting from the Word of Wisdom could accomplish. They spoke of the Word of Wisdom as providing the power to resist temptation, as being essential to fulfilling one's earthly destiny, and as aiding in missionary work.

Notes

1. Conrad L. Bryner, "Interview with Fillmore Descendants II," October 7, 2011; Judith Bryner Pobanz, Kathleen Stewart Holbrook, and Eloise, "Interview with Fillmore Descendants," October 3, 2011.

2. Leonard J. Arrington, ed., "Oliver Cowdery's Kirtland, Ohio, 'Sketchbook,'" *BYU Studies* 12, no. 4 (Summer 1972): 416.

3. Steven C. Harper, *The Word of Wisdom* (Orem, UT: Millennial Press, 2007), 58.

4. Paul H. Peterson, "An Historical Analysis of the Word of Wisdom" (master's thesis, Brigham Young University, 1972), 71.

5. "Minutes of the Salt Lake School of the Prophets," September 28, 1883, 52, Vault Corporate Records, Church History Library, The Church of Jesus Christ of Latter-day Saints, Salt Lake City.

6. John D. T. McAllister and David H. Cannon to President John Taylor, "Letterpress Copybook, 1881–1887," November 24, 1886, Secure Stacks Corporate Records, Church History Library.

7. Thomas G. Alexander, *Mormonism in Transition: A History of the Latter-day Saints, 1890–1930* (Urbana: University of Illinois, 1996), 259–60.

8. Robert J. McCue, "Did the Word of Wisdom Become a Commandment in 1851?," *Dialogue* 14, no. 3 (September 1, 1981): 70.

9. To reach the highest levels of salvation after death, members of the Church must make specific covenants with God in an LDS temple. They also receive the crowning blessings of earthly life during a temple endowment ceremony. Church members who live far from a temple might save money for years to visit the temple just once. Church employees throughout the world must be worthy of a temple recommend, from the gardeners at Temple Square in Salt Lake City to the faculty at BYU–Hawaii to Church administrators in Mexico City.

10. Lester Bush argued that this delay in compliance actually worked in favor of the Saints' health because in many cases drinking alcohol, or tea or coffee made with boiled water, was safer than drinking unboiled water. Fresh water often carried the causes of diarrhea, cholera, dysentery, and typhoid—which could result in death. In addition, smoking (the most dangerous form of tobacco) was not really widespread until the twentieth century, and smoking-related deaths tend to occur a little later in life, past the general life span of people in the nineteenth century. "Whatever merit or function the Word of Wisdom had for the nineteenth century Mormons, in retrospect we know that circumstances changed around the turn of the century in such a way that its guidelines could unquestionably promote better physical health (i.e., there was more cigarette smoking, and less serious infectious disease). That this development—the implications of which were not apparent to the medical scientists for decades—coincided with a decision by the church leadership to require firm adherence to the Word of Wisdom is quite remarkable." Lester E. Bush Jr., "The Word of Wisdom in Early Nineteenth-Century Perspective," *Dialogue* 14, no. 3 (September 1, 1981): 60.

11. Thomas G. Alexander, "The Word of Wisdom: From Principle to Requirement," *Dialogue* 14, no. 3 (September 1, 1981): 82. See also Alexander, *Mormonism in Transition*, 258–71.

12. Anecdotal evidence abounds about faithful Church members who drank coffee or iced tea. An October 3, 1942, message from the First Presidency, read over the pulpit at general conference, suggests leaders were concerned over a diminishing, but still persistent, lack of compliance. "For more than half a century President Grant has on every appropriate occasion admonished the Saints touching their obligation to keep the Word of Wisdom. . . . But his admonitions have not found a resting place in all our hearts. We, the First Presidency of the Church of Jesus Christ of Latter-day Saints, now solemnly renew all these counsels, we repeat all these admonitions, we reinvoke obedience to God's law of health given us by God Himself. . . . We urge the Saints to quit trifling with this law and so to live it that we may claim its promises." James R. Clark, comp., *Messages of the First Presidency of The Church of Jesus Christ of Latter-Day Saints* (Salt Lake City: Bookcraft, 1965), 6:170–71.

13. Neither Mayo Clinic researchers nor Church leaders believe the potential benefits of these substances outweigh the negative health effects of drinking. Mayo Clinic staff, "Red Wine, Antioxidants and Resveratrol: Good for Your Heart?" Mayo Foundation for Medical Education and Research, http://www.mayoclinic.com/health/red-wine/HB00089.

14. For example, Elder Simpson quotes this scripture and promises, "We are blessed by obedience to law. Transgression of the law always brings unhappiness." Robert L. Simpson, "God's Law of Health," *Improvement Era*, 1963, 488. See also Milton R. Hunter, "A Letter to My Son Michael," *Improvement Era*, 1963, 472.

15. Frederick J. Pack, "Should LDS Drink Coca Cola?," *Improvement Era*, March 1918, 432–35.

16. Joseph Fielding Smith, "Use of Cola Drinks and Playing Games of Chance," *Improvement Era*, September 1965, 759.

17. Doris T. Charriere, *Hidden Treasures of the Word of Wisdom* (Salt Lake City: Hawkes Publishing, 1978), 17–18.

18. Alan K. Parrish, *John A. Widtsoe: A Biography* (Salt Lake City, Utah: Deseret Book, 2003), 61–64, 101–3; *In a Sunlit Land, the Autobiography of John A. Widtsoe* (Salt Lake City: Deseret News Press, 1953), 28–41, 222.

19. John A. Widtsoe and Leah D. Widtsoe, *The Word of Wisdom: A Modern Interpretation* (Salt Lake City: Deseret Book, 1950).

20. James B. Allen and Glen M. Leonard, in *The Presidents of the Church: Biographical Essays*, ed. Leonard J. Arrington (Salt Lake City, Utah: Deseret Book, 1993), 298.

21. Leah D. Widtsoe, *How to Be Well: A Health Handbook and Cook-book Based on the Newer Knowledge of Nutrition* (Salt Lake City: Deseret Book, 1943).

22. Widtsoe, *How to Be Well*, 5.

23. Leah D. Widtsoe, "Widtsoe Oral History Interview," 1965, L. Tom Perry Special Collections, Brigham Young University, Provo, UT, 40.

24. Widtsoe, *How to Be Well*, 33.

25. R. Marie Griffith, *Born Again Bodies: Flesh and Spirit in American Christianity* (Berkeley: University of California Press, 2004).

26. However, Heather Curtis argues that the divine healing movement among charismatics had pushed toward that direction in the late nineteenth and early twentieth centuries. Heather D. Curtis, *Faith in the Great Physician: Suffering and Divine Healing in American Culture, 1860–1900* (Baltimore: Johns Hopkins University Press, 2007).

27. Widtsoe, "Widtsoe Oral History Interview," 36, 40.

28. Deidra Boyack Jeffries, *The Word of Wisdom: A Weight-loss Diet* (Salt Lake City: Hawkes Publishing, 1984), 20. "Perhaps it is time that we as a people recognize that the Word of Wisdom is as profound a forerunner in nutritional prescriptions as it has proven to be medically prophetic regarding the consequences of the use of coffee, tea, alcohol and tobacco."

29. Widtsoe and Widtsoe, *Word of Wisdom*, 288.

30. Leah D. Widtsoe, "Word of Wisdom Menus and Recipes," *Millennial Star Supplement* 93, no. 10 (1931): 1.

31. Widtsoe, "Widtsoe Oral History Interview," 38–39.

32. Simpson, "God's Law of Health," 488.

33. Marion D. Hanks, "How Fortunate Can We Be?," *Improvement Era*, June 1965, 526.

14

Illuminating the Text of the Doctrine and Covenants through the Gospel of John

Nicholas J. Frederick

It may surprise some readers of the Doctrine and Covenants just how prominent a role the Bible plays in the construction of the revelations. Philip Barlow has observed how Joseph Smith's nineteenth-century revelations "remained intimately linked to the Bible. Some dealt directly with biblical themes, and quoted or closely paraphrased traditional scripture. All were saturated with KJV words, phrases, and concepts: for every two verses of the revelations recorded in the Doctrine and Covenants, approximately three phrases or clauses parallel some KJV phrase or clause."[1] Although the Lord revealed through Joseph Smith information and doctrines designed for this dispensation, he employed the Bible as a means of constructing the revelations, utilizing ancient biblical "building blocks" to create a modern mosaic. Some of these "building blocks" are lengthy quotations, such as the excerpts from the book of Revelation found in section 88. Other occurrences may be quotations or paraphrases of only four or five words. Some of the clearest of these quotations and allusions (over three hundred in all) in the Doctrine and Covenants come from the Gospel of John, the Gospel most filled with unique

---

Nicholas J. Frederick is an adjunct professor of ancient scripture at Brigham Young University.

language and imagery.² This paper will explore the possibility that one key to interpreting the Doctrine and Covenants may come through isolating and examining the many passages of the Bible, specifically from the Gospel of John, found throughout the Doctrine and Covenants. While it is common to view Restoration scripture as something of a window into the Bible, this method reverses that interpretive approach and suggests that there is value in using the Bible as a window into the Doctrine and Covenants. In particular, this paper will examine how both Johannine Christology and anthropology are employed throughout the revelations as a way of crafting a unique Mormon theology.³

Christology

The Word. John begins his Gospel with a prologue known as the *logos* hymn, a rather dense section of 18 verses through which John attempted to poetically illustrate the divine nature of Jesus Christ prior to his arrival on earth—Jesus is the preexistent *logos*, or "Word," who mediates between the transcendent God and the mortal realm of earth.⁴ Throughout these eighteen verses, the grand images of light and darkness, reception and rejection, life and glory are woven into the tale of the descent of the Word to earth, and they signify the divine beginnings of Christ's earthly ministry. In a way, John's prologue represents an encapsulation of the entire Gospel, "that in the life and ministry of Jesus of Nazareth the glory of God was uniquely and perfectly disclosed."⁵

In the Doctrine and Covenants, several passages refer directly (with small changes) to the prologue of John's Gospel. Seven of these—D&C 6:21; 10:57–58; 11:11, 29; 34:2; 39:2–3; 45:7–8; and 88:48–49—utilize the language of John 1:5 and 11, which read: "And the light shineth in darkness; and the darkness comprehended it not. . . . He came unto his own, and his own received him not." A closer examination of the sections in which this language occurs suggests that the choice of language may have significance. First, there is the sense of new creation implicit throughout the prologue, particularly the allusion to Genesis 1:1 in John 1:1. By invoking the language of the prologue, the Lord is announcing that a similar creation is taking place; just as the era of Christianity was a "new creation" in the midst of the world of the Jews, the Mormon epoch will be a "new creation" amongst a world of Christians. The fact that in both verses there is a scene with a rejected figure, the "light" in

John 1:5 and the Word himself in John 1:11, reinforces the idea of a restoration following a period of apostasy, or "darkness."

This restoration allusion finds further support through a more literal reading of John 1:11. In Greek, this verse contains a play on words. It could be rendered "He came unto his own *things* [τὰ ἴδια] and his own *people* [οἱ ἴδιοι] received him not." While for John, this wordplay may have represented the Jewish rejection of Jesus, for Joseph Smith, it works equally well in signifying the Christian rejection of Jesus, who must once again restore his gospel following a period of "darkness." Finally, with the exception of section 88, the revelations in which the language of John 1:1–18 is found all pertain to the growth and expansion of the early Church. This may indicate that the appropriation of these specific verses was intended to signify for the readers that a new Christianity, or a second attempt by the Word to "dwell among us," was about to commence. This idea is bolstered by the presence of several imperfect verbs (signifying uncompleted action) in John 1:1–4, suggesting an action that has begun but is not yet completed. Thus this hymn becomes the ideal pericope for the Restoration, as it signifies that this creative process is still ongoing and has not been fully completed.

"I Am." One of the peculiar qualities of John's Gospel is his use of the title "I Am." Throughout the Fourth Gospel, Jesus consistently identifies himself with the phrase "I Am" followed by some variation of a predicate nominative. For example, to a crowd of hungry listeners, Jesus declared, "I am [*egō eimi*] the bread of life" (John 6:35). To the Apostles, gathered together for one last feast, Jesus declared, "I am the way, the truth, and the life" (John 14:6). Other instances of the use of "I Am" include "light of the world" (John 8:12), the "good shepherd" (John 10:11, 14), "the resurrection and the life" (John 11:25), and the "true vine" (John 15:1, 5). At times, Jesus didn't even bother adding a predicate nominative, declaring simply, "I Am," as he does with the Samaritan woman (John 4:26), when announcing that "before Abraham was, I am" (John 8:58), or when facing the officers sent to arrest him (see John 18:5, 8). This identification of Jesus as "I Am" held great sacral significance for the Jews. In the Septuagint account of Moses' theophany at the burning bush, Jehovah identified himself as *egō eimi ho on*, literally "I am the one who exists" (Exodus 3:14).[6] Isaiah employed the "I Am" as a more explicit theological proclamation: "I, even I, am the Lord; and beside me there is no saviour. I have declared, and have saved, and I have shewed, when there was no strange god among you: therefore ye are my witnesses, saith the Lord, that I am God. Yea, before the day was I am he; and there is none that can deliver out of my hand: I will work, and who shall let it?" (Isaiah 43:11–13). The fact that Jesus adopts this same terminology serves to connect him with the Old Testament deity,[7] either as the Messiah or Jehovah himself.[8]

The Jesus who reveals himself to Joseph Smith also employs this same "I Am" title.[9] At various times throughout the Doctrine and Covenants, he identifies himself as "I am" plus "Jesus Christ, the Son of God" (D&C 6:21; 10:57; 14:9; 35:2; 49:28; 51:20), "the light" (D&C 10:58; 11:11), "the true light" (D&C 88:50), "the life and the light" (D&C 11:28), "the light and the life" (D&C 12:9; 34:2; 45:7), "the good shepherd" (D&C 50:44), "the Great I Am" (D&C 29:1; 38:1; 39:1), "endless" (D&C 19:4, 10), "your advocate" (D&C 29:5; 32:3; 110:4), "the stone of Israel" (D&C 50:44), "the first and the last" (D&C 110:4), "he who said—Other sheep have I which are not of this fold" (D&C 10:59), "the beginning and the end" (D&C 19:1; 35:1; 38:1; 45:7), and "the Alpha and Omega" (D&C 19:1; 45:7; 63:60; 68:35; 84:120; 112:34; 132:66). It could be argued that since Jesus is speaking in the first person in these revelations, the use of "I am" is merely a grammatical necessity. However, many of the usages of "I am" in the revelations are distinctly Johannine and thus point the readers directly toward the "I Am" formula. For example, the references to "light" and "life" reflect the language of John's prologue, particularly John 1:4. The predicate nominative "good shepherd" in D&C 50:44 evokes John 10:11 and 14, while the somewhat awkward "I am he who said—Other sheep have I which are not of this fold" in D&C 10:59 explicitly brings to mind John 10:16. Additionally, the specific usage of "the Great I Am" and "the stone of Israel" recalls usages of "I Am" in the Old Testament.[10]

All in all, there are over thirty occurrences of the "I Am" formula found throughout the Doctrine and Covenants. Understood as the divine title of the Johannine Jesus, a passage from D&C 11:28–29 states, "Behold, I am Jesus Christ, the Son of God. I am the life and the light of the world. I am the same who came unto mine own and mine own received me not." This passage can now be understood as working on multiple levels. First, the title "I am" identifies the speaker with the Old Testament God or the Messiah. Second, the predicate nominative and subsequent appositive, "Jesus Christ, the Son of God," identifies the speaker with the New Testament God. The fact that the speaker also incorporates the phrase "the life and light of the world," a passage clearly invoking John's preface, appropriates the creative "Word" into this figure as well. Finally, this speaker is revealing himself through Joseph Smith. The combination of Old Testament, New Testament, and Restoration elements in these verses serves to claim that the divine figure speaking through Joseph Smith is the Word, Jehovah, the Jewish Messiah, and Jesus Christ. Interestingly, this type of language in the revelations both appropriates the entire biblical tradition and constrains the reader to accept the revelation produced through Joseph Smith as either true revelation or gross blasphemy. Additionally, if the usage of the "I Am" language in the Gospel of John was to signify to potential believers that Jesus was the incarnation or representation of the Old Testament God, then its recurrence in latter-day revelation may have a similar intent. Potential converts to Mormonism are invited to listen to the words of God and find at the head of the Church the same divine being who occupies the Fourth Gospel, again linking together the Latter-day Saint Jesus, the Christian Jesus, and the Jewish Jehovah.[11]

Anthropology

Sons of God. We have seen how the Doctrine and Covenants utilizes the Johannine prologue as a means of correlating the Jesus of the New Testament with the Jesus of the Restoration. Now we turn to examining how Johannine language in the revelations explicates the true nature of humankind. In four revelations, sections 11, 34, 39, and 45, the references to John 1:5 and 11 that were examined previously are followed up by another verse from John's prologue, John 1:12, which reads: "But as many as received him, to them gave he power to become the sons[12] of God, even to them that believe on his name."[13] It is difficult to know exactly what John meant by "sons of God," and some commentators have chosen to interpret this passage as a spiritual awakening or rebirth. F. F. Bruce writes that "to enter God's family one must receive his Word—in other terms, one must believe in his name."[14]

Furthermore, in Doctrine and Covenants 34:3, Christ says to Orson Hyde, "[I am he] who so loved the world that he gave his own life, that as many as would believe might become the sons of God. Wherefore you are my son," suggesting that a form of belief in Jesus' name is sufficient to be called his son or daughter.[15] In D&C 35:2, Sidney Rigdon and Edward Partridge are told that the "sons of God" are "even as many as will believe on [Christ's] name." Section 39, given to James Covill in January 1831, specifies that receiving Jesus means to receive the gospel, specifically repentance, baptism, and the Holy Ghost (D&C 39:5–6). In both the Book of Mormon and at least the Restoration revelations received by March 1831, Joseph seems to have understood the title "son of God" to refer to a spiritual renewal brought about by accepting the redemption of Jesus Christ.[16] Whereas the prologue of John's Gospel announced to the first-century world that a new era had dawned, one in which God "was made flesh" and even "dwelt among us," the strong presence of the prologue in these early revelations signified a similar new era, where God would once again dwell with men and symbolically make them his sons.

However, the concept of becoming the "sons of God" has meaning beyond a spiritual renewal. Raymond Brown has noted that it is in the Gospel of John that "our present state as God's children on this earth comes out most clearly."[17] Augustine, bishop of Hippo, wrote, "But he himself that justifies also deifies, for by justifying he makes sons of God. 'For he has given them power to become the sons of God.' If then we have been made sons of god, we have also been made gods."[18] There is present in the Gospel of John the idea that the divinity of God overflows to mankind and that through following Jesus Christ, we somehow tap into that mystical union. Jesus' intercessory prayer, spoken at the point at which his hour had come, alludes to this relationship. Prior to entering into the Garden of Gethsemane, Jesus prayed "that they all may be one; as thou, Father, art in me, and I in thee, that they also may be one in us: that the world may believe that thou hast sent me. And the glory which thou gavest me I have given them; that they may be one, even as we are one" (John 17:21–22).

This second hermeneutical model for understanding John 1:12 becomes particularly relevant in the one allusion to John's prologue that has not been examined yet, D&C 88:48–50, which reads:

> I say unto you, he hath seen him; nevertheless, he who came unto his own was not comprehended. The light shineth in darkness, and the darkness comprehendeth it not; nevertheless, the day shall come when you shall comprehend even God, being quickened in him and by him. Then shall ye know that ye have seen me, that I am, and that I am the true light that is in you, and that you are in me; otherwise ye could not abound.

Here the reader notes the appropriation of language from the prologue, with its image of darkness and light, but this usage has now moved beyond the use of a verbatim quotation to signify a new age. These verses promise to believers a time when they will be "quickened in him and by him," where they will know that "[Christ is] the true light that is in [them], and that [they] are in [him]." This additional appropriation of the Johannine prologue hints at an emerging divine anthropology, similar to what Augustine had declared, that mankind shares some element with God and is to some extent literally one with both the Father and the Son. The emphasis of the Johannine language is no longer so much about a contrasting light and darkness but about the light that all believers have within them, originating in Christ and linking mankind with him. The Gospel of John, with its emphasis upon humankind's divine nature, provides appropriate language for expressing this fundamental concept.

Exaltation. Starting in 1832, Joseph began to receive, in rapid succession, what Richard Bushman has termed the "four exaltation revelations,"[19] specifically sections 76, 84, 88, and 93. As Joseph's doctrinal insights grow and evolve through the course of these revelations, so does the prominence of Johannine language.[20] Sections 88 and 93 in particular demonstrate the influence of language and imagery from the Gospel of John. Section 88, termed "the Olive Leaf," opens with the voice of the Lord proclaiming, "Wherefore, I now send upon you another Comforter, even upon you my friends, that it may abide in your hearts, even the Holy Spirit of promise; which other Comforter is the same that I promised unto my disciples, as is recorded in the testimony of John" (v. 3). This verse refers to and even quotes from John 14:26, where Jesus had said, "But the Comforter, which is the Holy Ghost, whom the Father will send in my name, he shall teach you all things, and bring all things to your remembrance, whatsoever I have said unto you." Jesus clearly identifies this "Comforter" to be the Holy Spirit, whose task for the early Christian Church was to "bring to [their] remembrance" the words of Jesus, functioning as an additional witness that would point Christians toward the truth once Jesus had been resurrected and had ascended to the Father.

In section 88, this reference to a second "Comforter" evolves from the reception of a simple witness imparted through the Holy Ghost to a figure pivotal for obtaining exaltation. This "Holy Spirit of promise" is a "promise which I give unto you of eternal life, even the glory of the celestial kingdom; Which glory is that of the church of the Firstborn, even of God, the holiest of all, through Jesus Christ his Son" (D&C 88:4–5). Joseph Smith would later issue the invitation to "Come to God weary him until he blesses you. . . . Obtain that holy Spirit of promise—Then you can be sealed to Eternal Life."[21] Joseph Smith elaborated further on the specific function of the Holy Spirit of promise, stating that it was one of the duties of the Holy Spirit to act as a "ratifier" or "sealer" of eternal covenants, and thus an important figure in the progression of men and women toward exaltation (D&C 132:7).

Section 93, also received in 1833, again adopts and modifies Johannine scripture specifically to demonstrate the pathway to individual salvation. Notice how the language from the Gospel of John (in italics) is carefully woven throughout the first fifteen verses of section 93:

> Verily, thus saith the Lord: It shall come to pass that every soul who forsaketh his sins and cometh unto me, and calleth on my name, and obeyeth my voice, and keepeth my commandments, shall see my face and *know that I am* [John 8:28];
>
> *And that I am the true light that lighteth every man that cometh into the world* [John 1:9];
>
> *And that I am in the Father, and the Father in me, and the Father and I are one* [John 14:11]—
>
> The Father because he gave me of his fulness, and the Son because I was in the world and *made flesh* my tabernacle, and *dwelt among* the sons of men [John 1:14].
>
> I was in the world and received of my Father, and the works of him were plainly manifest.
>
> And John saw and bore record of the fulness of my glory, and the fulness of John's record is hereafter to be revealed.
>
> And he bore record, saying: I saw his glory, that he was in the beginning, before the world was [John 1:1];
>
> Therefore, *in the beginning the Word was* [John 1:1], for he was the Word, even the messenger of salvation—
>
> The light and the Redeemer of the world; the *Spirit of truth* [John 14:17; 16:13], who came into the world, because the world was made by him, *and in him was the life of men and the light of men* [John 1:4].
>
> The worlds were made by him; men were made by him; *all things were made by him*, and through him, and of him [John 1:3].

> And I, John, bear record that I *beheld his glory, as the glory of the Only Begotten of the Father, full of grace and truth*, even the *Spirit of truth*, which came and dwelt *in the flesh, and dwelt among us* [John 1:14].
>
> And I, John, saw that he received not of the fulness at the first, but received *grace for grace* [John 1:16];
>
> And he received not of the fulness at first, but continued from grace to grace, until he received a fulness;
>
> And thus he was called the Son of God, because he received not of the fulness at the first.
>
> And I, John, bear record, and lo, the heavens were opened, *and the Holy Ghost descended upon him in the form of a dove, and sat upon him* [John 1:32], and there came a voice out of heaven saying: This is my beloved Son.

In these opening verses of section 93, an assortment of verses originally located throughout the Gospel of John are reworked by God into a unique theological statement. In the Gospel of John, no mention is made about the Son not receiving of the fulness; rather, it is we who receive "grace for grace" due to our encounter with him. But the way the Johannine language of section 93 is recast now establishes that the Son was the party who received not of the fulness at first, and thus Jesus Christ progresses "grace to grace" until achieving a fulness.

A parallel scenario then follows. Just as Jesus progressed until partaking of the fulness, so men and women can progress in a similar fashion until they also receive of his fulness:

> I give unto you these sayings that you may understand and know how to worship, and know what you worship, that you may come unto the Father in my name, and in due time receive of his fulness.
>
> For if you keep my commandments you shall receive of his fulness, and be glorified in me as I am in the Father; therefore, I say unto you, you shall receive grace for grace.
>
> And now, verily I say unto you, I was in the beginning with the Father, and am the Firstborn;
>
> And all those who are begotten through me are partakers of the glory of the same, and are the church of the Firstborn. (D&C 93:19–22.)

Again, the revelations appropriate the *language* of John but have reshaped the *context*. What was an ancient hymn praising the divine, premortal glory of Jesus Christ has become in the latter days a fascinating elaboration of humankind's divine potential.

Eternal families. Finally, one additional place where the revelations utilize Johannine language to elaborate upon the doctrines of exaltation is section 132.[22] In chapter 17 of John's Gospel, Jesus offered the "intercessory prayer," intended to formally announce that he "finished the work that [the Father] gave [him] to do" (John 17:4). He begins the prayer in the following manner: "Father, the hour is come; glorify thy Son, that thy Son also may glorify thee: as thou hast given him power over all flesh, that he should give eternal life to as many as thou hast given him. And this is life eternal, that they might know thee the only true God, and Jesus Christ, whom thou hast sent" (John 17:1–3). The latter verse, verse 3, provides a definition of eternal life, namely, to achieve knowledge of God and Jesus Christ. To provide this knowledge of the "only true God" was one of the stated purposes of Jesus' ministry: "If ye had known me, ye should have known my Father also: and from henceforth ye know him, and have seen him. . . . He that hath seen me hath seen the Father" (John 14:7, 9). Apparently, when people have gained this knowledge of the Father and the Son, they recognize the divinity that exists within themselves; they recognize that they share some unity with God and Jesus. It is the hope for this understanding and subsequent unification between God and his children that serves as the occasion for the prayer: "That they all may be one; as thou, Father, art in me, and I in thee, that they also may be one in us: that the world may believe that thou hast sent me. And the glory which thou gavest me I have given them; that they may be one, even as we are one: I in them, and thou in me, that they may be made perfect in one; and that the world may know that thou hast sent me, and hast loved them, as thou hast loved me" (John 17:21–23). Both the high Christology and the high anthropology of John come through explicitly in these verses: not only is Jesus "one" with the Father, but so are his children.

Once again, the language of John is adopted and refashioned in the text of the Doctrine and Covenants. Framed around a discussion of the Abrahamic covenant, section 132 elaborates on the nature of those who become exalted, specifically noting that those sealed "by the Holy Spirit of promise" will achieve a degree or kingdom of glory that "shall be a fulness and a continuation of the seeds forever and ever" (D&C 132:19). This idea of a "continuation of the seeds" becomes for Joseph Smith the ultimate meaning in the Abrahamic covenant, the proper interpretation of the promise that "[God] will multiply thy seed as the stars of the heaven, and as the sand which is upon the sea shore" (Genesis 22:17; see also 32:12). This promise was not restricted to the descendants of the patriarchs on earth but was also granted to all those who become exalted and begin to raise spiritual offspring of their own.[23] It is this vision of eternal increase referred to when, a few verses later, we read, "This is eternal lives—to know the only wise and true God, and Jesus Christ, whom he hath sent. I am he. Receive ye, therefore, my law" (D&C 132:24). While Jesus' statement in John 17:3 seemed to imply that "eternal life" meant knowing that one shared something with God and Jesus, that the potential for some sort of unity was available, D&C 132:24 goes beyond John. True knowledge of God and Jesus Christ comes through *eternal lives*, namely the propagation of eternal increase.[24] If one wants to truly *know* and *understand* what it is like to be God, then one must become exalted, create worlds, and bear the children to inhabit those worlds, for that is the teleological nature of God's existence, his "work and his glory" (Moses 1:39).

Conclusion

This paper began with the intention of demonstrating that an examination of places where the Doctrine and Covenants utilized passages from the Gospel of John would provide one window through which we could observe and interpret the text. What of use has been unearthed from this interpretation? The Johannine prologue and the "I Am" passages proved useful in illustrating how Mormonism was a restoration of the ancient Church. The "I Am" passages also linked the Jesus of the New Testament and Christianity with the latter-day Jesus, while the Johannine prologue's emphasis upon light and darkness proved to be the perfect depiction of apostasy and the Restoration. Later revelations introduced deeper theological concepts but maintained the same Johannine language. Images from John such as "another Comforter," "light," and "life eternal" became useful building blocks for Restoration theology. Significantly, the revelations did not just borrow or copy John's language but often reimagined it, molding and crafting the words and ideas of John into a whole new theology, one that maintained John's high Christology and anthropology but allowed room for God to expand on biblical concepts while introducing new and innovative doctrinal developments. At one point, Joseph Smith said, "To know God learn to become God's [sic]."[25] The Fourth Gospel, a text that presented Jesus Christ as a deity who came to earth and offered the words of eternal life, served perfectly as a text from which to "vocalize" Jesus, to allow latter-day followers of Jesus the opportunity to know God by having him speak in a familiar fashion. Through incorporating the words of John's Gospel, with their emphasis upon becoming "sons of God," into revelations given through the Prophet Joseph Smith, God laid out a path by which his children could "learn to become Gods" themselves.

While observing that Mormons typically view the Bible through "the lens of modern revelation," Robert L. Millet noted that Latter-day Saints "need to be just as attentive to those occasions when Bible passages serve as a hermeneutical lens through which we can expand our understanding of teachings contained in the Book of Mormon, the Doctrine and Covenants, and the Pearl of Great Price."[26] This is a daunting task. It is difficult enough to master Restoration scripture, such as the Book of Mormon, but to master both Restoration scripture and the Bible to the point where we can use them to interpret and interrogate each other requires a great deal of work, study, and dedication. But if we truly desire to uncover and understand all the wondrous depths of truth that God has spread throughout the scriptures, it behooves us to do so. The text of the Doctrine and Covenants provides us with one excellent example of how this search can be exercised. We can isolate the biblical texts that contribute to the construction of the Doctrine and Covenants as well as examine both the original context of biblical passages and how phrases and passages have been minutely (or explicitly) altered by God in the Doctrine and Covenants. By doing so, we are able to gain important insights and observe key nuances that might have been easily missed otherwise. The use of the Bible in the Doctrine and Covenants also emphasizes that God views the Bible not as an artifact of the past but as a tool for the future. The reality of continuing revelation is that God can take scripture given two millennia ago and adapt, utilize, and rework it into something that is relevant for the present and future success of the Church. The prominence of the Bible within the Doctrine and Covenants provides to us as readers the chance to participate in an intertextual dialogue, one that promises to reward those readers who take the time and make the effort to engage it, who attempt to locate the truths contained therein.

Notes

1. Philip L. Barlow, *Mormons and the Bible: The Place of the Latter-day Saints in American Religion* (New York: Oxford University Press, 1991), 62. Barlow's statement relies heavily upon work done by Ellis T. Rasmussen, "Textual Parallels to the Doctrine and Covenants and Book of Commandments as Found in the Bible" (master's thesis, Brigham Young University, 1951); and Lois Jean Smutz "Textual Parallels to the Doctrine and Covenants (Sections 65 to 133) as Found in the Bible" (master's thesis, Brigham Young University, 1971). Rasmussen concluded that the median for appearances of the Bible within the Doctrine and Covenants was 1.3 (5), while Smutz's later study confirmed Rasmussen's with a median of 1.33 (62). See also Eric D. Huntsman, "The King James Bible and the Doctrine and Covenants," in *The King James Bible and the Restoration*, ed. Kent P. Jackson (Provo, UT: Religious Studies Center, Brigham Young University, 2011), 187.

2. In addition to the language of the revelations being heavily influenced by Johannine language, Joseph Smith also interacted with the Johannine corpus in other ways. Upon inquiring as to the fate of John the Beloved, Joseph Smith saw in a vision "a translated version of the record made on parchment by John and hidden up by himself." *History of the Church of Jesus Christ of Latter-day Saints*, ed. B. H. Roberts, 2nd ed. rev. (Salt Lake City: Deseret Book, 1981), 1:35–36. Section 76, Joseph Smith's vision of the different levels of heaven and hell, was inspired by a reading of John 5:29. Section 77 contains a dialogue between Smith and an unknown interlocutor regarding some of the more curious images from the book of Revelation, such as the meaning of the "sea of glass" or the identity of the "four beasts." Finally, Smith's most famous sermon, the King Follett Discourse, delivered three months prior to his death, was inspired by a reading of John 5:19.

3. "Christology" is the study of the divinity of Jesus Christ, usually looking specifically at how his divinity interacts with his humanity, as well as his origins. "Anthropology" is the study of how humanity is presented in a text. Did humans preexist? Do they have agency? What kind of afterlife might they obtain?

4. This stands in contrast to the synoptic Gospels, which begin their narratives with the birth (Matthew and Luke) or baptism (Mark) of Jesus.

5. F. F. Bruce, *The Gospel of John* (Grand Rapids, MI: William B. Eerdmans, 1994), 28.

6. Additional usages of this title in the LXX include Exodus 6:6; 20:1, 5; Leviticus 17:5; Hosea 13:4; Joel 2:27, as well as several instances in Isaiah.

7. One scholar writes that the parallels between Isaiah 43 and the Johannine *egō eimi* "are so close that they can hardly be considered accidental." Philip B. Harner, *The "I Am" of the Fourth Gospel* (Philadelphia: Fortress Press, 1970), 61.

8. Thomas L. Brodie notes, "Jesus' self-identification as the expected Messiah is so formulated that it indicates the presence of God." *The Gospel According to John: A Literary and Theological Commentary* (Oxford: Oxford University Press, 1997), 224. Raymond Brown examines the use of *egō eimi* at the arrest in John 18 and notes that "throughout the Gospel John has played on the *egō eimi* without an expressed predicate giving voice to Jesus' divine claims. . . . The name seems to have the power to keep the

disciples safe" as well as having "the power to paralyze his enemies." *The Death of the Messiah: From Gethsemane to the Grave* (New York: Doubleday, 1994), 1:260–261.

9. Significantly, the idea that Jesus speaks with a Johannine "voice" is not unique to the Doctrine and Covenants. Krister Stendahl has observed that the Jesus of 3 Nephi compared most closely to the Johannine Jesus of the New Testament, even though on the surface the temple sermon in 3 Nephi correlates most closely with the Matthean Sermon on the Mount. Krister Stendahl, "The Sermon on the Mount and Third Nephi," in *Reflections on Mormonism*, ed. Truman G. Madsen (Salt Lake City: Bookcraft, 1978), 139–54.

10. Significantly, the "I Am" sayings in the revelations that don't come directly from the Fourth Gospel are found in other texts of the Johannine corpus. Jesus' claims in D&C 29:5; 32:3; and 110:4 that he is our "advocate" with the Father are clearly an allusion to 1 John 2:1, while the titles of "Alpha and Omega," "the beginning and the end," and "the first and the last" come from a third contribution of John, the book of Revelation (D&C 1:11; 22:13).

11. Steven C. Harper makes a similar observation regarding the use of "I Am" in section 110 of the Doctrine and Covenants. See *Making Sense of the Doctrine and Covenants: A Guided Tour Through Modern Revelation* (Salt Lake City: Deseret Book, 2008), 407.

12. "Sons" is a translation of the Greek τέκνα, which is better rendered as "children."

13. The tenses of the verbs in both the prologue of John and the revelation of Joseph Smith are quite interesting. In John 1:12, the author uses the aorist ἔδωκεν, suggesting that this "power" has already been given and is not merely a future possibility. D&C 34:3 and 45:8 both follow in English the sense of the aorist tense, but D&C 11:30 reads: "But verily, verily, I say unto you, that as many as receive me, to them *will I give* power to become the sons of God, even to them that believe on my name. Amen" (emphasis added), suggesting that the bestowal of this "power" is a future event.

14. Bruce, *Gospel of John*, 38.

15. The first clause of this verse is an allusion to John 3:16.

16. Compare Mosiah 5:7.

17. *The Gospel According to John I–XII*, ed. Raymond E. Brown, vol. 29 of the Anchor Bible Series (Garden City, NY: Doubleday, 1966), 11.

18. Augustine, *On the Psalms*, 50.2.

19. Richard Lyman Bushman, *Joseph Smith: Rough Stone Rolling* (New York: Knopf, 2005), 195.

20. Although section 76 does not employ strict Johannine language per se, "The Vision," as previously noted, was apparently inspired by Joseph's translation of John 5:29. See *History of the Church*, 1:245.

21. *The Words of Joseph Smith*, ed. Lyndon W. Cook and Andrew F. Ehat (Orem, UT: Grandin Book, 1991), 15.

22. Although space did not allow an appropriate analysis, another verse where John interacts with the revelation and deals with the question of exaltation is D&C 98:18: "Let not your hearts be troubled; for in my Father's house are many mansions, and I have prepared a place for you; and where my Father and I am, there ye shall be also." Compare John 14:2.

23. Smith later declared, "Except a man and his wife enter into an everlasting covenant and be married for eternity, while in this probation, by the power and authority of the Holy Priesthood, they will cease to increase when they die; that is, they will not have any children after the resurrection." *History of the Church*, 5:391.

24. Joseph Fielding Smith stated, "Those who are married in the temple for all time and eternity obtain the blessing of *eternal lives*. I put stress on *eternal lives*. Eternal life is God's life, that is, to be like him. *Eternal lives* means eternal increase—the continuation, as the revelation says, of the seeds forever. To be married outside of the temple is for time only." *Answers to Gospel Questions* (Salt Lake City: Deseret Book, 1963), 4:197.

25. *Words of Joseph Smith*, 361.

26. Robert L. Millet, "What the Bible Means to Latter-day Saints," in *The King James Bible and the Restoration*, ed. Kent P. Jackson (Provo, UT: Religious Studies Center, Brigham Young University, 2011), 5.

15

Treasures, Witches, and Ancient Inhabitants (D&C 111)

Craig James Ostler

After more than 175 years, a certain mystique continues to surround the revelation in Doctrine and Covenants section 111.[1] This is partly due to evidence that the Prophet Joseph Smith and his companions Oliver Cowdery, Sidney Rigdon, and Hyrum Smith traveled in the summer of 1836 to Salem, Massachusetts, where the revelation was received, seeking to find hidden treasure. Both the reminiscence of a disaffected former member of the Church, Ebenezer Robinson, and collaboration in a letter written by Joseph to his wife Emma[2] indicate that a man named Burgess informed the Prophet that he knew of money available in Salem, Massachusetts. According to Robinson, Burgess "stated that a large amount of money had been secreted in the cellar of a certain house in Salem, Massachusetts, which had belonged to a widow, and he thought he was the only person now living, who had knowledge of it, or to the location of the house."[3] Sadly, misusing the events surrounding the revelation received in Salem and misconstruing the results of the journey, enemies of the Prophet have helped fulfill Moroni's warning that Joseph's "name should be had for good and evil among all nations . . . or that

---

Craig James Ostler is a professor of Church history and doctrine at Brigham Young University.

it should be both good and evil spoken of among all people" (Joseph Smith—History 1:33). In the "notes" section of *A Comprehensive History of the Church*, B. H. Roberts referred to the Salem trip. "Another circumstance connected with this Kirtland period," Elder Roberts explained, "and in a way related to the financial difficulties of the times, is dwelt upon by anti-'Mormon' writers to the disadvantage of the Prophet and of the church."[4] Since the time of B. H. Roberts's *Comprehensive History*, misunderstandings of the Salem trip and its subsequent revelation have continued to be cited in discrediting the Prophet.[5]

A day or two after arriving in Salem, Massachusetts, Sunday, August 6, 1836, Joseph received the revelation recorded as section 111 in our current Doctrine and Covenants. The Lord assured those who had traveled to Salem, "I have much treasure in the city for you, for the benefit of Zion" (D&C 111:2). In addition, he promised that "its wealth pertaining to gold and silver shall be yours" (D&C 111:4). References in the revelation to treasure have only served to place greater emphasis on treasure seeking. For example, several articles and commentaries examining section 111 have addressed the Prophet's debts and involvement in looking for buried treasure, focusing on the Lord's seeming play on words as he referred to "treasure," "gold and silver," and "debts" (D&C 111:2, 4–5, 10). Dr. Donald Q. Cannon summarized the expedition's experience: "Apparently they divided their time between preaching, sightseeing, and looking for the treasure."[6]

Those that traveled to Salem were desperate to pay their debts and made the journey to this eastern seaboard city to find treasure. Nevertheless, the Prophet and his companions spent precious little time during the month they lodged in Salem looking for buried treasure, and preaching was not the focus of their journey either. Further, a closer examination of the revelation suggests that subsequent visits to museums, libraries, and historical sites in Salem and the surrounding areas had greater import than sightseeing. Indeed, much might be gained from focusing on the Lord's statement that "there are more treasures than one for you in this city" (D&C 111:10). For example, there are significant questions to be answered regarding the time that the Prophet and his companions spent in Salem fulfilling the Lord's commands to "inquire diligently concerning the more ancient inhabitants and founders of this city" (D&C 111:9). The Lord specifically commanded these brethren to "tarry in this place, and in the regions round about" (D&C 111:7), apparently, to fulfill this command. This article will seek to answer questions concerning (1) the context of the journey to Salem, (2) what the Lord commanded Joseph and his companions to do, (3) what they accomplished, and (4) the lessons they learned from their time in Salem and the surrounding country.

Context of the Revelation: Concerns for Debt

Joseph Smith traveled to Salem, Massachusetts, in July through the first week of August 1836, while on a journey from Kirtland, Ohio, to the eastern seaboard.[7] At that time, heavy debt weighed upon the leaders of the Church due to loans secured to purchase land, to acquire goods for the mercantile establishments of the Church, and to build the Kirtland Temple. In addition, in 1833, when mobs expelled the Saints from Jackson County, Missouri, they also took control of the Church-owned printing press and goods from the Church-owned store. Earlier, leaders in Ohio and in Missouri formed a joint business to manage the Church's assets. This joint business was given the name of the United Firm.[8] Joseph counted on both of the Missouri enterprises—the printing press and the store—to raise funds to help repay creditors in New York City. With the loss of the income-producing printing press and store commodities, the Church was unable to pay for the goods that members of the United Firm had purchased on credit. In 1834 the Lord temporarily relieved the Church leaders in Kirtland of responsibility to pay the Missouri debt by dissolving the United Firm and commanding them to organize into two separate orders "called the United Order of the Stake of Zion, the city of Kirtland," and "the United Order of the City of Zion" (D&C 104:48). Furthermore, the Lord commanded Joseph Smith to "write speedily to New York and write according to that which shall be dictated by my Spirit; and I will soften the hearts of those to whom you are in debt, that it shall be taken away out of their minds to bring affliction upon you" (D&C 104:81). Notwithstanding his promise to soften the hearts of the United Firm's creditors, the Lord also made it very clear that "it is my will that you shall pay all your debts" (D&C 104:78). Thus, members of the United Firm in Kirtland had the moral responsibility to pay back the debt, albeit they had been given a reprieve for a short time. Accordingly, Joseph and other leaders planned a trip to meet with their creditors in New York City and make arrangements for payment. As cited previously, Ebenezer Robinson asserted that in the summer of 1836, "a brother in the Church, by the name of Burgess, had come to Kirtland and stated that a large amount of money had been secreted in the cellar of a certain house in Salem, Massachusetts, which had belonged to a widow, and he thought he was the only person now living, who had knowledge of it, or to the location of the house."[9]

The report of prospective Salem treasure must have appeared tailor-made for the trip to meet with creditors in New York City. The Church leaders could provide their creditors with assurances of payment and then to travel to Salem, where they could, providentially, obtain the funds to pay their debts.

As planned, before arriving in Salem, Joseph, his brother Hyrum, Oliver Cowdery, and Sidney Rigdon traveled to New York City to meet with creditors. "From New York we continued our journey to Providence, on board a steamer," the Prophet wrote, "from thence to Boston, by steam cars, and arrived in Salem, Massachusetts, early in August, where we hired a house, and occupied the same during the month, teaching the people from house to house, and preaching publicly, as opportunity presented; visiting occasionally, sections of the surrounding country."[10] According to Robinson, after arriving, "Brother Burgess met them in Salem, evidently according to appointment, but time had wrought such a change that he could not for a certainty point out the house, and soon left. They however, found a house which they felt was the right one, and hired it."[11] Apparently, Robinson had some misinformation. On August 19, 1836, Joseph wrote from Salem to his wife Emma in Kirtland, Ohio, "We have found the house since Bro. Burgess left us, very luckily and providentially, as we had one spell been most discouraged. The house is occupied, and it will require much care and patience to rent or buy it."[12] It is evident, since the group had been in Salem for more than two weeks before the letter was written and left soon thereafter, that the home in which the treasure was supposedly secreted and the house hired by Joseph and his companions could not be one and the same as asserted by Robinson. In addition, the *Essex Register* reported that the Prophet and his companions did not actually rent a home, let alone the alleged treasure home, but rather referred to "the tenement leased by them in Union Street."[13] Thus there may also be other aspects of Robinson's report that are not entirely accurate.

The Lord's Commandment: Revelation in Salem (D&C 111)

As aforesaid, the revelation published as Doctrine and Covenants 111 came soon after the Prophet's arrival in Salem, Massachusetts. The Lord assured Joseph and his companions, "I . . . am not displeased with your coming this journey, notwithstanding your follies" (D&C 111:1). Furthermore, he acknowledged their concerns regarding their debts and promised, "I will give you power to pay them" (D&C 111:5). Rather than summarily dismissing them to return home to Kirtland, Ohio, the Lord commanded them to "tarry in this place, and in the regions round about" (D&C 111:7). Most importantly, he instructed them to "inquire diligently concerning the more ancient inhabitants and founders of this city; For there are more treasures than one for you in this city" (D&C 111:9–10). Past articles and commentaries on this revelation have made assertions that tied the Lord's command to inquire "concerning the more ancient inhabitants" (D&C 111:9) to genealogical research regarding the Prophet's ancestors, who lived in nearby Topsfield, Massachusetts.[14] However, as Kenneth W. Godfrey noted, there are no evidences or references provided in the notes of these articles for this assertion.[15] On the other hand, there is ample evidence that the brethren that received the revelation identified the "more ancient inhabitants" as the Puritans, who founded the city of Salem, Massachusetts.[16] Consequently, Joseph and his companions set out to learn the history of Salem and the surrounding areas.

Inquiring Diligently Concerning the Ancient Inhabitants and Founders of Salem[17]

Perhaps Salem is best, or rather worst, known for the court trials held there accusing citizens of being witches. In 1692, reports from a group of young girls fueled an inquisition to rid the town of evil influences in which they accused innocent people of using the power of the devil to torment them. Local religious and municipal leaders joined this misdirected crusade, which led to the deaths of more than twenty individuals and horror for more than two hundred who were accused of being in league with Satan. Eventually, the girls confessed their fatal mischief and expressed sorrow for their roles in the tragedy. For years a specter of shame hung over the families of those involved in sentencing innocent people to death.[18]

During the approximately three weeks that they remained in the Salem area, in obedience to the Lord's command, Joseph and his companions learned much regarding the early history of New England. For example, they visited the East India Marine Society Museum in Salem. The guest register for the museum exhibits the names of Oliver Cowdery, Sidney Ridgon, and Joseph Smith. Cowdery and Rigdon visited the museum on August 6, 1836, and Joseph on August 9, 1836. Both visits were within one week of receiving the Lord's instructions to inquire after the ancient inhabitants of Salem.[19] They also traveled to the nearby countryside rich with tales of religious fervor and patriotism.

As editor of the Church's newspaper, Oliver Cowdery wrote to his brother[20] in the Kirtland, Ohio, area concerning the corruption and wickedness that he witnessed in traveling to the East Coast before they arrived in Salem. In addition, Oliver Cowdery addressed the activities and information they learned in and around Salem. Two of Oliver's letters were published in the *Latter Day Saints' Messenger and Advocate* concerning his experiences and thoughts during the time he spent in and around Salem, Massachusetts. These letters offer insight into the locations visited and the lessons learned from obeying the Lord's command to inquire after the founders of Salem and its ancient inhabitants. "During my tarry in this country," Oliver wrote, "I have visited Salem, 15 miles from this city [Boston]. I viewed the hill, immediately to the north-west of the town, on which they used, in olden times when they were very righteous, to hang people for the alleged crime of witchcraft—it still bears the name of 'witch hill,' and looks down upon this ancient town like a monument set up to remind after generations of the folly of their fathers."[21]

In addition, it is evident that Oliver and possibly other members of the party visited the library or purchased books on the history of Salem's "ancient inhabitants." In the following lengthy quotation from the *Messenger and Advocate*, Oliver gave attention and detail to this aspect of the visit to Salem. Based on his descriptions, it becomes clear that Oliver considered the "ancient inhabitants" mentioned in the revelation to refer to the early Puritan settlers in Salem. Furthermore, the time that Oliver dedicated to researching the ancient inhabitants and his lengthy letter documenting his research manifest that he gave great importance to his findings. He wrote,

> This witch business began in 1691, and was so effectually carried on for about two years that the innocent blood of hundreds moistened the earth to gratify the vile ambition of jealous mortals.
>
> It may not be wholly uninteresting to the readers of the Messenger, to give a short account of this disgraceful affair, as found in some of the ancient writings on that subject. I am aware that the *fact* is familiar with us all, but the *matter* of fact is not. The first appearance of any thing of this nature, was in the family of a priest, by the name of Parris, who, it is said, could not make money fast enough by merchandizing, therefore undertook the traffic in men's souls—he lived in Salem. After preaching about two years, he contrived to get "a grant from a part of the town, that the house and land occupied, and which had been allotted by the whole people to the ministry, should be and remain to him, &c. as his own estate in fee simple."[22] At this many of the good people revolted, upon which strife and contention were stirred up. Soon a number of Mr. Parris' children were sorely tormented—bewitched—thrown down—scratched—pinched—bitten—squeezed, and many other grievous things, by some of the neighbors. The result was, prosecution, imprisonment and death. Remember, by the way, that none of these were afflicted by corporeal hands, but could see the persons' spirits or appearances coming to, and tormenting them—sometimes in the form of cats, dogs, hogs, &c.
>
> A deeper laid plan for the purpose of satiating revenge, upon such a principle, I think I never read of. In the family of this Parris, resided an Indian and his wife: the latter, as appears, was the first complained of by Parris' children. She was committed to prison, and her master (P) refusing to pay the fees, suffered her to be sold for the same. The account is not a little astonishing, while it discloses the grand secret of the matter. Speaking of her being sold for the fees, the historian says . . .[23]

Oliver proceeded to quote liberally—four columns of newsprint—without identifying who "the historian" might be.

Further investigation has revealed that Oliver Cowdery had access to Robert Calef's volume, *More Wonders of the Invisible World*. Calef challenged the presumptions and accusations in the previously published volume by Cotton Mather, the similarly named *Wonders of the Invisible World*. Originally published in London in 1700, Calef's work had been reprinted in Salem in 1823.[24] Thus, while in Salem, Oliver either spent considerable time with a volume from the library, copying page after page into his notes, or he purchased a personal copy for himself. It seems clear that Oliver saw his searching this volume as fulfillment of the Lord's command to inquire after the ancient inhabitants of the city.

Oliver concluded his extensive quotations from Calef's work with a few observations and additional notes: "I presume your patience is exhausted in reading this horrid affair," he wrote, "one which spreads, and must, while the account remains upon the page of history, or in the minds of men, a dark gloom over Salem, with all its modern politeness, refinement and religion."[25]

Cowdery further wrote of nearby locations that he visited. From his references to other areas and events, it appears that he, and possibly Joseph, Hyrum, and Sidney, visited Lexington, the Bunker Hill monument (then being erected),[26] the State House in Boston, the navy yard in Charleston, and Cambridge, Massachusetts. After visiting the Charleston navy yard, Oliver recounted, "From this we went to Bunker hill, viewed the ground which, on the 17th of June, 1775, was drenched with blood for the liberty I enjoy. . . . The history of this battle is so familiar in the minds of the readers of the Messenger, that it would be occupying space unnecessarily, to give even a detail; but judge of the feelings of my heart, when I viewed, from the top of the monument, the entire theater on which was fought one of the most important battles ever recorded in history."[27]

Lessons Learned in Obeying the Revelation: Visiting the "Areas Round About" Salem

From visits to the surrounding areas, Oliver gained additional understanding of the harm that a misplaced religious zeal might inflict on others. He shared with readers of the *Messenger and Advocate*, "In this place and in Boston, you know, the poor Baptists and Quakers, suffered, also, because their religion was better than their neighbors', of the good *steady* habits order. Undoubtedly you have read of their sufferings and are prepared to decide upon the injustice of their persecutors as well as the cause." Oliver referred to the area around Boston as "the cradle of liberty—where the first germ of American independence was seen to sprout."[28]

One particular visit to the vicinity of Charleston made a poignant impression upon the brethren during their time in Salem. They visited the ruins of the recently burned Catholic Ursuline Convent. Built in an area of ardent Protestantism, the compound included a convent, a school, a chapel, gardens, and other buildings. Most of the students at the private school were from Protestant families. Anti-Catholic sentiment, fired by rumors of nuns held against their will, led to mob-inspired terrorism, ultimately resulting in the August 11, 1834, burning of the entire compound. After the Church leaders walked through the grounds and observed the destruction, Oliver Cowdery wrote his thoughts.

> It was a religious persecution—a disgraceful, shameful religious persecution—one, or more, religious societies rising up against another. Is this religion? The good people here, being very tenacious of right, as well as the tradition of their ancestors, thought it doing God service to burn a Catholic convent, because the Catholic religion was different from their own. The Author of my existence knows the sorrowing of my heart, on the reflection that our country has come to this, that the weak must be trodden down by the strong, and disorder, confusion and terror, must distract our land and sow the discordant seeds of party strife and party animosity in the hearts of ignorant men, led on by infatuated priests, to overwhelm the continent with blood, and spread destruction and devastation throughout our happy asylum, and expose us to the fire, the sword, the rack and to death! I confess I retired from this scene of mobbery with a heavier heart than from the far-famed Bunker hill, rendered doubly so, by the patriotism, virtue, integrity, connected with the righteousness of the cause in which our fathers died![29]

History of the Church includes the following summary of the time spent in and around Salem: "[we] arrived in Salem, Massachusetts, early in August, where we hired a house, and occupied the same during the month, teaching the people from house to house, and preaching publicly, as opportunity presented; visiting occasionally, sections of the surrounding country, which are rich in the history of the Pilgrim Fathers of New England, in Indian warfare, religious superstition, bigotry, persecution, and learned ignorance."[30]

The Prophet Joseph Smith was equally affected by this visit to the Ursuline Convent. Expressing his thoughts and feelings regarding that experience, he wrote,

> Well did the Savior say concerning such, "by their fruits you shall know them." And if the wicked mob who destroyed the Charleston convent, and the cool, calculating religious lookers on, who inspired their hearts with deeds of infamy, do not arise, and redress the wrong, and restore the injured four-fold, they in turn, will receive of the measure they have meted out till the just indignation of a righteous God is satisfied. When will man cease to war with man, and wrest from him his sacred rights of worshiping his God according as his conscience dictates? Holy Father, hasten the day.[31]

Conclusion

The journey to Salem, Massachusetts, brought forth fruits much more valuable than treasure hunting. On one hand, it is difficult to determine with absolute certainty this journey's influence on the Prophet Joseph Smith and the other three leaders of the Church. On the other hand, it appears to be clear that they had many opportunities to learn about the need for the Latter-day Saints to welcome into their communities individuals of goodwill from all faiths or even of no membership to any particular faith. The lessons of justice, equality, fairness, tolerance, and inclusion, so important to the fledgling restored Church, were further imprinted upon the minds of its leaders during their time in Salem.

It appears highly likely that the Lord sought to insure that these brethren learned the distinction between intolerance for wickedness and tolerance for differing religious beliefs. Later in Nauvoo, the Prophet would write to welcome individuals of all religious persuasions or no religious persuasions to join with the Saints in building up that city[32]—a city that had similar aspirations to the Salem of the founders and ancient inhabitants about whom the Lord commanded Joseph to inquire. The Salem dream was shattered when its early inhabitants became overzealous in their attempts to establish a New Jerusalem, persecuting innocent people. Evidently, the Lord hoped to warn and educate the early leaders of his Church concerning the tendency of some in religious societies to establish their own righteousness by excessively crusading against real and supposed evils among them. When this occurs, innocent individuals suffer at their hands and religion becomes a stink in the land. The kingdom of God has needed and will continue to need to put into practice these important lessons. Consequently, the revelation in Doctrine and Covenants section 111 has had more influence on the building up of the kingdom of God than it has previously been given credit for. The Lord has worked and will continue to work by small and simple means to bring to pass his purposes (see Alma 37:6–7; D&C 64:33). In summation, there continue to be more treasures than one to be gleaned from the revelation received in Salem, Massachusetts.

Notes

1. Section 111 was not included in the Doctrine and Covenants until the 1876 edition. It was first published in the *Deseret News* (December 25, 1852). See Lyndon W. Cook, *The Revelations of the Prophet Joseph Smith* (Salt Lake City: Deseret Book, 1985), 221.

2. Joseph wrote, "With regard to the great object of our mission, you will be anxious to know. We have found the house since Bro. Burgess left us, very luckily and providentially, as we had one spell been most discouraged. The house is occupied, and it will require much care and patience to rent or buy it. We think we shall be able to effect it; if not now within the course of a few months. We think we shall be at home about the middle of September." Joseph Smith, "To Emma Smith, August 19, 1836," *The Personal Writings of Joseph Smith*, comp. and ed. Dean C. Jessee (Salt Lake City: Deseret Book, 1984), 349–50.

3. Ebenezer Robinson, "Items of Personal History of the Editor. Including Some Items of Church History Not Generally Known," *The Return* 1, no. 7 (1889): 105, http://www.sidneyrigdon.com/RigWrit/M&A/Return1.htm. Robinson wrote that he left the Church over the seeming preoccupation of Church leaders with temporal financial concerns.

4. B. H. Roberts, *A Comprehensive History of the Church of Jesus Christ of Latter-day Saints* (Provo, UT: Brigham Young University Press, 1965), 1:410.

5. The main published sources of criticism of the Prophet's trip to Salem are Fawn Brodie, *No Man Knows My History: The Life of Joseph Smith, the Mormon Prophet* (New York: Alfred A. Knopf, 1945), 192–93; Jerald and Sandra Tanner, *Mormonism—Shadow or Reality?* (Salt Lake City: Modern Microfilm Company, 1972), 49; and Richard N. Ostling and Joan K. Ostling, *Mormon America: The Power and the Promise* (New York: HarperCollins, 1999), 31. Brodie asserts that upon hearing of treasure in Salem, Massachusetts, Joseph Smith was overcome by an irresistible force to treasure hunt and left his prophetic duties to look for buried gold. She also mistakenly asserts that Joseph considered this a "missionary tour." Jerald and Sandra Tanner refer to section 111 as

"The Treasure Hunt Revelation" and suggest that any explanation of the revelation is "an attempt to keep from facing reality." The Ostlings imaginatively assert that Joseph hoped to use a seer stone to tell him where the reported treasure lay, but "the seer stone failed again, and his money-digging was no more successful than before."

6. Donald Q. Cannon, "Joseph Smith in Salem: D&C 111," *Studies in Scripture*, vol. 1, *The Doctrine and Covenants*, ed. Robert L. Millet and Kent P. Jackson (Salt Lake City: Deseret Book, 1989), 435. In citing Cannon's work, I in no way wish to disparage his research, as he has been an esteemed colleague in the department of Church history and doctrine at Brigham Young University and graciously opened and shared with me all of his research files on the Prophet's journey to Salem, Massachusetts.

7. "Section 111, received on Sunday, 6 August 1836 . . . departed for Kirtland, about 25 August 1836. . . . [and] arrived back in Kirtland sometime in September 1836." Lyndon W. Cook, *The Revelations of the Prophet Joseph Smith* (Salt Lake City: Deseret Book, 1985), 221. Also see *History of the Church of Jesus Christ of Latter-day Saints*, ed. B. H. Roberts, 2nd ed. rev. (Salt Lake City: Deseret Book, 1973), 2:464–66.

8. See Craig J. Ostler, "The Laws of Consecration, Stewardship, and Tithing," *Sperry Symposium Classics: The Doctrine and Covenants* (Salt Lake City: Deseret Book; Provo, UT: Religious Studies Center and Brigham Young University, 2004), 155–75; Max H. Parkin, "Joseph Smith and the United Firm: The Growth and Decline of the Church's First Master Plan of Business and Finance, Ohio and Missouri, 1832–1834," *BYU Studies* 46, no. 3 (2007): 5–66; Lyndon W. Cook, *Joseph Smith and the Law of Consecration* (Provo, UT: Grandin Book, 1985).

9. Robinson, *Return*, 105. Ebenezer indicated that "[they] saw the brother Burgess, but Don Carlos Smith told [them] with regard to the hidden treasure."

10. *History of the Church*, 2:464. Interestingly, no mention of the treasure is made in *History of the Church*. On the other hand, Joseph made reference to the house and Brother Burgess in his letter to Emma (see endnote 3).

11. Robinson, *Return*, 106.

12. Smith, "To Emma Smith," 350.

13. *Essex Register* (Salem, MA), August 25, 1836. The tenement, a complex of apartments identified with that leased by the brethren, evidently still remains and is located on the northwest corner of Union Street as it makes a *T* with Herbert Street. As such, it does not meet the description of a home in which a treasure was hidden. There is only one tenement building on Union Street.

14. See Cannon, "Joseph Smith in Salem: D&C 111," 432–37; Kenneth W. Godfrey, "More Treasures Than One," in *Hearken O Ye People: Discourses on the Doctrine and Covenants* (Sandy, UT: Randall Book, 1984), 191–202; Leaun Otten, "Applying the Doctrine and Covenants to Daily Life," in *Sidney B. Sperry Symposium*, January 27, 1979, 37–49; Hyrum M. Smith and Janne M. Sjodahl, *Doctrine and Covenants Commentary*, rev. ed. (Salt Lake City: Deseret Book, 1958), 729; Sidney B. Sperry, *Doctrine and Covenants Compendium* (Salt Lake City: Bookcraft, 1960), 610; Stephen E. Robinson and H. Dean Garrett, *A Commentary on the Doctrine and Covenants* (Salt Lake City: Deseret Book, 2005), 4:76; Joseph Fielding McConkie and Craig J. Ostler, *Revelations of the Restoration* (Salt Lake City: Deseret Book, 2000), 897; Steven C. Harper, *Making Sense of the*

Doctrine and Covenants (Salt Lake City: Deseret Book, 2008), 412–13; Richard Lyman Bushman, *Joseph Smith: Rough Stone Rolling* (New York: Alfed A. Knopf, 2005), 328–29.

15. Godfrey, "More Treasures Than One," 196, 203n23. I found that most authors quote one another in a circular fashion. The earliest inference to the ancient inhabitants referring to genealogical research in the Smith line that I have been able to locate is that of Hyrum M. Smith and Janne M. Sjodahl, *Doctrine and Covenants Commentary*, cited above. It appears that all others have taken their lead from Smith and Sjodahl's work.

16. In addition to Oliver Cowdery's references to Salem in "olden times" and "this ancient town," I found other publications that referred to the homes and cemetery of the early Puritans as an "ancient house," "ancient leanto houses," and the "ancient burying ground." See *Essex Antiquarian* (Salem, MA), February, July, August, and September, 1901. Also, Webster's 1828 dictionary defines *ancient* as follows: "*Ancient* is opposed to *modern*. . . . When we speak of a thing that existed formerly, which has ceased to exist, we commonly use *ancient*." Noah Webster, *An American Dictionary of the English Language*, facsimile of the 1828 edition (San Francisco: Foundation for American Christian Education, 1995), "ancient."

17. Puritan Roger Conant is credited as being the founder of Salem. The Prophet and the other leaders who traveled to Salem left no writings mentioning Conant nor any other specific founders. It may be that the Lord referred to "the more ancient inhabitants and founders of this city" as a group and not as individuals for which to search. On the other hand, important lessons can be learned from a study of Roger Conant's life. His steadfast faith in the establishment and even the naming of Salem as the "city of peace," is worthy of study. The standard biography of Conant's life is Clifford K. Shipton, *Roger Conant: A Founder of Massachusetts* (Cambridge, MA: Harvard University Press, 1945). Modern historian Jim McAllister has also provided insightful tribute to the efforts of Roger Conant. See Jim McAllister, *Salem: From Naumkeag to Witch City* (Beverly, MA: Commonwealth Editions, 2000); Joseph Flibbert et al., *Salem: Cornerstone of a Historic City* (Beverly, MA: Commonwealth Editions, 1999); and Jim McAllister, "Roger Conant: Salem's Founder," http://www.salemweb.com/tales/conant.shtml.

18. For detailed accounts and analysis of the Salem witch trials, see *Salem-Village Witchcraft: A Documentary Record of Local Conflict in Colonial New England*, ed. Paul Boyer and Stephen Nissenbaum (Boston: Northeastern University Press, 1993); and Frances Hill, *A Delusion of Satan* (Cambridge, MA: Da Capo Press, 1995).

19. See Alexander L. Baugh, "A Historical Note on Joseph Smith's 1836 Visit to the East India Marine Society Museum in Salem, Massachusetts," *Mormon Historical Studies* 11, no. 1 (2010):143–50.

20. Likely, this was Oliver's eldest brother, Warren, who shouldered much of Oliver's responsibilities as an editor for the *Latter Day Saints' Messenger and Advocate* while Oliver journeyed to New England.

21. Oliver Cowdery, "Prospectus," *Latter Day Saints' Messenger and Advocate*, (October 1836), 388. "No one knows for certain where nineteen people condemned as witches were hanged. But all the evidence contained in the surviving records, including death warrants, Samuel Sewall's diary, and Robert Calef's *More Wonders of the Invisible World*, points to the lower ledges of what is now called Gallows Hill." Frances

Hill, *Hunting for Witches: A Visitor's Guide to the Salem Witch Trials* (Beverly, MA: Commonwealth Editions, 2002), 93.

22. Quoted from Robert Calef, *More Wonders of the Invisible World, or The Wonders of The Invisible World Displayed* (London, 1700, reprinted Salem, MA: John D. and T. C. Cushing, Jr. for Cushing and Appleton, 1823), 187.

23. Cowdery, "Prospectus," 388–89.

24. I am indebted to Richard Lloyd Anderson for identifying that Oliver Cowdery quoted Robert Calef in his letters published in the *Messenger and Advocate*. Richard Lloyd Anderson, "Joseph Smith's Journeys," *Church Almanac 2006* (Salt Lake City: Deseret News, 2005), 146. Cowdery quotes from Calef, *More Wonders of the Invisible World*, 187, 189, 192, and, nearly in their entirety, 197–206. A copy of the 1823 reprint in Salem, Massachusetts, is located in the Harold B. Lee Library, Brigham Young University, Provo, UT.

25. Cowdery, "Prospectus," 391.

26. Cowdery identified that the monument had reached eighty feet in height at the time of his visit. The granite obelisk currently stands 221 feet tall, honoring the group of bedraggled farmers who fought the British troops in the first major battle of the Revolutionary War, June 17, 1775. It is located across the Charles River from Boston, on top of Breed's Hill.

27. Cowdery, "Prospectus," 392.

28. Cowdery, "Prospectus," 391.

29. Cowdery, "Prospectus," 393. Oliver took in the principles of religious and personal liberty like fire in his soul. He wrote to his brother and to the Saints regarding the sacred rights of individuals. I wonder if this fire burned out of control in his defense of his actions as he faced excommunication from the kingdom less than two years later in Missouri. Note that his defense for selling his lands in Jackson County is couched in terms of his rights as an American citizen trumping his covenants as a consecrated member of the Church of Jesus Christ.

30. *History of the Church*, 2:464.

31. *History of the Church*, 2:465. No one was ever brought to justice and held responsible for the burning of the convent.

32. *History of the Church*, 4:273.

16

From Obscurity to Scripture: Joseph F. Smith's Vision of the Redemption of the Dead

Mary Jane Woodger

I was one of those who casually participated in one of the most significant acts of common consent of my generation. I excuse my lack of understanding because I was young when in the April 1976 general conference I sustained and approved the actions of the First Presidency and Council of the Twelve in adding two new sections to the Pearl of Great Price, formally enlarging the official body of the standard works of the Church.[1] Though Elder Boyd K. Packer of the Quorum of the Twelve called that time a day of "great events relating to the scriptures,"[2] my reaction to the addition of scripture was nonchalant. I was not alone in that response. Indeed, Elder Packer felt that most Church members had the same reaction. He said: "I was surprised, and I think all of the Brethren were surprised, at how casually that announcement of two additions to the standard works was received by the Church. But we will live to sense the significance of it; we will tell our grandchildren and our great-grandchildren, and we will record in our diaries, that we were on the earth and remember when that took place."[3] This paper will seek to attach

---

Mary Jane Woodger is a professor of Church history and doctrine at Brigham Young University.

the proper significance to the inclusion of Joseph F. Smith's vision of the redemption of the dead in the standard works.

Today, more is known about how this scriptural passage came to be than what is known about probably any other section found in the Doctrine and Covenants. Most members are aware of the circumstances surrounding President Joseph F. Smith when he received this revelation. During his final illness in October 1918, President Smith was stricken by age and was undoubtedly pondering the recent death of his son and other family members. With his own looming death, which took place a few weeks after, he may have been "[wondering] about the nature of the ministry that would be his in the spirit world."[4]

There has been some research about the global and personal context surrounding Joseph F. Smith's vision.[5] Latter-day Saint scholars Thomas G. Alexander, Richard E. Bennett, and George S. Tate have described the context in which the revelation was received, citing the influence of the Great War, the 1918 influenza pandemic, and President Joseph F. Smith's personal experiences with death as events that brought him to ponder the significant passages of 2 Peter. This paper, however, will examine the process by which this vision was eventually canonized as part of the standard works. While the vision affirms the great love of God, the timing of the vision's canonization also clarifies and reiterates God's great love for his children, especially his love for his valiant and obedient children who, as members of The Church of Jesus Christ of Latter-day Saints, shoulder the responsibility of performing ordinances for the dead.

The text of Joseph F. Smith's vision of the redemption of the dead sets forth with remarkable clarity the manner in which the Savior before his Resurrection declared liberty to the captives in spirit prison. This revelation revises the Bible: Christ himself did not go personally to the spirits in prison; rather, he organized others to teach. It also discloses the pattern by which the doctrines of the gospel are shared with those who have died without that knowledge. The vision itself answered many questions that had perplexed not only Latter-day Saint communities but the entire Christian world. Joseph F. Smith's vision of the redemption of the dead answers many difficult theological questions, such as, what becomes of those who die without the opportunity to accept Christ while they lived? Of particular interest to Saints is the message of how the gospel is taught to the dead in the spirit world. Many religious scholars have made serious efforts at analyzing and expanding on the vision's text, which answers those questions.[6]

The vision of the redemption of the dead went through an incubation period until it was formally added to the Pearl of Great Price, and later to the Doctrine and Covenants. Church members had to mature in doctrines involving temple work before they could comprehend the responsibility to their kindred dead implicated in Joseph F. Smith's vision. Later, General Authorities began referring to the doctrine in the vision in general conference addresses. The revelation was then taught, accepted, and ultimately applied by Church membership. When technological advancements made genealogical research practical, the Saints could more fully live by the teachings in President Smith's revelation, and it was canonized as part of the standard works.

The research provided in this paper is "a thorough study of the historical process that brought this doctrinal statement out of obscurity and into the realm of modern Mormon scripture."[7] This study centers on the use of this vision by General Authorities in general conference, exploring who quoted the text, the context of use, and the interpretation of the doctrinal insights shared.

Section 138 of the Doctrine and Covenants now serves as one of the foundational documents for the current practices and doctrines of the vicarious temple ordinances for The Church of Jesus Christ of Latter-day Saints. With this in mind, it is important to understand the process that took place from the announcement of the vision in 1918 to its canonization in 1976 and the use of the canonized version by General Authorities thereafter. This paper will explore the factors that led to the vision's canonization and will hypothesize why 1976 became the watershed year for the vision to become scripture. Making this revelation scripture before this time would have caused unnecessary hardship for the Saints, who lacked the technology and ability to accomplish the necessary family history work.

Announcement

Joseph F. Smith never described his vision in general conference. In October 1918, most Saints did not expect to see their prophet take the stand at general conference, since the prophet "[had] been undergoing a siege of very serious illness for the last five months."[8] At the time, Joseph F. Smith was too ill to speak very long. However, it appears President Smith had every intention of sharing his vision at a future time when he was more capable of standing before a congregation. He said, "I shall postpone until some future time, the Lord being willing, my attempt to tell you some of the things that are in my mind, and that dwell in my heart. I have not lived alone these five months. I have dwelt in the spirit of prayer, of supplication, of faith and of determination; and I have had my communication with the Spirit of the Lord continuously."[9] President Smith's entire address may have lasted a total of five minutes, and the above statement was all that he said regarding the future new scripture. According to his son Joseph Fielding Smith, the prophet expressed "the fact that during the past half-year he had been the recipient of numerous manifestations, some of which he had shared with his son, both before and following the conference."[10] At the close of the October 1918 conference, the prophet then dictated the vision of the redemption of the dead to Joseph Fielding Smith.[11]

Acknowledgment

On October 31, 1918, the dictated manuscript was presented to the First Presidency, the Quorum of the Twelve, and the Church Patriarch in a council meeting. At the time, the prophet was too ill to attend, so he asked his son Joseph Fielding Smith to read the revelation to the gathering. President Anthon H. Lund recorded in his journal, "In our Council Joseph F. Smith, Jr. read a revelation which his father had had in which he saw the spirits in Paradise and he also saw that Jesus organized a number of brethren to go and preach to the spirits in prison, but did not go himself. It was an interesting document and the apostles accepted it as true and from God."[12] Elder James E. Talmage also wrote about the event in his journal:

> Attended meeting of the First Presidency and the Twelve. Today President Smith who is still confined to his home by illness, sent to the Brethren the account of a vision through which, as he states, were revealed to him important facts relating to the work of the disembodied Savior in the realm of departed spirits, and of the missionary work in progress on the other side of the veil. By united action the Council of the Twelve, with the Counselors in the First Presidency, and the Presiding Patriarch accepted and endorsed the revelation as the word

of the Lord. President Smith's signed statement will be published in the next issue (December) of the Improvement Era, which is the organ of the Priesthood quorums of the church.[13]

The text of the vision then appeared in the November 30 edition of the *Deseret Evening News*. It was also printed "in the December *Improvement Era*, and in the January 1919 editions of the *Relief Society Magazine*, the *Utah Genealogical and Historical Magazine*, the *Young Woman's Journal*, and the *Millennial Star*."[14] General Authorities seemed anxious for the Saints to have access to the text of the vision in a timely manner.

President Smith's physical condition worsened, and on November 19, 1918, he died of pleuropneumonia. In his funeral address for President Joseph F. Smith, Elder Talmage mentioned the vision. He reminded the audience: "[President Smith] was permitted shortly before his passing to have a glimpse into the hereafter, and to learn where he would soon be at work. He was a preacher of righteousness on earth, he is a preacher of righteousness today. He was a missionary from his boyhood up, and he is a missionary today amongst those who have not yet heard the gospel, though they have passed from mortality into the spirit world. I cannot conceive of him as otherwise than busily engaged in the work of the Master."[15]

Obscurity

Considering the prominence of the vision during the last weeks of Joseph F. Smith's life and at his funeral, one has to wonder how it drifted into obscurity over the next twenty-seven years. There is no documentation of the vision being discussed by any Church leader in general conference until 1945. One has to wonder why the contemporaries of Joseph F. Smith, those closest to him, those who had sat in a council room and declared the revelation to be the word of God, did not speak of it in general conference. There must have been a reason for this neglect. Even the prophet's own son Joseph Fielding Smith did not, as a General Authority, use the vision in his sermons, though he included it in his father's biography (published in 1938) and also in the volume *Gospel Doctrine*.[16] Likewise, Elder Talmage did not discuss the vision in front of the Church congregations at general conference, despite speaking on the importance of genealogical work. It is interesting to note that a few weeks before Joseph F. Smith's announcement that he had had a vision, Elder Talmage had given a talk in the Tabernacle, where he said:

> The purpose ... is that of promoting among the members of the Church a vital, active interest in the compilation of genealogical records, in the collating of items of lineage and in the formulation of true family pedigrees, so that the relationship between ancestry and posterity may be determined and be made readily accessible....
>
> It is a notable fact that the last seven or eight decades have witnessed a development of interest in genealogical matters theretofore unknown in modern times.... There is ... an influence operative in the world, a spirit moving upon the people, in response to which the living are yearningly reaching backward to learn of their dead.[17]

And yet, after the prophet received a revelation just a few weeks later which detailed the activity of the spirit world, James E. Talmage never mentioned the vision in general conference.

After Joseph F. Smith's death, his contemporaries simply did not refer back to the vision of the redemption of the dead. During Heber J. Grant's administration, other pressing issues such as Prohibition, the Great Depression, and World War II dominated the teachings of the General Authorities. However, although World War II would take millions of lives, General Authorities said nothing about the revelation which so clearly outlined what would happen in the spirit world to the victims of the war.

Mentioning

It was not until April 1945 that Elder Joseph L. Wirthlin was the first to mention in general conference President Joseph F. Smith's vision of the redemption of the dead. Elder Wirthlin used the revelation to counter the teachings of Cardinal Gibbons, a leading ecclesiastical leader of the day. Cardinal Gibbons taught "that the ordinance of baptism was changed from that of immersion to sprinkling for convenience's sake." Elder Wirthlin used President Smith's vision to refute the premise of "convenience's sake" and emphasized the validity of modern prophetic revelation over human deduction. He also answered the question of what would happen to those not born of the water and the spirit. Elder Wirthlin emphasized that the vision of the redemption of the dead showed the great kindness of a Father in Heaven who instituted a plan "whereby all his children, be they alive or dead, might have the privilege of accepting or rejecting the gospel of his beloved Son."[18] This emphasis on God's kindness was the first time the vision of the redemption of the dead had been used as a metaphor in general conference.

It would be another nineteen years before President Smith's vision of the redemption of the dead would again be mentioned during general conference. In April 1964, Elder Marion G. Romney simply stated: "Another medium of revelation is visions. You know about Nephi's vision, the Prophet's great vision recorded in the 76th section of the Doctrine and Covenants, and President Joseph F. Smith's vision of work for the dead in the spirit world." It is interesting that Elder Romney said to the congregation, when referring to the vision, "you know about it" even though the vision had not been spoken of in general conference for nearly two decades.[19]

Two years later, in 1966, Elder Spencer W. Kimball spoke of continuing revelation, and merely said, "The visions of Wilford Woodruff and Joseph F. Smith would certainly be on a par with the visions of Peter and Paul."[20] Elder Kimball then declared that the vision of the redemption of the dead a "most comprehensive" example of the revelation available to Latter-day Saints.[21] In the three addresses listed above, the vision is mentioned but the text of the revelation itself is not quoted. At this time, General Authorities made no attempt to connect the vision's doctrine to the lives of the Saints.

Canonization

In October 1975, just six months before the vision's canonization, Elder Boyd K. Packer made an interesting introduction to his general conference address: "I have reason, my brothers and sisters, to feel very deeply about the subject that I have chosen for today, and to feel more than the usual need for your sustaining prayers, because of its very sacred nature."[22] One of the subjects Elder Packer felt strongly about was the vision of the redemption of the dead. For the first time in a general conference, a General Authority quoted directly from the vision. It had been fifty-seven years since the vision had been acknowledged to be the word of God; this was the first time words from the text were shared in conference.

This was also to be the first time that the vision would make the pivotal link to genealogical research. After quoting two verses from the future scripture, Elder Packer stated, "Here and now then, we move to accomplish the work to which we are assigned.... We gather the records of our kindred dead, indeed, the records of the entire human family; and in sacred temples in baptismal fonts designed as those were anciently, we perform these sacred ordinances." Elder Packer may have sensed that the vision would soon become scripture for the Church. He taught that only through temple ordinances can spirits be released from bondage, which ordinances can only be realized after conducting genealogical research.[23]

Joseph Fielding McConkie believes that his father, Elder Bruce R. McConkie of the Quorum of the Twelve, was instrumental in introducing the subject of the vision's canonization to the First Presidency. Joseph says that his father drew heavily upon the vision while writing his six-volume series on the Messiah: "Because of his position on the Scriptures Publication Committee and his love of the revelations of the Restoration, Elder McConkie was in a position to recommend that Joseph Smith's vision of the celestial kingdom and Joseph F. Smith's vision of the redemption of the dead be added to the canon of scripture." At the time, Elder McConkie also desired to add other historical manuscripts to the canon, including the Wentworth letter, the *Lectures on Faith*, the Doctrinal Exposition of the First Presidency on the Father and the Son issued in 1916, the King Follett Discourse, and a similar discourse given by the Prophet Joseph Smith in the Grove at Nauvoo in June of 1844. The fact that the vision of the redemption of the dead and Joseph Smith's vision of the celestial kingdom were canonized while the other manuscripts were not reveals the documents' importance as Latter-day Saint doctrine.[24]

Additionally, President Kimball's son Edward L. Kimball discloses that his father had "long wished for official recognition of two revelations dealing with the state of the dead" because of the significance they would accord genealogy work.[25] There is no doubt that President Kimball, in his sacred calling as prophet, felt a spirit of urgency to include these two visions in the standard works.

Non-Church stimuli at the time also incited Churchwide interest in the concept of life after death. With the publication of Alex Haley's book *Roots* in 1975 and its dramatization as a television miniseries in January 1977, interest in family history increased nationally. A "genealogy mania" was sweeping the nation, and the Church certainly had enhanced the reason that this surge of genealogy was taking place.[26] Bicentennial celebrations in 1976, which fostered national pride and presentations of local history, may have also contributed to the Saints' enthusiasm to accept the vision as scripture.[27]

At the April 1976 general conference, President N. Eldon Tanner, First Counselor in the First Presidency, stood at the pulpit and concluded the sustaining of the General Authorities and general officers of the Church by stating:

> At a meeting of the Council of the First Presidency and Quorum of the Twelve held in the Salt Lake Temple on March 25, 1976, approval was given to add to the Pearl of Great Price the following two revelations:
>
> First, a vision of the celestial kingdom given to Joseph Smith, the Prophet, in the Kirtland Temple, on January 21, 1836, which deals with the salvation of those who die without a knowledge of the gospel.
>
> And second, a vision given to President Joseph F. Smith in Salt Lake City, Utah, on October 3, 1918, showing the visit of the Lord Jesus Christ in the spirit world and setting forth the doctrine of the redemption of the dead.
>
> It is proposed that we sustain and approve this action and adopt these revelations as part of the standard works of The Church of Jesus Christ of Latter-day Saints.[28]

The congregation voted affirmatively, and the two visions were immediately added to the Pearl of Great Price. With that addition, the Pearl of Great Price received its first new scriptures since its own acceptance as a standard work in 1880. Five years later, these visions were transferred to the new 1981 edition of the Doctrine and Covenants as sections 137 and 138. Church administration followed the pattern of canonization of Doctrine and Covenants 87, which had also been a part of the Pearl of Great Price before it was moved to the Doctrine and Covenants. No changes were made in the text of section 138 as it moved from the Pearl of Great Price to the Doctrine and Covenants. Both sections 137 and 138 shed light on the salvation of the dead, so their addition to the scriptural canon was timely, arriving in "an era of unprecedented temple-building activity."[29] Elder McConkie noted the timeliness of the canonization of section 138 with regards to temple work for the dead. In the August 1976 *Ensign*, he related:

It is significant that the two revelations which the Brethren chose at this time to add to the canon of scripture both deal with that great and wondrous concept known and understood only by the Latter-day Saints: the doctrine of salvation for the dead. With the recent dedication of new temples in Ogden, Provo, and Washington, D.C.; with the complete remodeling of the Mesa, St. George, and Hawaii Temples; and with the building of new temples in Japan, Brazil, Mexico, and Seattle, this basic Christian doctrine, which shows the love of a gracious Father for all his children, is receiving an emphasis never before known.[30]

As the vision became scripture, most Saints little understood that it would promote temple and genealogy work as never before. It appears that the revelation had not been canonized before because in 1976, hardly any genealogical technology existed, making the process impractical and tedious. After the revelation was accepted by the congregation, its doctrine became binding. The Saints had made a covenant to fulfill their obligation to save their dead as outlined in the vision of the redemption of the dead. General Authorities began to use section 138 on a more regular basis to better teach the Saints about this sacred responsibility.

Teaching the Vision

In the April 1981 general conference, Elder Royden G. Derrick of the First Quorum of the Seventy extensively reviewed what Joseph F. Smith saw in the spirit world in order to emphasize the urgency of temple work for the dead. He quoted verses 11–12, 14, 18, 20, 30–32, and 57–59. Never before had a General Authority quoted so comprehensively from the vision. At the end of his talk, Elder Derrick very clearly outlined how the scripture had become binding on the Saints, associating the scripture with the responsibilities of finding names, building temples, and performing ordinances. He said, "One of the major missions of the Church is to uniquely identify these individuals who have died and perform the necessary saving ordinances in their behalf, for they cannot do it for themselves. Once these ordinances are performed, if the individual accepts the gospel in the great world of spirits, then this work will be effective."[31] For the first time, a General Authority in general conference stressed the necessity of doing individual family history research to produce the needed data for temple work.

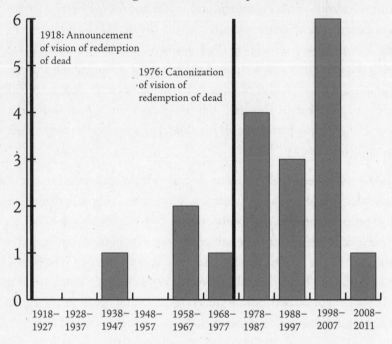

Other Apostles have since taught of this responsibility of the living, but they have also suggested that joy would come to the dead who benefit from vicarious saving ordinances. In October 1992, President Thomas S. Monson of the First Presidency quoted Joseph F. Smith as he instructed, "Through our efforts in their behalf [the dead] their chains of bondage will fall from them, and the darkness surrounding them will clear away, that light may shine upon them and they shall hear in the spirit world of the work that has been done for them by their children here, and will rejoice with you in your performance of these duties."[32] Likewise, Robert D. Hales of the Quorum of the Twelve Apostles restated the joy the dead felt because their deliverance was at hand, intimating that the Saints would also feel joy in completing ordinances for the dead.[33]

In April 1993, President Ezra Taft Benson noted the timeliness of the vision of the redemption of the dead and its significance to living Latter-day Saints. He explained, "There has been considerable publicity and media coverage recently on the reporting of experiences that seemingly verify that 'life after life' is a reality."³⁴ In his address, President Benson used Joseph F. Smith's vision as the absolute declaration of the reality of life after life, reminding Church members that the vision of the redemption of the dead had been accepted as holy scripture and therefore truth from heaven.

In the October 2005 general conference, Elder Paul E. Koelliker of the First Quorum of the Seventy connected the vision with temple work, stating, "There is still available time in many temples to accommodate the counsel of the First Presidency to put aside some of our leisure time and devote more time to performing temple ordinances. I pray that we will be responsive to this invitation to come to the door of the temple."³⁵ He used the doctrine in President Smith's vision to emphasize to members the importance of temple work, especially above leisure activities.

General Authorities also used the vision of the redemption of the dead to show a pattern for personal revelation. Elder Joseph B. Wirthlin of the Quorum of the Twelve Apostles, in May 1982, and President Henry B. Eyring of the First Presidency, in October 2010, used the vision as a pattern for receiving revelation. They encouraged Church members to take the same approach that President Joseph F. Smith had taken to seek personal revelation. Before introducing the vision, Elder Wirthlin began his address by saying, "It is about pondering and what can be gained therefrom that I should like to address my remarks today."³⁶ Likewise, President Henry B. Eyring used the vision as instruction for personal revelation: "For me, President Joseph F. Smith set an example of how pondering can invite light from God."³⁷ These General Authorities used the vision to illustrate a pattern of pondering and revelation that all Saints can follow.

General Authorities also used the vision to show how God values women. In his vision, Joseph F. Smith saw Eve and her daughters involved in missionary work in the spirit world. In October 1993, Elder Dallin H. Oaks of the Quorum of the Twelve Apostles emphasized Eve and her role in the plan of salvation.³⁸ In October 1999, President James E. Faust validated Latter-day Saint women in their "lasting legacy" of blessing the lives of "all men and women," both living and dead.³⁹ Joseph F. Smith's vision served to show how women too preach the gospel and bring lost souls to a knowledge of their God.

Fulfilling the Scripture

The great mercy of the Lord can be seen in the timing of making the vision of the redemption of the dead a binding covenant. The Lord appears to have waited until the means would be available to realize the work of saving the dead. Through his servant Joseph F. Smith, the Lord seemed to take preliminary steps in preparing the Saints for the inclusion of the vision of the redemption of the dead in the standard works. For instance, while dedicating the Washington DC Temple in November 1974, President Spencer W. Kimball prophesied that "the day is coming, not too far ahead of us, when all the temples on this earth will be going night and day."[40] In his October 1975 conference address, Elder Packer stated that President Kimball's prophecy represented "our signal that the great work necessary to sustain the temples must be moved forward." He assessed, "Genealogical work has, I fear, sometimes been made to appear too difficult, too involved, and too time-consuming to really be inviting to the average high priest."[41]

In the past, genealogy work had been slow, monotonous, and difficult. "Latter-day Saints had been encouraged for decades to research their kindred dead and provide completed family group sheets, which were verified by the Temple Index Bureau before the vicarious temple ordinances could be performed. This was a slow and tedious hand-checking process, and often information provided was incorrect and the sheets had to be rejected."[42] An "acute shortage of names" had also plagued the Genealogical Society's "efforts to keep the temples supplied."[43] Although the Saints were encouraged to do their own genealogy and not be dependent on temple files for names, the names at the temples available for temple work were often insufficient for those wanting to serve. As Church membership increased, "the situation was critical, and solutions had to be found as quickly as possible."[44]

Elder Packer and the other members of the Temple and Genealogy Executive Committee prayed and studied to understand "why the work was not going forward. . . . In these efforts Elder Packer worked closely with Elder Bruce R. McConkie in exploring and discussing the scriptural basis for the sure direction in which the committee was moving."[45] The canonization of the vision of the redemption of the dead would play a large part in moving the work for the dead forward.

From Obscurity to Scripture   247

By assignment from the First Presidency, Elder Packer addressed the employees of the Genealogical Society on November 18, 1975, and pleaded for their cooperation: "Now I'm appealing to you all to set your minds to the task of simplifying basic genealogical research and of streamlining, in every way possible, the process by which names come from members of the Church and are ultimately presented in the temple for ordinance work."[46]

On December 10, 1975, the Genealogical Society became the Genealogical Department of the Church. This action fully integrated the department as part of the Church's central administration for the first time.[47] In addition, during the first part of 1976, all General Authorities visiting stake conferences were to instruct Church members "to prepare a life history and to make a record of events which had transpired in their lives."[48] In this way the First Presidency encouraged personal participation in genealogical work, paving the way for even more hands-on participation in the process.

With the preliminary measures paving the way, the announcement that the two revelations were to become scripture was significant in moving the work ahead. Immediately after the vision of the redemption of the dead was canonized, genealogical work was simplified in major strides. In 1976, the year the vision became scripture, the Genealogical Department adopted long-range goals to simplify the process for the first time.[49] Before, long-range planning had been informal. The plan presented to and cleared by the First Presidency included the "creation of multiple automated data files" and "the widespread distribution of genealogical information through personal computers."[50] The First Presidency envisioned that these goals would return the responsibility of finding names to the Church members, with whom the responsibility had resided until 1927. Elder J. Richard Clarke said this decision would "revolutionize family history work." He hoped to "make family history work easy for anyone who would try"; this would "propel the Church into a new era of family history activity."[51]

Lucille Tate, Elder Packer's biographer, shows how the Genealogical Department took measures to make family history work easier after the vision became scripture:

> By April 1 that year [1977], they had gained approval from the First Presidency for long-range goals that would move "a church and a people" nearer to what the Lord expected of them in redeeming

their dead. The Genealogical Department was tooling up to enter the age of computers, and in order to become conversant with them Elder Packer attended a one-week crash course at IBM in San Jose, California.

By assignment from the committee, Elder Packer in a talk titled "That They May Be Redeemed," said: "Billions have lived and we are to redeem all of them. . . . Overwhelming? Not quite! For we are the sons and daughters of God. He has told us that He would give 'no commandments unto the children of men, save he shall prepare a way for them that they may accomplish the thing which he commandeth them'" (1 Nephi 3:7).[52]

Up to the canonization of President Smith's vision, the majority of Church members did not have a way to perform vicarious temple work. However, in 1977, Elder Packer summed up the process as follows: "It is as though someone knew we would be traveling that way . . . and we find provision, information, inventions . . . set along the way waiting for us to take them up, and we see the invisible hand of the Almighty providing for us."[53]

In general conference two years after the canonization, President Spencer W. Kimball asserted, "I feel the same sense of urgency about temple work for the dead as I do about the missionary work for the living, since they are basically one and the same. . . . We are introducing a Churchwide program of extracting names from genealogical records."[54] In an interview with the *Ensign*, George H. Fudge of the Genealogical Department clearly stated that "new technology had been made available to mankind which can help us accomplish the Lord's purposes at a much faster pace and with much greater accuracy than ever before."[55] Fudge continued:

> December 1978 marks the end of the current four-generation program for individuals and the beginning of the four-generation program for families. . . .
>
> Now we come to a very significant idea associated with this thrust: as has been announced, original research beyond the four-generation level will be accepted but will no longer be required of individual members of the Church. Instead, the Church feels the responsibility to begin a massive records gathering and extraction program in order to prepare names for temple work. . . . By using computers, temples

will be able to record their own information. And rather than sending tons of paper back to Salt Lake City, they will send a concise computerized record of all their work. Consequently, our indexes will be easier to compile.[56]

The computer would become the indispensable tool in genealogical research, allowing Church members to fulfill the responsibility that General Authorities had linked to section 138.

The Genealogical Department aimed to streamline and simplify. As a result, the material necessary to do genealogical research became available more easily and in greater quantity than ever before. Branch libraries were computerized in 1975. By March 1976, genealogical films circulated numbered 22,127, "a 45 percent increase from March 1975."[57] The Family History Library in Salt Lake City was "flooded with an average of 3,500 visitors daily during the summer of 1977, up from a high of 2,000 per day in the previous year."[58] In 1977, the stake record extraction program was introduced, and the program was declared "phenomenally successful."[59] In 1981, just five years after Joseph F. Smith's vision was canonized, the International Genealogical Index (IGI) was published. According to Eleanor Knowles, "Members could submit single-entry forms with individual names, without having to wait until the individual could be linked to a family."[60] The IGI grew substantially with each edition, expanding by 34 million names in 1975, 81 million in 1981, 108 million in 1984, 147 million in 1988, and 187 million in 1992. The number of names increased by an average of 9 million names each year.[61] The *Church News* referred to the widespread interest as an "international genealogy mania."[62]

Conclusion

The vision of the redemption of the dead has become central to the theology of the Latter-day Saints. It confirms and expands earlier prophetic insights concerning work for the dead and introduces doctrinal truths that were unknown before October 1918 and not fully instituted until 1976.[63] As religious scholar Trever R. Anderson describes, "Latter-day Saints view the words of the Prophet and Apostles as the words of God, yet canonized scripture still stands on a higher plane. Canonization of a revelation or vision validates its authority, prominence, and doctrinal power." By being canonized, this 1918 vision "was elevated from obscure Church history to central core doctrine."⁶⁴

Since canonization, Doctrine and Covenants 138 has been linked by General Authorities to temple, genealogical, and family history work. Section 138 is now a major part of Church doctrine and has become the basis of Church teachings about salvation of the dead.

The process by which Joseph F. Smith's vision of the redemption of the dead became part of the Doctrine and Covenants serves as an example of how revelation becomes canonized. Not until Church members were capable of fulfilling their responsibility to the dead did the revelation become binding as a scriptural command. Over time, Church leaders have gradually taught about the significance of section 138, and Latter-day Saints have accordingly lived by this doctrine in stages. Practices such as building temples and performing saving ordinances for the living and the dead demonstrate that the doctrines associated with the vision were first considered authoritative by the leadership of the Church in 1918 but are now binding to all the members of the Church.

The remarkable process of bringing this vision to scripture is worthy of sharing with our grandchildren and great-grandchildren now that the work of salvation for the dead is achievable. This doctrinal foundation will yet provide the way in which, as Elder Boyd K. Packer has expressed, "we can redeem our dead by the thousands and tens of thousands and millions and billions and tens of billions. We have not yet moved to the edge of the light."⁶⁵

Appendix A

1976 Long-Range Goals

No.	Summary of Goal	Current Implementation
1	Develop and maintain a central genealogical file that shows family relationships and temple ordinance data for individuals	FamilySearch, Ancestral File
2	Design all name entry systems to place individuals in their proper family order	Ancestral File
3	Prepare a single index to all temple work for a given individual	International Genealogical Index
4	Make information in the central genealogical file available to Church members as a beginning point for their own genealogical research	FamilySearch
5	Establish genealogical service centers in temple districts, particularly overseas, and involve members in a records extraction program	Family History Service Centers, Family Record Extraction
6	Use modern technology in temple recording and enable service centers to process names locally	Ordinance Recording System, TempleReady
7	Transfer to families and local priesthood leaders the burden of determining the accuracy of name submission and responsibility for avoiding duplication of temple ordinances	TempleReady
8	Develop and maintain a family organization register to aid members in contacting other persons researching their same lines	Family Registry, Ancestral File
9	Provide a service to assist priesthood leaders in more difficult areas of genealogical research	Published research outlines
10	Continue the present program of gathering records of genealogical interest from around the world	Expansion of microfilm acquisitions

Adapted from James B. Allen, Jessie L. Embry, and Kahlile B. Mehr, *Hearts Turned to the Fathers* (Provo, UT: BYU Studies, 1995), 271.

Notes

1. N. Eldon Tanner, "The Sustaining of Church Officers," *Ensign*, May 1976, 19.
2. Boyd K. Packer, "Teach the Scriptures" (address to CES religious educators, October 14, 1977), 4.
3. Packer, "Teach the Scriptures," 4.
4. Craig J. Ostler and Joseph Fielding McConkie, *Revelations of the Restoration* (Salt Lake City: Deseret Book, 2000), 1143.
5. See Richard E. Bennett, "'And I Saw the Hosts of the Dead, Both Small and Great': Joseph F. Smith, World War I, and His Visions of the Dead," in *By Study and by Faith: Selections from the "Religious Educator,"* ed. Richard Neitzel Holzapfel and Kent P. Jackson (Provo, UT: Religious Studies Center, Brigham Young University, 2009), 113–35; George S. Tate, "'The Great World of the Spirits of the Dead': Death, the Great War, and the 1918 Influenza Pandemic as Context for Doctrine and Covenants 138," *BYU Studies* 46, no. 1 (2007): 5–40; and Thomas G. Alexander, *Mormonism in Transition: A History of the Latter-day Saints, 1890–1930* (Urbana: University of Illinois Press, 1986), 282, 299.
6. See H. Dean Garrett and Stephen E. Robinson, *A Commentary on Doctrine and Covenants*, vol. 4 (Salt Lake City: Deseret Book, 2001); Lyndon W. Cook, *Revelations of the Prophet Joseph Smith: A Historical and Biographical Commentary of the Doctrine and Covenants* (Salt Lake City: 1981); Ostler and McConkie, *Revelations of the Restoration*; and Donald W. Parry and Jay A. Parry, *Understanding Death and the Resurrection* (Salt Lake City: Deseret Book, 2003).
7. Bennett, "'And I Saw the Hosts of the Dead,'" 113.
8. Joseph F. Smith, in Conference Report, October 1918, 2.
9. Joseph F. Smith, in Conference Report, October 1918, 2.
10. Cited in Robert L. Millet, "Salvation beyond the Grave (D&C 137 and 138)," in *Studies in Scripture*, vol. 1, *The Doctrine and Covenants*, ed. Robert L. Millet and Kent P. Jackson (Salt Lake City: Deseret Book, 1989), 554.
11. See Joseph Fielding Smith, *Life of Joseph F. Smith* (Salt Lake City: Deseret News, 1938), 466.
12. Anthon H. Lund, journal, October 31, 1918, Church History Library, The Church of Jesus Christ of Latter-day Saints, Salt Lake City.
13. James E. Talmage, diary, October 31, 1918, L. Tom Perry Special Collections, Harold B. Lee Library, Brigham Young University, box 5, folder 6, 62.
14. Millet, "Salvation Beyond the Grave," 561.
15. James E. Talmage, in Conference Report, April 1919, 60.
16. *Gospel Doctrine: Selections from the Sermons and Writings of Joseph F. Smith* (Salt Lake City: Deseret Book, 1946), 472–75; and Smith, *Life of Joseph F. Smith*, 466–69.
17. James E. Talmage, "Genealogical Work Is Essential to Redemption of the Dead in the Holy Temples of the Lord" (address delivered in the Tabernacle, Salt Lake City, September 22, 1918).
18. Joseph L. Wirthlin, in Conference Report, April 1945, 69, 71.
19. Marion G. Romney, in Conference Report, April 1964, 124.

20. Spencer W. Kimball, in Conference Report, October 1966, 23.
21. Spencer W. Kimball, in Conference Report, October 1966, 26.
22. Boyd K. Packer, "The Redemption of the Dead," *Ensign*, November 1975, 97.
23. Packer, "Redemption of the Dead," 99.
24. Joseph Fielding McConkie, *The Bruce R. McConkie Story: Reflections of a Son* (Salt Lake City: Deseret Book, 2003), 383, 389, 391.
25. Edward L. Kimball, *Lengthen Your Stride: The Presidency of Spencer W. Kimball* (Salt Lake City: Deseret Book, 2005), 377.
26. Kimball, *Lengthen Your Stride*, 377.
27. Kip Sperry, "From Kirtland to Computers: the Growth of Family History Record Keeping," in *The Heavens Are Open: 1992 Sperry Symposium on the Doctrine and Covenants and Church History*, ed. Byron R. Merrill (Salt Lake City: Deseret Book, 1993), 294.
28. Tanner, "Sustaining of Church Officers," 19.
29. Richard O. Cowan, *The Doctrine and Covenants: Our Modern Scripture* (Salt Lake City: Deseret Book, 1984), 208.
30. Bruce R. McConkie, "A New Commandment: Save Thyself and Thy Kindred!," *Ensign*, August 1976, 8.
31. Royden G. Derrick, "Moral Values and Rewards," *Ensign*, May 1981, 68.
32. Quoted in Thomas S. Monson, "The Priesthood in Action," *Ensign*, November 1992, 48.
33. See Robert D. Hales, "Faith through Tribulation Brings Peace and Joy," *Ensign*, May 2003, 18; and Robert D. Hales, "Your Sorrow Shall Be Turned to Joy," *Ensign*, November 1983, 66.
34. Ezra Taft Benson, "'Because I Live, Ye Shall Live Also,'" *Ensign*, April 1993, 2.
35. Paul E. Koelliker, "Gospel Covenants Bring Promised Blessings," *Ensign*, November 2005, 95.
36. Joseph B. Wirthlin, "Pondering Strengthens the Spiritual Life," *Ensign*, May 1982, 23.
37. Henry B. Eyring, "Serve with the Spirit," *Ensign*, November 2010, 60.
38. Dallin H. Oaks, "'The Great Plan of Happiness,'" *Ensign*, November 1993, 73.
39. James E. Faust, "What It Means to Be a Daughter of God," *Ensign*, November 1999, 101.
40. Quoted in Lucille C. Tate, *Boyd K. Packer: A Watchman on the Tower* (Salt Lake City: Bookcraft, 1995), 198.
41. Quoted in Tate, *Boyd K. Packer*, 198.
42. Eleanor Knowles, *Howard W. Hunter* (Salt Lake City: Deseret Book, 1994), 188.
43. James B. Allen and others, *Hearts Turned to the Fathers: A History of the Genealogical Society of Utah, 1894–1994* (Provo, UT: BYU Studies, 1995), 174.
44. Knowles, *Howard W. Hunter*, 188.
45. Tate, *Boyd K. Packer*, 199.
46. Quoted in Tate, *Boyd K. Packer*, 199.
47. Allen et al., *Hearts Turned to the Fathers*, 267.
48. Boyd K. Packer, "Someone Up There Loves You," *Ensign*, January 1977, 10.

49. See appendix A.
50. Allen and others, *Hearts Turned to the Fathers*, 271.
51. Allen and others, *Hearts Turned to the Fathers*, 308.
52. Tate, *Boyd K. Packer*, 201; compare Boyd K. Packer, "That All May Be Redeemed" (Regional Representatives Seminar, Tabernacle, Salt Lake City, April 1, 1977).
53. Packer, "That All May Be Redeemed," as cited in Tate, *Boyd K. Packer*, 202.
54. Quoted in "New Directions in Work for the Dead," *Ensign*, June 1978, 62.
55. "New Directions in Work for the Dead," 62.
56. "New Directions in Work for the Dead," 64, 67.
57. Allen and others, *Hearts Turned to the Fathers*, 286.
58. Allen and others, *Hearts Turned to the Fathers*, 291.
59. R. Scott Lloyd, "New Effort to 'Harvest' Millions of Names," *Church News*, May 27, 1989, 5.
60. Knowles, *Howard W. Hunter*, 191.
61. Allen and others, *Hearts Turned to the Fathers*, 318.
62. Quoted in Allen and others, *Hearts Turned to the Fathers*, 291.
63. See Robert L. Millet, *Life after Death* (Salt Lake City: Deseret Book, 1999), 85.
64. Trever R. Anderson, "Doctrine and Covenants Section 110: From Vision to Canonization" (master's thesis, Brigham Young University, August 2010), 154.
65. Quoted in Tate, *Boyd K. Packer*, 203.

Index

Aaronic Priesthood: in account of priesthood restoration, 55–59; early understanding of, 170; explained in Section 84, 176–77
Abrahamic covenant, 215
Agency, 137, 140, 142, 143
Alexander, Thomas G., 235
Allen, Graham, 106n4
America, language of nineteenth-century, 98–99
Anderson, James: on John the Baptist, 37; on double prophetic meaning, 38–39; on prophecy, 41, 45; on great and dreadful day, 42; on turning hearts of fathers to children, 44
Anderson, Richard Lloyd, 83, 166n39
Anderson, Trever R., 249
Angels, ministering, 57
Anthropology: divine, 184–85, 187–89; Johannine, 209–15
Apostasy, in early Church, 154–55
Apostleship, 103–4
Armor of God, 82, 83, 84–89
Atonement: sacrament and, 77–79; intertextuality and, 102; Fall and, 161
Augustine, 210

Baby, help with, at fireside, 4–5
Baptism, authority for, 60
Barlow, Philip, 205
Bates, Paulina, 116, 117, 133n30
Bednar, David A.: on revelation, 20; on pure hearts, 85; on conduct, 86
Bennett, Richard E., 235

Benson, Ezra Taft: on law of chastity, 87; on Zion, 137; on agency, 143; on vision of redemption of dead, 244–45
Bible: revisions to, 25, 30; and revelation construction, 205; expanding understanding through, 216. *See also* Joseph Smith Translation of Bible
Biblical intertextuality: overview of, 92–95; reasons for, 95–100; functions of, 100–104; appreciating, 104
Billings, Titus, 144
Bishops, responsibilities of, 173
Body, 201–2. *See also* Word of Wisdom
Book of Commandments: publication of, 22–23; witnesses of, 23–24; revisions to, 24–27; rearrangement of, 50–51
Book of Mormon: introduction to, 1; preparation of, 7, 9; ministry of Jesus Christ in, 7–9; references to Godhead in, 12–13; revisions to, 25, 30; intertextuality and, 96, 100, 106n3; Isaiah passages in, 113–14, 129nn9–10; teachings on priesthood in, 170
Booth, Ezra, 176
Breastplate of righteousness, 85–86
Brodie, Thomas L., 217n8
Brother, love for, 157–58
Brown, Raymond, 210, 217–18n8
Bruce, F. F., 209
Burder, Samuel, 37, 47n10
Bush, Lester, 203n10
Bushman, Richard, 67

Calef, Robert, 226–27
Calmet, Antoine Augustin, 39
Campbell, Alexander, 116, 131n20, 170–71
Cannon, David H., 194
Cannon, Donald Q., 221
Cannon, George Q.: on sacrament in early Church, 64; as convert from Methodism, 67; on worthiness to take sacrament, 71
Carpenter, Benjamin, 52
Carpenter, David, 21
Carter, Jared, 172
Carter, Simeon, 172
Catholic Ursuline Convent, 228, 229
Chain of Being/Chain of Belonging, 184–85, 187–89
Chandler, Edward, 42, 48n38
Charriere, Doris T., 196
Chastity, 86–88
Children of God, 209–11
Christofferson, D. Todd, on Zion, 139, 145
Christology, Johannine, 206–9
Churchill, Winston, 198
Church of Jesus Christ of Latter-day Saints, The. *See* Early Church
Clark, Adam, 62n22
Clarke, J. Richard, 247
Coca-Cola, 196
Coe, Joseph, 169
Cola drinks, 196
Coltrin, Zebedee, 169
Commandments, obedience to, 85–86
Communication: in revelation, 20–22, 25–26; through Holy Ghost, 29
Compendium of the Doctrines of the Gospel, 51
Conant, Roger, 232n17
Conduct, protecting, 85–86
Consecration: Zion and, 137; parable of twelve sons and, 157–58; parable of nobleman and tower and, 160–61; high priesthood and, 172
Cook, Quentin L., 12
Covill, James, 210
Cowdery, Oliver: revelation for, 2, 135; and publication of D&C, 22; revision of revelations and, 26; Elijah appears to, 35, 42–43; account of priesthood restoration, 51–60; as convert from Methodism, 67; vision given to, 71; translation process and, 96–97; marvelous work through, 100; as Apostle, 103; missionary work and, 141; looks for treasure, 223; researches New England history, 225–28
Cowley, Matthias F., 41
Crawford, Alexander, 170–71
Cyril, 65

Dead, redemption of. *See* Redemption of dead, vision of
Debt, of early Church leaders, 222–24
Degrees of Glory, vision of, 185, 186
Derrick, Royden G., 243
Disciples of Christ, 170–71
Divine anthropology, 184–85, 187–89

Early Church: sacrament in, 64–71; apostasy in, 154–55; unity in, 157–58, 160–61; Word of Wisdom in, 193–95, 203nn10, 12; growth of, 207; debt in, 222–24
Earth, 186
Edwards, Jonathan, 116, 131n22
Elect, 102–3
Elias, 36–38, 53, 56, 58–59. *See also* Elijah, return of
Elijah, return of: prophecies on, 34–35; method of, 35–42; timing of, 42–43; reason for, 43–44; blessings of, 44–45; John the Baptist and, 53
Emblems, of sacrament, 78–79
Endowment, 52
Endurance, salvation through, 6, 12
Enoch, 40
Eternal families, 214–15
Eternal life, 214–15, 219nn23, 24
Eve, 245
Everett, Edward, 36, 46–47n7
Exaltation, 211–14, 219nn23, 24
Eyring, Henry B.: on return of Elijah, 43; on sin, 87; on personal revelation, 245

Fall, Atonement and, 161
Family: and Chain of Belonging, 184–85, 187–89; and Johannine anthropology, 209–15; eternal, 214–15. *See also* Genealogy
Faust, James E., 245
Feet, shod with preparation, 88–89
Fig tree, parable of, 151–53
Fillmore, Lizzie Belle Gardner, 193, 195
Finney, Charles G., 116, 131–32n23
Fireside, fellowshipping at, 4–5
Foundation, Jesus Christ as, 9–10
Fry, John, 40, 42, 48n28
Frye, Northrup, 150
Fudge, George H., 248–49
Fundamentalism, 30

Gathering, of righteous, 154, 155
Gause, Jesse, 154, 168
Genealogical Department, 247–48
Genealogy, 239, 240–41, 243, 246–49
Gibbons, Cardinal, 239
Girdle of truth, 86–88
Glory, vision of degrees of, 185, 186
God: relationship between Jesus Christ and, 16; nature of, 95–96; and Chain of Belonging, 188–89; children of, 209–11; knowing, 216; love of, 235
Godhead, 12–13
Grant, Heber J.: on distribution of sacrament, 68; Word of Wisdom and, 194, 195
Great Chain of Being/Chain of Belonging, 184–85, 187–89
Greswell, Edward, 40, 48n26
Griffith, Marie, 198

Hafen, Bruce C., 89
Hales, Robert D.: on Zion, 134; on ordinances for dead, 244
Haley, Alex, 241
Hamilton, C. Mark, 69–70
Hancock, Levi, 171
Hanks, Marion D., 201–2
Harris, Martin, 137, 138
Health, Word of Wisdom and, 192–93, 195–202

Heart, pure, 85, 86, 138, 143–44
Helmet of salvation, 84
High priesthood, 169–74, 177–78
Hinckley, Gordon B., 140
Hodge, Charles, 116, 117, 132n24
Holy Ghost, 29, 211
Holy Spirit of promise, 211–12
Homes, Nathaniel, 39–40
Hunter, Howard W.: on return of Elijah, 41; on sacrament, 83
Hyde, Orson: as convert from Methodism, 67; and Isaianic language in D&C, 116, 130–31n18; revelation for, 173–74; called son of God, 209
Hymnbook, 70

I Am, 207–8, 215, 217–18nn8, 10
IGI (International Genealogical Index), 249
Independence, Missouri, as Zion, 136
Indirect communication, parables as, 150
Inspiration: acting on, 4–5, 15–16; for minister's questions, 13–14. *See also* Revelation(s)
International Genealogical Index (IGI), 249
Intertextuality. *See* Biblical intertextuality
Irenaeus, 65
Isaianic language, in D&C: method of, 108–12; reasons for, 112–17; summary of, 117–18; occurrences of, 119–27t

Jeffries, Deirdra Boyack, 204n28
Jesus Christ: coming to know, 3; as foundation, 9–10; relationship between God and, 16; administers sacrament, 79–80; remembering, 84; taking upon name of, 88–89; in Gospel of John, 206–9; progression of, 213; preaches in spirit prison, 235. *See also* Atonement; Messiah, name of; Personal ministry of Jesus Christ; Second Coming
Jewish traditions, Elijah's return and, 39–41, 42

John, Gospel of: overview of, 205–6, 215–16; Christology of, 206–9; anthropology of, 209–15; influence of, on Joseph Smith, 217n2
Johnson, Luke, 173–74
Johnson, Lyman E., 71, 173–74
Johnson, Seth, 70
Johnstone, Edward, 40–41, 48n31
John the Baptist: as Elijah, 35–38, 40; accounts of priesthood restoration and, 51–53, 54–60; prophecies on, 53–54
Joseph of Egypt, 86
Joseph Smith Papers: Manuscript Revelation Books, 30
Joseph Smith Translation of Bible, 114–15, 129n11, 135, 175

Kimball, Edward L., 241
Kimball, Spencer W.: on remembrance, 77, 78; on temptation, 87; on revelation and redemption of dead, 240; vision of redemption of dead and, 241; on temples, 246; on temple work, 248
Kirtland Temple, 52, 69–70
Knight, Joseph, Sr., 100, 135, 139
Knight, Newel, 76, 139
Knight, Polly, 139
Knight, Sally, 76
Knowles, Eleanor, 249
Koelliker, Paul E., 245

Laborers in the field, parable of, 158–59, 187–88
Language, of revelation, 21–25, 96–97, 107n7. *See also* Biblical intertextuality
Latter days, prophecies on, 101–2
Lee, Harold B.: on sacrament and armor of God, 84; on learning future from scriptures, 128n5
Levi, sons of, 58, 59–60
Lewis, C. S., 89
Light of Christ, 186
Little, James A., 51
Loins, 86
Lord's Supper. *See* Sacrament
Love: for others, 157–58; of God, 235
Lund, Anthon H., 237

Marriage, 44–45, 219nn23, 24
Marsh, Thomas B., 67
"Marvelous work," 93, 100–101
Materialism, 144
Matthews, Robert J., 175
Maxwell, Neal A., 144
McAllister, John D. T., 194
McConkie, Bruce R.: on sacrament at Second Coming, 80, 81–82; on prophetic quotes, 128n4; on parables, 149, 150; vision of redemption of dead and, 241; on revelations regarding salvation for dead, 242–43
McConkie, Joseph Fielding, 241
McElhaney, Lee, 15
McKiernan, F. Mark, 163n11
McLellin, William: as scribe, 23; as witness, 24; on Joseph Smith as prophet, 26–27; on priesthood, 171; revelation for, 173–74
Melchizedek, 170, 175
Melchizedek Priesthood: in account of priesthood restoration, 55–56, 59; developments in understanding, 175–76; explained in Section 84, 176–77
Messiah, name of, 54–55, 62n20. *See also* Jesus Christ
Messianic prophecies, of Isaiah in D&C, 110–12
Miller, Perry, 98
Miller, William, 116, 132n27
Millet, Robert L., 161, 216
Minister, as Church investigator, 13–14
Ministering angels, 57
Missionary work: Zion and, 137, 141–42; reports on, 168–69; high priesthood and, 173–74, 177; and Chain of Belonging, 187–88; Word of Wisdom and, 199–200; in spirit prison, 235
Missouri, as Zion, 136
Monson, Thomas S., 244
More Wonders of the Invisible World (Calef), 226–27
Morley, Isaac, 144
Moroni, foretells Elijah's return, 34
Murdock, John, 141, 169

Nauvoo, Illinois, tolerance in, 229–30
Nephites, Christ's ministry among, 7–8
Nettleton, Asahel, 116, 132n26
New England, history of, 224–27
New Testament, parables from, 151–56
Nobleman and the tower, parable of, 159–62
Noise, interrupting communication, 20–21

Oaks, Dallin H.: on revelation, 3, 17; on taking upon name of Christ, 89; on sacrament, 89–90; on teaching gospel principles, 140–41; on parables, 151; on application of scriptures, 156; on Eve and plan of salvation, 245
Obedience: to commandments, 85–86; Zion and, 137, 139–41; to Word of Wisdom, 196
Ogden, D. Kelly, 159
Old Testament, 98, 129n11
Olive Leaf: parable of laborers in field and, 158; overview of, 182–83; historical setting for, 183–85; text of, 186–89; salvation and, 211–12
Onderdonk, Benjamin T., 116, 131n21
Ordinances, authority for, 60
Ottley, Thane, 13–14

Pack, Frederick J., 196
Packer, Boyd K.: on revisions made to revelations, 26; on parables, 150; on additions to Pearl of Great Price, 234; on vision of redemption of dead, 240–41; on genealogy, 246, 247, 248; on redemption of dead, 250
Parables: overview of, 149–50, 162; power of, 150–51; from New Testament, 151–56; classifying, 163n3; and Chain of Belonging, 187–88
Partridge, Edward, 25–26, 146, 209
Patoch, Mr. (Church investigator), 13–14
Patrick, Simon, 36–37
Patten, David W., 67
Perfection, of revelations, 21–27, 30–31
Personal ministry of Jesus Christ: D&C as witness of, 1–3; use of personal pronouns and, 3–9, 11–17

Peterson, Paul, 194
Phelps, William W., 70, 138
Pratt, Orson: and rearrangement of D&C, 50–51; on John the Baptist, 53–54; on Aaronic Priesthood, 58; on restoration of priesthood, 61–62n15; and Isaianic language in D&C, 116, 131n19; on parable of laborers in field, 158; on consecration, 160
Pratt, Parley P.: on revelation process, 96; and Isaianic language in D&C, 116, 130n16; Olive Leaf and, 189
Prayer: sacrament, 66–68, 81; parable of unjust judge and, 155
Preparation, feet shod with, 88–89
Price, P., 37
Priesthood: parable of wheat and tares and, 154; overview of Section 84 and, 167–68, 178; early understanding of, 170–72; developments in understanding, 172–76; Section 84's contributions to understanding, 176–78
Priesthood restoration: Elijah and, 45; prophecies on, 50–51, 53–54; accounts of, 51–53, 54–60
Pronouns, personal, in D&C, 2, 3–9, 11–17
Psychological noise, 20–21
Pure hearts, 85, 86, 138, 143–44

Qahal Qadosh Gadol Synagogue, 43

Rebukes, of Isaiah in D&C, 110
Redemption of dead, vision of: overview of, 234–36, 249–50; announcement and acknowledgement of, 236–38; drifts into obscurity, 238–40; canonization of, 240–43; teaching, 243–45; fulfillment of, 245–49
Remembrance, 77
Restoration: doctrine of, 11–13; Isaiah's prophecies on, 110–12
Revelation(s): Dallin H. Oaks on, 3, 17; as process, 19–20, 29–31; imperfections in, 20–24; revisions to, 24–27; to understand revelation, 27–29; Holy Ghost and, 29; translation of, 96–97,

106n4; language of, 107n7; receiving personal, 245. *See also* Inspiration
Revision of revelations, 24–27, 30–31
Richards, Franklin D., 51
Richards, LeGrand, 44
Rigdon, Sidney: and revision of revelations, 26; on endowment, 52; and Isaianic language in D&C, 116, 130n15; consecrates and dedicates Zion, 138–39; missionary work and, 141; fig tree parable and, 151–52; impact of, 163n11; and background to Section 84, 168; high priesthood and, 172; called son of God, 209; looks for treasure, 223; researches New England history, 225
Righteousness, 85–86
Roberts, B. H., 77, 221
Robinson, Ebenezer, 220, 222–23
Rock, Jesus Christ as, 9–10
Romney, Marion G., 240
Roots (Haley), 241

Sabbath, honoring, 140, 147n15
Sacrament: background of, 64–66; administration of, 66–68, 75; frequency of, 68–69; meaning of, 69–71; textual connections regarding, 76–77; as act of remembrance, 77–79; following Second Coming, 79–82; as protection, 82–89; blessings of, 89–90
Sacrifice, of sons of Levi, 58, 59–60
St. Michael's seminary, 9–10
Salem revelation: overview of, 220–22, 229–30; context of, 222–24; content of, 224; New England history and, 224–27; lessons learned from, 227–29
Salem witch trials, 224
Salvation: through endurance, 6, 12; Olive Leaf and, 187
Satan, tactics of, 87
Sawyer, T. J., 37
Scale of Nature, 184
School of the Prophets, 183
Scriptures: personalizing and internalizing, 2–5; revisions to, 25, 30–31; intertextuality of, 96; learning future from, 128n5; application of, 156

Sealing, 44–45, 219nn23, 24
Second Coming, 58, 80–81, 152–54
Section 111. *See* Salem revelation
Section 138. *See* Redemption of dead, vision of
Section 76, 185
Section 84: overview of, 167–68, 178; content and background to, 168–69; contributions to priesthood understanding, 176–78
Section 88. *See* Olive Leaf
Semantic noise, 20
Shoes, 88–89
Sickness, 198–99
Simeon, Charles, 37, 46n4
Simpson, Robert L., 201
Sin, 87
Smith, Emma, 70, 76, 99–100, 135
Smith, Hyrum: on sacrament, 69; marvelous work through, 100; missionary work and, 141, 142; as high priest, 169; looks for treasure, 223; researches New England history, 225
Smith, Joseph: on revelation, 19, 21; revelation given to, 20, 28–29; and revision of revelations, 24–27, 31; as prophet, 26–27; Moroni teaches, 34; Elijah appears to, 35, 42–43; on sealing, 44, 219n23; on Elijah, 44–45; account of priesthood restoration, 51–53, 54–60; administration of sacrament and, 64, 68; on sacrament, 70; vision given to, 71; and sacrament at Second Coming, 80; and translation process, 96–98; writing abilities of, 99–100; marvelous work through, 100–101; and Isaianic language in D&C, 112–16, 118; Zion and, 134, 139; on Polly Knight, 139; missionary work and, 141, 142–43; and parable of wheat and tares, 153, 154–55; parable of unjust judge and, 156; background to Section 84 and, 168–69; high priesthood and, 172–74; Chain of Belonging and, 184–85; on Holy Spirit of promise, 211–12; on knowing God, 216; Gospel of John's influence on, 217n2; treasure hunting and,

220–21; Church debt and, 222; looks for treasure, 223; researches New England history, 225; on Ursuline Convent, 229
Smith, Joseph F., 194–95. *See also* Redemption of dead, vision of
Smith, Joseph Fielding: on return of Elijah, 35, 41–42; on Elijah and temple work, 44; on prophecy on Elijah, 45; on angelic visitors to Kirtland Temple, 46n2; on section 4, 93; on parable of wheat and tares, 153–54; on cola drinks, 196; on temple marriage, 219n24; on visions of Joseph F. Smith, 237
Smith, Joseph, Sr., 92, 100, 169
Smith, Lucy Mack, 92
Smith, Hyrum, 135
Snodgrass, Klyne R., 150, 163n3, 164n17
Snow, Lorenzo, 189, 194
Sons, parable of twelve, 156–58
Sons of God, 209–11
Sperry, Sidney B., 160
Spirit prison, 235
Spirit world. *See* Redemption of dead, vision of
Stendahl, Krister, 218n9
Stewart, Philemon, 116, 133n29
Sunday, as day to administer sacrament, 68. *See also* Sabbath, honoring
Sunderland, La Roy, 189

Talmage, James E., 237–38, 239
Tanner, N. Eldon, 242
Tate, George S., 235
Tate, Lucille, 247–48
Taylor, John: as convert from Methodism, 67; on sacrament, 79; on parable of laborers in field, 165n31
Tea, 195–96. *See also* Word of Wisdom
Teachings of the Prophet Joseph Smith (Smith), 115
Technology, genealogy and, 248–49
Temple marriage, 44–45, 219nn23, 24
Temples and temple work: Elijah and, 44–45; parable of nobleman and tower and, 166n41; Word of Wisdom and, 194–95; ordinances of, 203n9; Spencer W.

Kimball on, 246. *See also* Redemption of dead, vision of
Temptation, 87
Ten virgins, parable of, 152–53
Thayer, Ezra, 169
Thompson, Robert B., 58
Thoughts, protecting, 84
Tokens, of sacrament, 78–79
Tolerance, 227–30
Transubstantiation, 65
Treasure hunting, 220–21, 223
Tribulation: revelation foretelling, 28; Zion and, 137, 139; parable of nobleman and tower and, 159–60
Truth, girdle of, 86–88
Twelve Apostles, 103–4
Twelve sons, parable of, 156–58

Uchtdorf, Dieter F., 3
Underwood, Grant, 27
United Firm, 168, 222
Unity, of Saints, 157–58, 160–61
Unjust judge, parable of, 155–56

Van Wagoner, Richard S., 163–64n14
Virgins, parable of ten, 152–53
Virtue, 86–88
Vision of February 1832, 185
Voice, in Isaiah's prophecies, 112

Wait, Daniel Guildford, 37, 47n9
Wesley, John, 116, 132n25
Wheat and tares, parable of, 153–55
White, Ellen G., 116, 133n28
Whitlock, Harvey, 141
Whitmer, David: revelation given to, 2; marvelous work through, 100; as Apostle, 103; missionary work and, 141
Whitmer, John, 136, 156
Whitmer, Peter, Jr., 168
Whitney, Newel K., 68, 168, 169
Whitney, Orson F., 144
Widtsoe, John A., 194, 196–98
Widtsoe, Leah, 194, 196–201
Wight, Lyman, 171
Williams, Frederick G., 103, 169
Wirthlin, Joseph B., 245

Wirthlin, Joseph L., 239–40
Witch trials, 224
Witnesses, of D&C, 23–24
Woman and unjust judge, parable of, 155–56
Women: and preparation of sacrament, 66; value of, 245
Woodruff, Wilford: on sacrament, 69; on worthiness to take sacrament, 71; on honoring Sabbath, 147n15; on Word of Wisdom, 194
Word, the, 206–7
Word of Wisdom: Biblical intertextuality and, 94; overview of, 192–93; in early Church, 193–95, 203nn10, 12; as health law, 195–202
Words of Joseph Smith, The (Ehat and Cook), 115

Worlds, 158
Worthiness, to take sacrament, 70–71

Young, Brigham: on revelation, 21–22; on sacrifice of sons of Levi, 59–60; as convert from Methodism, 67; on sacrament, 67, 70; and Isaianic language in D&C, 116, 130n17; on Zion, 145; on honoring Sabbath, 147n15; Word of Wisdom and, 194

Zion: revelation on, 28; overview of, 134–35, 145–46; location of, 135–36; pattern for establishing, 136–39; implementing principles to establish, 139–44; parable of twelve sons and, 158; redemption of, 159–60; securing, 161–62